ABSOLUTE BEGINNER'S GUIDE

TO

Microsoft® Windows® XP

Shelley O'Hara

201 West 103rd Street,
Indianapolis, Indiana 46290

Absolute Beginner's Guide to Microsoft® Windows® XP

International Standard Book Number: 0-7897-2856-7

Library of Congress Catalog Card Number: 2002110532

Printed in the United States of America

First Printing: December 2002

05   04   03   02   4   3   2   1

Trademarks

Warning and Disclaimer

Associate Publisher
Greg Wiegand

Acquisitions Editor
Stephanie J. McComb

Development Editor
Mark Cierzniak

Managing Editor
Thomas Hayes

Project Editor
Tricia Liebig

Production Editor
Benjamin Berg

Copy Editor
Geneil Breeze

Indexer
Ken Johnson

Proofreader
Carla Lewis

Technical Editor
Vince Averello

Team Coordinator
Sharry Lee Gregory

Interior Designer
Anne Jones

Cover Designer
Anne Jones

Page Layout
Julie Parks

Graphics
Tammy Graham
Oliver Jackson

Contents at a Glance

Table of Contents

About the Author

Shelley O'Hara is the author of more than 100 books, mostly dealing with computers. She has written some of the all-time best-selling computer books, including *Easy Windows XP Home Edition* and *Easy Windows 98*. She also does computer training and teaches writing classes. In addition to tech writing, O'Hara has also published a romantic comedy called *The Marriage Trifecta*.

Dedication

To my father, Raymond N. Ball, who has taught me how to be a person of integrity (and much, much more) simply from the way he delights in his life and family.

Acknowledgments

Just like there are dream teams in sports, there are dream teams on book projects. I was fortunate enough to work with my own particular editing dream team, the people and staff who made writing this book so much easier. (You can't imagine all the work the editors do, yet it's only my name on the cover.)

My particular dream team includes Greg Wiegand for inviting me to do this project; my favorite acquisitions editor, Stephanie McComb for negotiating the details; my favorite do-it-all team coordinator, Sharry Lee Gregory (using your full name to make your mom happy); Mark Cierzniak for excellent developmental; Vince Averello for his savvy, smart, excellent technical editing (thanks especially for help with many of the figures in this book); Tricia Liebig, a perfect project editor; and the other production and copy editors who worked on this project, Benjamin Berg and Geneil Breeze.

We Want to Hear from You!

As the reader of this book, *you* are our most important critic and commentator. We value your opinion and want to know what we're doing right, what we could do better, what areas you'd like to see us publish in, and any other words of wisdom you're willing to pass our way.

As an associate publisher for Que Publishing, I welcome your comments. You can email or write me directly to let me know what you did or didn't like about this book—as well as what we can do to make our books better.

Please note that I cannot help you with technical problems related to the *topic* of this book. We do have a User Services group, however, where I will forward specific technical questions related to the book.

When you write, please be sure to include this book's title and author as well as your name, email address, and phone number. I will carefully review your comments and share them with the author and editors who worked on the book.

Email: feedback@quepublishing.com

Mail: Greg Wiegand
Que Publishing
201 West 103rd Street
Indianapolis, IN 46290 USA

For more information about this book or another Que title, visit our Web site at www.quepublishing.com. Type the ISBN (excluding hyphens) or the title of a book in the Search field to find the page you're looking for.

INTRODUCTION

If you are new to Windows XP or to Windows in general, this is the book for you. In easy-to-understand language and with step-by-step explanations, this book covers all the key tasks for using Windows XP.

Windows is an operating system. You don't need to know the hows and whys of an operating system. You just need to know there is one. And that the operating system is like the behind-the-scenes manager who takes care of all the basic computing tasks such as saving your work, printing a document, starting a program, and so on.

Therefore, you only need to learn how to perform these basic actions once. That is, once you learn how to print, you follow the same basic steps to print in all Windows programs. Once you learn how to start a program, you can start *any* program. Once you learn how to move or resize a window, you can perform this action for *any* window.

You'll find that learning how to use Windows is the same thing as learning how to use your computer.

Some Key Terms

To use Windows, you need to know the basic terminology used for common actions:

- *Point*—Move the mouse on the desk to move the pointer onscreen. The tip of the arrow should be on the item to which you are pointing. To open a menu or an icon, you point to the item you want.

- *Click*—Press and release the left mouse button once. You use click to select commands and toolbar buttons, as well as perform other Windows tasks.

- *Double-click*—Press and release the left mouse button twice in rapid succession. Double-clicking opens an icon. (See the next section for exceptions or changes to double-clicking.)

- *Right-click*—Press and release the right mouse button once. You often right-click to display a shortcut menu.

- *Drag*—Hold down the mouse button and drag the pointer across the screen. Release the mouse button. Dragging is most often used for selecting text.

Some Things to Keep in Mind

You can personalize many features of Windows so that it is set up the way you like to work. That's one of the benefits of Windows. For consistency, though, this book makes some assumptions about how you use your computer. When working through steps and especially when viewing the figures in this book, keep in mind the following distinctions:

- Windows provides many ways to perform the same action. For instance, for commands, you can select a command from a menu, use a shortcut key, use a toolbar button, or use a shortcut menu. This book covers one main method (the most common for that particular task) and also mentions other methods, usually in a tip.

- Your particular Windows setup may not look identical to the one used in the figures in this book. For instance, if you use a desktop image, you see that. (The figures in this book use a plain background.) Don't let these differences distract you; Windows may look different, but it works the same way.

- Your computer setup is most likely different than the one used in the book. Therefore, you will see different programs listed on your Start menu, different fonts in your Font list, different folders and documents, and so on. Again, don't be distracted by the differences.

- To open folders and files, you double-click the icon. You can also set up Windows to work similar to an Internet browser. That is, you can single-click to open an icon. This book assumes the double-click setup. If you use single-click, keep in mind that you single-click instead of double-click. You can read more about changing Windows's working mode in Chapter 20, "Viewing and Finding Files."

The Basic Structure of This Book

This book is divided into six parts, each centered around a certain theme. The book builds on the skills you need, starting with the basics and then moving to more complex topics such as networking. You can read the book straight-through, look up topics when you have a question, or browse through the contents, reading information that intrigues you.

This section provides a quick breakdown of the parts.

Part I, "The Basics," explains all the key tasks for using your computer. If you read only this section, you would have enough skill knowledge to perform most basic computer tasks. This part covers upgrading (Chapter 1), understanding the Windows desktop (Chapter 2), starting programs (Chapter 3), saving your work (Chapter 4), printing (Chapter 5), handling files (Chapter 6), and troubleshooting (Chapter 7).

Part II, "Communications," includes five chapters, each devoted to a particular Windows communication feature, including getting set up for communication (Chapter 8), sending and receiving email (Chapter 9), browsing and searching the Internet (Chapters 10 and 11), and faxing (Chapter 12).

Part III, "Entertainment," centers on the various ways you can use Windows as an entertainment medium, including playing music and videos and working with photographs and movies.

Part IV, "Your Own Personal Windows," explores the many changes you can make to how Windows operates. As you become more proficient, you'll find that you may want to change certain Windows elements, such as adding a desktop image (covered in Chapter 15 with other desktop customizing options), adding new programs (Chapter 16), and customizing email and Internet (Chapter 17) and printing (Chapter 18).

Although you don't need to know the ins and outs of computer maintenance (the topic of Part V) as a beginner, you'll find that you do need a reference and guide for the various maintenance tasks. Even though you won't perform these daily, you should be familiar with how to organize files (Chapter 19), find files (Chapter 20), use security measures (Chapter 21), improve your disk performance (Chapter 22), schedule maintenance tasks (Chapter 23), and upgrade hardware or Windows (Chapter 24).

The final part, Part VI, "Windows XP for Special Situations," covers what the part's name implies: special features for special situations. This part includes chapters on the many Windows accessory programs (Chapter 25), multiple user accounts (Chapter 26), accessibility options for those with special needs (Chapter 27), and home networking (Chapter 28).

Enjoy your learning journey!

Conventions Used in This Book

There are cautions, tips, and notes throughout this book.

A *caution* will tell you to beware of a potentially dangerous act or situation. In some cases, ignoring a caution could cause you significant problems—so pay particular attention to them!

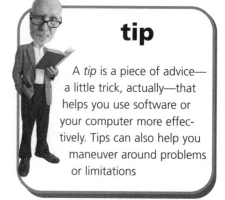

tip

A *tip* is a piece of advice—a little trick, actually—that helps you use software or your computer more effectively. Tips can also help you maneuver around problems or limitations

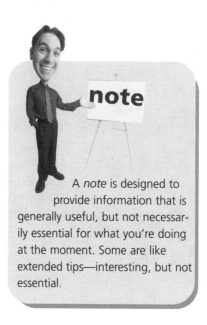

note

A *note* is designed to provide information that is generally useful, but not necessarily essential for what you're doing at the moment. Some are like extended tips—interesting, but not essential.

PART i

THE BASICS

1

UPGRADING TO MICROSOFT WINDOWS XP

Taking a Tour of What's New

If you have a brand-new computer, you might be interested in knowing what is different about Microsoft Windows XP, the most recent version of Windows. You might be curious especially if you have used other computer operating systems, such as Mac or Linux, or if you know someone who uses a different version, such as Windows 98 or Windows Me.

If you are upgrading to Windows XP, you want the same information: what's new and improved. This chapter gives an overview of most of the major changes as well as explains the basics of installing Windows XP, setting up user accounts, and transferring settings from another computer.

As mentioned, Windows XP, introduced in 2001, is the newest version of Windows. This version includes interface changes (how the operating system works and looks), new features (such as wizards and a movie-making program), behind-the-scenes changes (such as making your computer more stable), and others. Review this section to get a quick overview of what's different in Windows XP.

Revamped Start Menu

One of the first changes you notice with Windows XP is the revamped Start menu. The menu is now divided into two sections. The left section, by default, lists Internet and E-mail, two commonly used features. Below that, you see a list of the most often used programs. Rather than wade through the program menu, you can click one of these program icons to start that program (see Figure 1.1).

FIGURE 1.1

The structure of the Start menu is different, listing common programs and recently used programs on the left, folders and commands on the right.

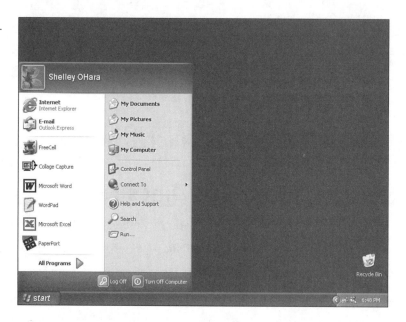

If the program is not listed, you can still start it by clicking the **Start** button and then the **All Programs** command. All your programs, within the program folders, are displayed. You learn more about starting programs in Chapter 3, "Starting Programs."

What else is new? When you install new programs, Windows highlights the new additions on the Start menu and also displays a pop-up ScreenTip noting that new programs have been added.

In the right pane, you see Windows XP folders and commands. Both **My Documents** and **My Computer** are listed on the **Start** menu rather than as desktop icons. In addition, the **Help** and **Support**, **Search**, and **Run** commands are part of the default **Start** menu.

At the bottom of the **Start** menu, you can use the **Log Off** button to turn off your computer, or switch to another user if multiple users are using the computer. The initial setup for multiple users is covered in this chapter. For complete details on managing user accounts, see Chapter 26, "Setting Up Windows XP for Multiple Users."

tip

You can change the menu, adding other programs to the left pane, for instance. See Chapter 16, "Setting Up Programs," later in this book.

Streamlined Desktop and Taskbar

The other obvious desktop change is the lone icon, the Recycle Bin. Although My Computer and My Documents are now listed on the Start menu rather than as desktop icons, you can add these icons as well as program icons to your desktop. See Chapter 16, "Setting Up Programs," for help with this change.

In addition to the newly styled desktop, the taskbar is a little different too. The clock always appears, but you can choose to hide or display other inactive status icons. Click the **arrow** button to expand the status bar area (usually called the *system tray*). Click the **arrow** button again to hide the inactive icons.

note

Look also for new messages from the system tray alerting you when a print job is finished, when new hardware is found and installed, when the printer is out of paper, and other behind-the-scenes status information.

Task Pane in Folder Windows

Windows XP now adds a task pane with common commands in file windows. These commands are context-sensitive. For example, if you select a folder, you see commands for working with folders. If you select a file, you see commands for working with files. If you select a picture, you see commands for working with pictures (see Figure 1.2).

FIGURE 1.2

Notice the new task pane as well as the new filmstrip view for the contents of a file window.

Windows XP also provides new views for displaying drive and folder contents. You can learn more about sorting, displaying, and customizing file windows in Chapter 20, "Viewing and Finding Files."

Redesigned Control Panel

To make most customization changes, you use the Control Panel. You can use the Control Panel icons to customize the display, change the mouse, add a new printer, and make other common changes.

In previous versions, all icons were listed in one window. As follows from the revamping of folder windows, the Control Panel now sports a different look. The default view groups icons by task (see Figure 1.3). Rather than find an icon by its category or feature, you can find it from a list of common tasks.

tip

For information on using the new task pane commands to manage files and folders, see Chapter 6, "Understanding the Basics of File Management."

tip

If you prefer to use the original view or if you can't find the Control Panel icon you need, switch to Classic View by clicking the **Switch to Classic View** command in the task pane of the Control Panel.

FIGURE 1.3

To display the Control Panel, click **Start** and then **Control Panel**. You can click any of the categories to display the features in that category.

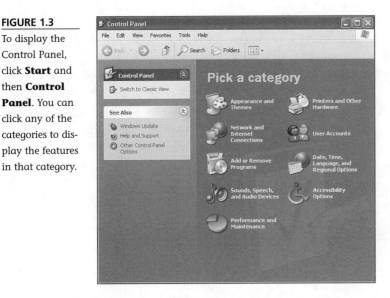

Internet Security and Privacy

Internet Explorer includes some new features designed to help make Web surfing more secure and more private. These features are especially critical as more people select alternative methods for connecting to the Internet. The top new Internet features include

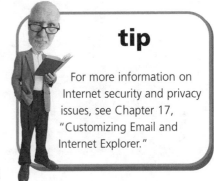

tip

For more information on Internet security and privacy issues, see Chapter 17, "Customizing Email and Internet Explorer."

- New Firewall protection feature for users on a network or with a 24/7 Internet broadband connection, such as cable and DSL
- New Privacy tab for setting privacy controls
- Command for deleting all cookies

Other Windows XP Highlights

In addition to the cosmetic changes, you will also find some behind-the-scenes changes that make Windows XP more stable, more secure, and easier to maintain. These features vary from simple wizards to help keep your files and desktop organized to more sophisticated wizards that set up home networking.

Here's a brief highlight of each feature as well as a reference for finding more information:

■ With Windows Movie Maker, a new program for editing videos, you can create storyboards and timelines, import video files, record videos, add narration, and perform all the other magic needed to create your own personal video films. Chapter 14, "Working with Photographs and Movies," covers not only this new movie program but also new features for working with pictures.

■ Use Windows Messenger to send and receive instant messages. You can add the names and email addresses of friends, co-workers, and family. When they are online, you are alerted. (You must also be online.) You can then type and send instant messages. Figure 1.4 shows the Windows Messenger window.

FIGURE 1.4

You can send instant messages using Windows Messenger.

■ Windows XP provides more support for digital cameras, with easier setup and a task list for the My Pictures folder that includes tasks for printing photos or ordering photo prints over the Internet. As another option, use the My Pictures folder links to email a favorite picture.

■ The Desktop Cleanup Wizard determines which desktop icons you are really using and which might be better off removed. You can access this wizard from the Desktop tab of the Display Properties dialog box. See Chapter 23, "Handling PC Maintenance," for more information.

■ Although speech recognition is not new, the availability of programs that take advantage of this technology are more common. More programs (in contrast to just specialized voice recognition programs) now take advantage of speech. For instance, in the new version of Office XP, you can dictate letters and access commands by speaking. Speech recognition is set up through Windows XP's Control Panel.

Installing Windows XP

If you purchased a new computer, Windows XP should already be installed. If you are upgrading, you need to install the new operating system.

The steps vary depending on your system and the choices you select, so step-by-step directions for each scenario are not provided. Keep in mind that installation is automated, so basically, you follow this process:

1. Insert the Windows XP disk into your drive. The setup program starts automatically (see Figure 1.5).

FIGURE 1.5

Use this menu to install Windows XP.

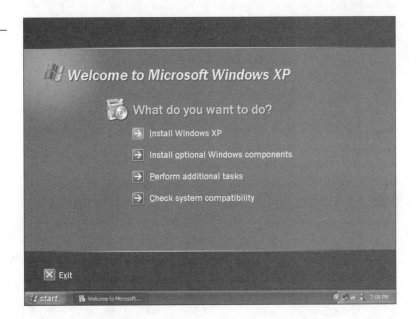

2. Select **Install Windows XP**.

3. For each step, make your selections and click **Next**. Each step is described in the wizard window, so use that as a guideline for making your choices. The setup program then installs Windows XP and sets up your hardware.

A key installation task with Windows XP is the Windows Product Activation. When you install Windows, you are prompted to activate your copy of Windows. You can do so online or via the phone line. You do not have to provide personal information (such as your address or phone number). At a minimum, you have to enter only the country or region in which you live.

If you don't activate the product during installation, you will be prompted to do so periodically (and frequently!). You have a grace period of 30 days. If you don't activate it by that time, you effectively are locked out of your computer. You can activate it through Microsoft and then start using the computer again.

Setting Up User Accounts

Because a computer—especially a home computer—is commonly used by more than one person, Windows XP makes it easy to set up accounts for each person, even remembering certain options for each person's setup, such as how the desktop appears, which Web sites are saved to a favorite list, and others. Each person can customize Windows XP to his or her liking without messing up someone else's choices.

When you install Windows XP, you are prompted to set up accounts. You can do so by entering the account names at the setup time. You can then make any changes using the Control Panel for User Accounts, covered in Chapter 26, "Setting Up Windows XP for Multiple Users."

Each time you turn on a computer, you see the list of the accounts. You can click your account to log on. When you are finished using your computer, you can log off by following these steps:

1. Click **Start**.

2. Click **Log Off**. You are prompted to confirm that you want to log off (see Figure 1.6).

3. Click **Log Off**. Windows logs you off and displays the logon screen listing all the icons and names for each user. Now another user can log on.

Windows XP might not set up all your hardware automatically. You might need to manually install drivers (files that tell Windows about a particular hardware device) after the Windows installation. Chapter 24, "Upgrading Windows," covers adding hardware.

tip

Microsoft periodically releases updates to Windows. You can update your version to the latest releases. You may also rerun the installation to install optional components. See Chapter 24 for information on these processes.

FIGURE 1.6

You can log off without restarting the computer.

To log on, click your username from the logon screen. All your personal settings are loaded, and you see the desktop and Start menu as you have set it up.

You can also go back and add new accounts, delete accounts, or change properties of an account. These user account features are covered in Chapter 28.

Transferring Settings

If you have an existing computer and purchase a new one, you don't need to go through the hassle of setting up all your preferences on the new computer. Instead, you can use the new Files and Settings Transfer Wizard to transfer files and settings from an old computer to a new one.

Desktop and display settings, settings for Internet Explorer and Outlook Express, and your dial-up connection information, and personal data such as the files and folders in My Documents are all transferred. You must establish a connection between the two computers either using a cable or through a network.

To use this feature, follow these steps:

1. Click **Start** and then click **All Programs**.

2. Click **Accessories**, **System Tools**, and then **Files and Settings Transfer Wizard**. You see the welcome screen; click **Next**. You are prompted to select which computer is which (see Figure 1.7).

FIGURE 1.7

Use the Files and Settings Transfer Wizard to copy key system settings from an old computer to the new one.

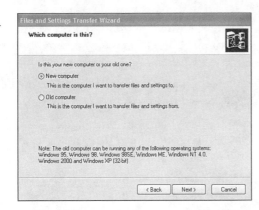

3. Make your selection and click **Next**. (Because the new computer has Windows XP and this new wizard, you most commonly select New computer for this step.) The wizard then displays a dialog box explaining that you need to run this wizard on your old computer. You can create a wizard disk or use your Windows XP disk (see Figure 1.8).

FIGURE 1.8

You can select how to get the wizard to run on the older computer.

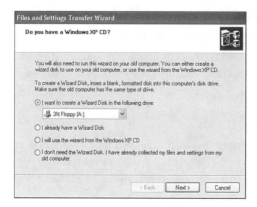

4. Make your selection on how to run the wizard on the old PC and click **Next**.

5. Continue making selections, clicking **Next** to advance to the next step. The dialog boxes explain the various choices you have. The exact steps you follow vary depending on your old computer and how you want to perform the transfer.

6. When the transfer is complete, click **Finish**. Your settings are now part of your new computer!

THE ABSOLUTE MINIMUM

This chapter provided an overview of what's new in Windows XP as well as covered how to install Windows, set up user accounts, and transfer settings (common tasks after the install). Keep in mind the following key points:

- Windows XP includes several interface changes including a redesigned Start menu, a desktop with just a single icon, and an expandable system tray (part of the taskbar).

- The file windows have also been revamped. They now include a task pane with commands pertinent to the contents in the window.

- Windows XP also includes new features such as wizards for cleaning up the desktop and a program for editing videos.

- You can start the install from the Windows XP CD. Follow the steps as out-lined in the installation wizard.

- You can set up accounts for each person who uses the computer. You can log off and then someone else can log on, all without restarting the computer.

- If you purchased a new computer and have an older computer, you can transfer some of your settings (such as your Internet connection) using the Files and Settings Transfer Wizard.

2

Getting Started With Windows XP

What's on the Desktop?

The Windows desktop is where all your work starts and ends. Getting familiar with the tools and features you can access from the desktop is the backbone of using a computer. Without these skills, you won't be able to do much. But with these skills, you will be able to start programs, work with files, check the status of any activities such as printing, and more. And luckily all these skills are easy to learn and practice.

The desktop is what you see when you first start your computer and Windows XP. The desktop provides access to all the programs and files on your computer (see Figure 2.1). Here's a quick overview of what you see:

Recycle Bin   Desktop

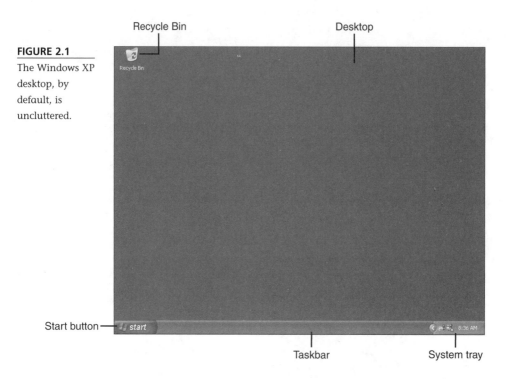

FIGURE 2.1

The Windows XP desktop, by default, is uncluttered.

Start button — start

Taskbar   System tray

■ The desktop is the background area. Think of this area as your computer "desk." You can place handy tools on the desktop so that you have fast access to them. For instance, you can add desktop icons.

■ Desktop icons provide access to commonly used programs, folders, and files. The only icon that appears by default is the Recycle Bin. You can place additional icons on the desktop for fast access to programs and folders. For instance, suppose that the program you use most often is Microsoft Word, a word processing program. You can add a program shortcut icon to the desktop so that you can quickly start the program. For more information on adding desktop icons, see Chapter 16, "Setting Up Programs." For information on rearranging the icons, see the section "Working with Icons."

tip

You can change the appearance of the desktop, selecting a different set of colors or using a picture for the background. See Chapter 15, "Customizing Windows XP," for more information.

■ The **Start** button is located in the lower-left corner and is used to display the **Start** menu. You learn more about this button in the following sections.

■ The taskbar displays a button for any open windows or programs. For instance, if you are working in a Word document, you see a taskbar for the program and document (see Figure 2.2). If you are viewing files in the My Documents folder, you see a button for that folder. The taskbar provides not only information about what's currently going on, but also provides a quick and simple way to switch among tasks. You do this by clicking the button for the program or window you want to make active.

FIGURE 2.2

The taskbar gives you a view of what you are currently working on.

■ The system tray includes status icons for current tasks. For instance, if you are printing, you see a printer icon. If you are connected to the Internet, you see a connection icon. For more on the system tray, see the section "Viewing the System Tray" later in this chapter.

The Start Menu

The **Start** menu provides a list of common programs and folder windows as well as buttons. Like its name implies, the **Start** menu is where you start! You can start programs or open common folders such as My Documents from this menu. To display the **Start** menu, click the **Start** button. The menu is displayed (see Figure 2.3).

FIGURE 2.3

Clicking the **Start** button reveals various commands; note also how different it looks from previous Windows versions.

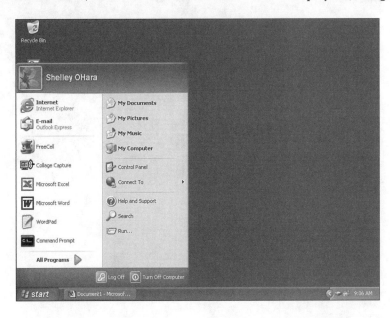

Lists Programs

At the top of the menu, you see the programs you use for the Internet and email. You can click the appropriate program icon to start the program. For instance, to start your email program, click **E-mail**.

Beneath the Internet and email programs is a list of several programs that you have recently used. What you see in your **Start** menu will be different from the list of programs that appear in Figure 2.3.

This list makes it easy to start frequently used programs: click the program name to start it. If a program is not listed, you can click the **All Programs** icon, which opens a list of programs installed on your computer (see Figure 2.4). You learn more about starting programs in Chapter 3, "Starting Programs."

note

By default, Windows XP lists Internet Explorer as the default Internet program and Outlook Express as the default mail program. If you use different programs, you can change the icon (see Chapter 16).

FIGURE 2.4

For access to all of the program folders and icons installed on your computer, use the **All Programs** command.

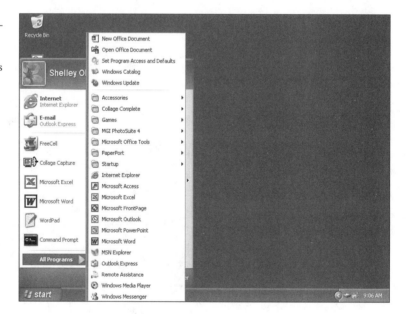

Includes Folders

On the right side of the **Start** menu, you see a list of default folders. You can click any of these folders—**My Documents**, **My Pictures**, **My Music**, **My Computer**—to open that folder. Figure 2.5, for instance, shows the results of clicking **My Computer**. Here you view all the drives and system folders on your computer. See Chapter 6, "Understanding File Management Basics," for more information on opening folders.

tip

You can turn the "last used program" feature off. Also, you can customize this list so that only your favorite programs appear as opposed to the last ones used. See Chapter 16, "Setting Up Programs," for more information.

FIGURE 2.5

You can use the **Start** menu to display My Computer.

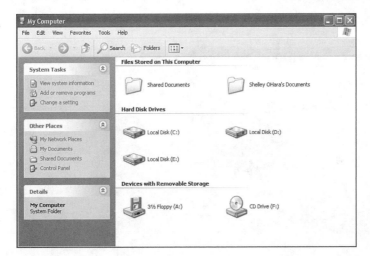

Displays Commands

In addition to folders, Windows XP lists commands such as **Control Panel**, **Connect To**, **Help and Support**, **Search**, and **Run on the Start** menu. You learn more about the purpose of these commands in later chapters in this book.

To select a command, follow these steps:

1. Click the command you want to execute. For instance, click **Control Panel** to

tip

Rather than include desktop icons for folders (as in previous versions), Windows XP lists the folders here on the Start menu. If you prefer the desktop icons, you can add them—see Chapter 15.

select this command. You see a window or dialog box that relates to this command.

For instance, if you click **Control Panel**, you see the Control Panel window listing common tasks (see Figure 2.6).

2. Do one of the following:

If you click **Run**, type the program you want to run.

If you click **Help and Support**, use the help window to display help information on a feature or topic. (Again, all these commands are covered later in this book.)

note

When you install new programs, Windows XP displays a ScreenTip on the **Start** menu. New programs also are highlighted in yellow.

FIGURE 2.6

The Control Panel provides "behind-the-scene" views of using Windows. You can use these features to customize how Windows works.

Enables You to Log or Turn Off

Along the bottom of the **Start** menu, you see some buttons: **Log Off** and **Turn Off Computer**.

When you are finished working with Windows, you can turn off your computer using the **Turn Off Computer** button. If someone else uses the computer, you can log off so that this person can log on. Use the **Log Off** button.

Working with Desktop Icons

By default, Windows XP displays the Recycle Bin on the desktop. This icon is usually located in the lower-right corner. You can use this icon to display (and possibly retrieve) files you have deleted. You can find out more about the Recycle Bin in Chapter 6, "Understanding File Management Basics."

If you prefer a clean, uncluttered desktop, you can keep it as is. If you are upgrading (and are used to the previous desktop layout, which includes icons for My Documents, My Computer, and others), you can add these icons, a process explained in this section.

You can add other shortcut icons so that you have convenient access to your most often used programs, such as Word, folders, and files. To add a program shortcut to the desktop, see Chapter 16.

Adding Folder Icons to the Desktop

To add My Documents, My Computer, or My Network Places icons to the desktop, follow these steps:

1. Right-click a blank area of the desktop to display the shortcut menu.

2. Click the **Properties** command. You see the Display Properties dialog box.

3. Click the **Desktop** tab to display these options.

4. Click the **Customize Desktop** button.

5. On the General tab, shown in Figure 2.7, check any of the Desktop icons you want displayed. For instance, to add the My Documents folder to the desktop, click the **My Documents** check box. You can select **My Documents**, **My Computer**, **My Network Places**, and **Internet Explorer**.

6. When you are finished, click **OK**. Any icon you checked now appears on the desktop.

tip

To close the **Start** menu without making a selection, click outside the menu or press the **Esc** key. As a shortcut, some keyboards include a Start key that you can press to display the **Start** menu.

If your computer freezes or if you make changes to key system features, you might need to restart. Click **Turn Off Computer** and then select **Restart**. For more information on shutting down the computer and restarting, see Chapter 7, "Troubleshooting Common Problems."

FIGURE 2.7

Use this dialog box to add desktop icons to the desktop and to change the appearance of these icons.

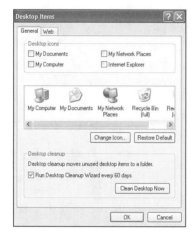

Moving Icons

You can place the icons on your desktop in any area. For instance, you might want to move the Recycle Bin from the lower-right corner to the upper-right so that it's the first thing you see. If you have added icons, you might want to rearrange them on the desktop.

You have two choices for moving: dragging the icon or having Windows arrange the icons. You can also keep the desktop icons equally spaced (or not evenly spaced) by using the **Align to Grid** command.

Follow these steps to drag an icon:

1. Position the mouse pointer over the icon.

2. Press and hold down the left mouse button and drag the icon to the location you want. The combination of press, hold, and drag is commonly referred to as simply "drag." That is, drag means to press and hold the mouse button while you move the mouse on the desktop.

3. When the icon is in the place you want, release the mouse button.

To have Windows arrange the icons, follow these steps:

1. Right-click a blank area of the desktop.

2. Click **Arrange Icons By** from the shortcut menu that appears and then select an order. You can arrange the icons by name, size, type, or modification date (see Figure 2.8).

   Or

Select **Auto Arrange**. Windows XP moves icons to the upper-left corner, spacing them equally down and then in a second column (to the right of the first column of icons) if needed.

Or

Select **Align to Grid**. When this command is checked, Windows XP keeps icons aligned to an underlying grid that spaces the icons automatically. To turn off this feature (if you want to place them closer together, for instance), uncheck the command.

> **tip**
>
> You can also use the shortcut menu to turn on or off desktop items, add and then lock Web items, and clean up the desktop using the Desktop Cleanup Wizard. You learn more about these features later in this book.

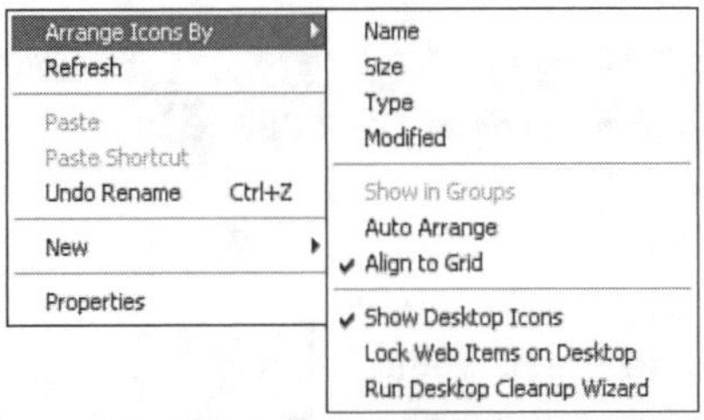

FIGURE 2.8

From the desktop shortcut menu, you can select arrangements for the icon.

Arrange Icons By ▶	Name
Refresh	Size
	Type
Paste	Modified
Paste Shortcut	
Undo Rename Ctrl+Z	Show in Groups
	Auto Arrange
New ▶	✓ Align to Grid
Properties	
	✓ Show Desktop Icons
	Lock Web Items on Desktop
	Run Desktop Cleanup Wizard

Viewing the Taskbar

The taskbar, as mentioned, contains buttons for all open windows and programs. The current window appears in a darker color. Any inactive windows use a button with a slightly lighter color as the taskbar. For instance, in Figure 2.9, the **My Computer** button is the active window (where you are currently working), and the Recycle Bin window is in the background.

The taskbar, then, gives you an idea of what you have running and which program or window is active (where you can work).

> **tip**
>
> If your desktop becomes too cluttered, you can delete icons. Note that if you delete a program shortcut icon, you are not deleting the program, just the icon. For more information on deleting and renaming icons or for uninstalling programs, see Chapter 16.

FIGURE 2.9

You can use the
taskbar to view
and change
among open
windows.

The taskbar also enables you to switch among
these open windows. To display a particular program or window, click the button in the taskbar.
For instance, to switch to the Recycle Bin window
in Figure 2.9, click the button for **Recycle Bin**.
That window becomes the active window.

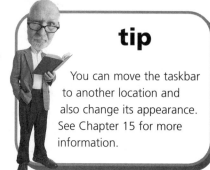

tip

You can move the taskbar
to another location and
also change its appearance.
See Chapter 15 for more
information.

Viewing the System Tray

The system tray is part of the taskbar and displays the current time as well as status icons. For
instance, Windows XP includes a notification
icon for automatic updates. You might also see icons for hardware components such
as a scanner (see Figure 2.10).

FIGURE 2.10

The system tray
displays notifi-
cation icons
highlighting
anything going
on with your
system.

Periodically, a notification message pops up from the system tray alerting you to events or suggesting actions. For instance, when a print job is successfully printed, you see a printer icon and then a message noting that the print job is complete. To close a message, click its **Close** button.

tip

You can hover the mouse pointer over the time to display the current date.

Windows XP also may prompt you to check for new updates or to try out certain features (especially MSN Messenger, which you can use to get and send Instant Messages). To access one of the highlighted features, click in the message.

Also, Windows XP can collapse the system tray to hide notification icons. To expand the area, click the left-pointing arrow next to the icons. The area will automatically return to the original view after a few seconds. You can also immediately hide the icons by clicking the now right-pointing icon.

Working with Windows

Windows XP displays all programs and content in a window on the desktop. When you start a program, for instance, you see the program window. When you open a folder, you see the contents in a window. Part of mastering XP is learning to manipulate the windows so that you can see and work with the area you want. For instance, you might want to move windows so that you can see more than one. You might want to maximize a window so that it fills the entire desktop area. You use the window controls as well as other window parts (title bar and border) to manipulate the window. This section covers common window tasks.

Opening and Closing Windows

To open a program window, start the program (as covered in Chapter 2, "Getting Started with Windows XP "). To open a content window, double-click the drive or folder icon from the desktop or select the folder from the **Start** menu. For instance, click **Start** and then **My Computer** to open this window (see Figure 2.11). The current window appears on top of any other open windows, and the title bar is brighter.

When a window is open, you see the controls for the window in the upper-right corner (from left to right: **Minimize**, **Maximize**, and **Close**). For example, to close a window, click its **Close** button as shown in Figure 2.11.

Title bar

Maximize button ——
Minimize button ——
Close button

FIGURE 2.11

All windows include common controls for working with that window.

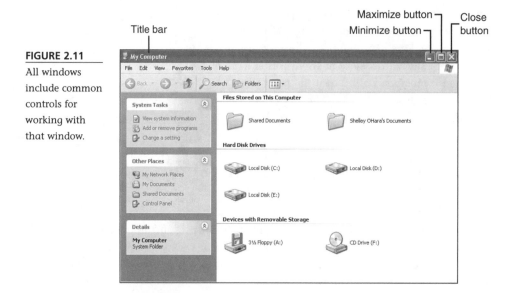

The window closes and disappears from the taskbar and desktop. If you close a program window, you also exit the program. (You learn more about programs in Chapter 3.)

Changing the Size of Windows

In addition to opening and closing, you can change the size of the windows. Windows XP uses special terms to describe the various sizes of a window including maximized, minimized, and restored. The changes you can make to the size of a window are covered here.

Maximizing a Window

A maximized window fills the entire desktop and does not have borders (see Figure 2.12). You commonly maximize program windows when you want to have the maximum display area for the work. To maximize a window so that it fills the entire screen, click its **Maximize** button.

When you maximize a window, the **Maximize** button changes to a **Restore** button which you can use to return the window to its original size.

FIGURE 2.12
Maximize a window when you want to make it as big as possible.

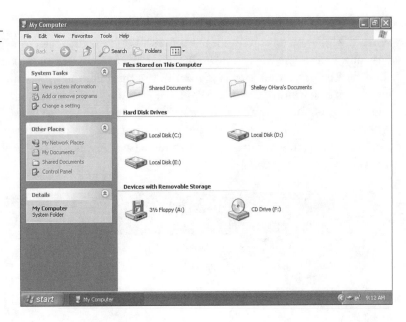

FIGURE 2.12
Maximize a window when you want to make it as big as possible.

Minimizing a Window

A minimized window is hidden from view (not closed) and is represented with a taskbar button (see Figure 2.13). To minimize a window (shrink it to a taskbar button), click its **Minimize** button. You can redisplay the window by clicking its button. You often minimize a window when you need handy access to it but don't want to use desktop space for the display of that window.

FIGURE 2.13
Minimizing a window hides it from view but still keeps it available.

Restoring a Window

When a window is open and not maximized, Windows uses the term "restore." Basically, you restore the window to its original size. To restore a maximized window, click the **Restore** button (see Figure 2.14). Use this size when you want to display more than one window on the desktop. For instance, if you are copying data from one program to another, you can view both windows and move between them. When a window is this size, it has borders so that you can resize it manually. You can also use the title bar to move the window (see "Arranging the Windows" later in this chapter.)

FIGURE 2.14

A restored window has borders that you can drag to resize.

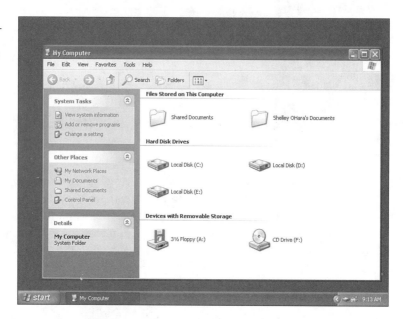

Resizing a Window

When a window is restored, you can change its size. To resize a window, put the mouse pointer on a border and then drag the border to resize the window. Remember that you can only resize restored windows. You cannot resize a maximized window.

Arranging the Windows

When you have more than one window open, you may need to arrange them on the desktop. As mentioned, you might copy data from one document or program to another. You might open several windows when you are doing file maintenance such as copying or moving a file. In any case, you can move the windows around the desktop by dragging, or you can have Windows XP arrange the windows.

To move a window, follow these steps:

1. Put the mouse pointer on the title bar.

2. Drag the window to the location you want. The window is moved.

tip

You can also display toolbars in the taskbar. For information on taskbar toolbars, see Chapter 15.

To have Windows XP arrange the windows, follow these steps:

1. Right-click a blank area of the taskbar to display the shortcut menu.

2. Select one of the commands for arranging the windows:

3. Click **Cascade Windows** to arrange the windows in a waterfall style, layered on top of each other from the upper-left corner down (see Figure 2.15).

FIGURE 2.15

The cascade view shows all open windows, one on top of the other.

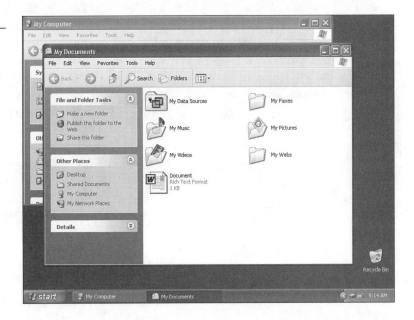

4. Click **Tile Windows Horizontally** to make all the windows the same size and place them horizontally next to each other.

5. Click **Tile Windows Vertically** to make all the windows the same size but place them vertically in order (see Figure 2.16).

FIGURE 2.16

Tiled windows is
another
arrangement
choice.

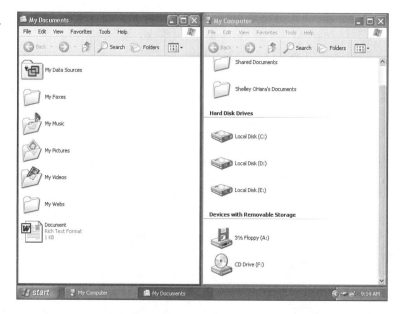

6. Click **Show the Desktop** to minimize
   all open windows. If you redisplay the
   taskbar shortcut menu, you can select
   Show Open Windows to redisplay the
   windows.

tip

You can undo the arrange-
ment and revert to the
original placement by right-
clicking the taskbar and
then selecting the **Undo**
command. The name of
the command varies
depending on the arrangement.
For instance, if you have tiled the
windows, the command is **Undo
Tile**.

THE ABSOLUTE MINIMUM

This chapter gave you a good basic framework for learning to manipulate windows. You can apply the skills you've learned here to all the programs you use and all the maintenance and file-keeping tasks you need to do while using the Windows XP operating system. In summary, keep these points in mind:

- The desktop is your starting place. Any programs you run or windows you open are displayed on the desktop.

- The **Start** menu is what it says—your starting place! Use this menu to start programs, open folders, access commands such as Help and Support, log off, and turn off and restart.

- You can place new desktop icons on the desktop. You can also move the icons around on the desktop.

- To see what programs and windows are open, check the taskbar. Also, to review any system notifications or information, check the system tray, the far-right corner of the taskbar.

- Everything you see in Windows will be displayed in a window (little w). For example, when you want to view the contents of a drive or folder or start a program, you open a window. Every window has controls so that you can place it and resize it in a way that is most convenient for the task at hand.

3

STARTING PROGRAMS

Starting a Program from the Start Menu

Most of your time on the computer will be spent working in some type of program—a word processing program to type letters, a spreadsheet program to create budgets, a database to keep track of contacts, and so on. So one of the most important skills is learning how to start a program.

Because different people prefer different ways of working, Windows XP provides many options for starting programs. What's the best way? The way *you* like. Pick the one that is easiest for you.

When you install a new Windows program, that program's installation procedure sets up a program icon (and sometimes a program folder if the program includes several components. For example, a scanning program may include a program for executing the scan as well as a program for working with and saving the scanned document). These are listed within the **Start** menu.

The **Start** menu provides two methods for starting a program. If you recently used a program, you can select it from the left pane of the **Start** menu. If the program is not listed, you can display all programs and then select the program from the longer menu. This section covers both of these methods.

Starting a Recent Program

Follow these steps to start a recently used program:

1. Click the **Start** button. The left pane displays the last several programs you used (see Figure 3.1).

FIGURE 3.1

If you recently used a program, select it from the short list on the **Start** menu.

2. Click the program. That program is started, and you see the program window.

Listing All Programs

Follow these steps to view and select from a list of all programs:

1. Click **Start** and then click **All Programs**. You see a list of all the program icons and program folders (see Figure 3.2).

FIGURE 3.2

You can access all installed programs by clicking the **All Programs** button on the **Start** menu.

2. If necessary, click the program folder. Any items with an arrow next to them are program folders rather than icons. When you click the program folder, you see the program icons within that folder. For instance, if you click **Accessories**, you see the Accessory programs included with Windows XP. Follow this step until you see the icon for the program you want to start.

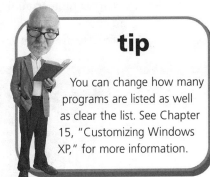

tip

You can change how many programs are listed as well as clear the list. See Chapter 15, "Customizing Windows XP," for more information.

3. Click the program icon to start the program. The program opens in its own window, and a taskbar button for the program appears in the taskbar. Figure 3.3 shows WordPad, a program included with Windows XP.

FIGURE 3.3

The program is opened in its own program window.

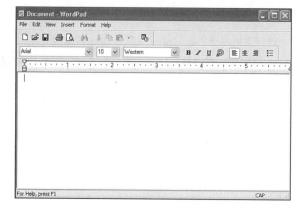

Starting a Program from a Shortcut Icon

In addition to the **Start** menu, you can also start programs from shortcut icons. Some programs automatically create shortcut icons, placing them on the desktop.

Figure 3.4 shows a shortcut icon for Outlook Express added to the desktop. Notice the little arrow on the icon; this indicates that the icon is a shortcut to that program. You can add shortcut icons to programs yourself, as covered in Lesson 16, "Setting Up Programs."

tip

To display a folder, you can simply point to it rather than click. If you have trouble getting the folder to stay open, it is easier to click than point.

FIGURE 3.4

You can place shortcut icons to programs on your desktop and then use these icons to start the program.

To start a program from a shortcut icon, double-click the shortcut icon on the desktop. The program starts and is displayed in its own window. A taskbar button appears for the program.

Switching Between Programs

You often work with more than one type of program at the same time. Windows XP enables you to quickly switch from one program to another. For example, you might want to review sales figures in a worksheet while at the same time creating a sales report in a word processing program. Switching between programs enables you not only to view data from several sources but also to share data among programs.

If the program doesn't start, you might not have double-clicked quickly enough. You must keep the mouse pointer in the same location and click twice. Sometimes beginners click, move, click the mouse, and this won't work. If you continue to have problems with clicking, change the mouse speed. See Chapter 15 for more information.

As mentioned, when you start a program, a button for that program is displayed in the taskbar. To switch to another program, simply click the button for that program. That program becomes the active program. For example, in Figure 3.5, Outlook Express is open as well as WordPad. You can tell that WordPad is the current program because its button is darkened. To switch to Outlook Express, click its button.

FIGURE 3.5

The taskbar buttons display the document and program name for each open program and window.

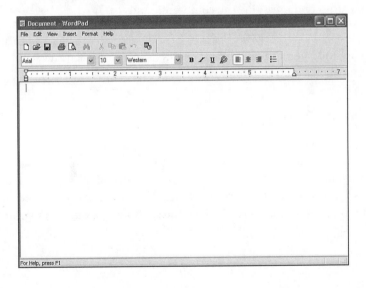

Trying Fancier Methods for Starting

So far this chapter has covered the most common ways to start a program. As you become more proficient, you might experiment with other ways of starting as explained in the following scenarios:

- You can start a program from the actual program file (not the same as a shortcut icon although you do the same thing: double-click the icon to start the program). When you install a program, the installation program copies the program file(s) to your hard drive. These programs are most often stored in the Program Files folder. (You learn more about navigating among your computer's folders in Chapter 6, "Understanding File Management Basics.") You can open this folder and double-click the program icon to start the program.

- You can start a program using the **Run** command on the **Start** menu. This command is often used to run installation programs or DOS programs.

- You can add a program to the Startup group. Windows XP automatically starts any programs in this special system folder each time you start Windows.

- You can assign a shortcut key to a program and press this key combination to start the program.

You can find out more about these methods in Chapter 16, "Setting Up Programs."

tip

You might hear different terms used to describe starting a program, including running, launching, and starting. These all mean the same thing. Also, programs can be referred to as programs, software, applications, or some combination (software application).

Working in a Program

When the program is started, you see the program window. A great thing about Windows XP is that all program windows share similar features (see Figure 3.6). Learning to use one program helps you master key skills for almost all other programs. For example, most programs include a menu bar that works the same in all programs. This section covers some basic skills for working in programs.

Toolbar   Menu bar

FIGURE 3.6

Get familiar
with the basic
program window
features.

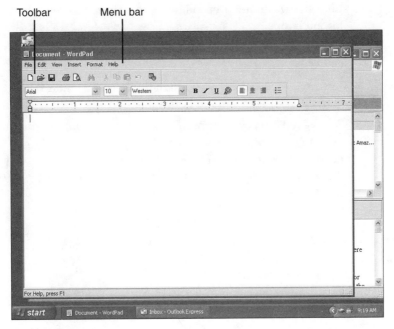

Selecting Commands

The top line of the program window is called the *title bar* and includes the name of
the document (or a generic name if the document has not been saved) and the program name.

Below the title bar, you see the menu bar. You use this to select commands. For
instance, open the **File** menu and select the **Save** command to save a document. To
use a menu, follow these steps:

1. Click the menu name. The menu drops down and displays a list of commands. For instance, in Figure 3.7, you see the **File** menu in WordPad.

FIGURE 3.7

To open a menu,
click its name in
the menu bar.

2. Click the command. Depending on the command you select, one of the following happens:

The command is executed. For instance, if you select File, Exit the program is closed.

You see a submenu. Any commands followed by an arrow display a submenu. Click the command in this menu to execute the selected command.

You see a dialog box prompting you for additional information about how to execute the command. For example, if you select File, Print you see the Print dialog box. You can select options for printing such as the printer to use and the number of copies to print. See the upcoming section "Selecting Dialog Box Options."

You'll find that not only do the menus work the same in most programs, but also many programs include the same commands. For example, you can commonly find a **File**, **Save** command for saving documents (covered in Chapter 4, "Saving Your Work"). **File**, **Print** is another common command; printing is covered in Chapter 5, "Printing." The **Edit** menu usually has commands for cutting text (**Cut**), copying text (**Copy**), and pasting cut or copied text (**Paste**). The **Help** menu provides access to online help; you can use the commands in this menu to look up help topics for the program. You learn more about help in Chapter 7, "Troubleshooting Common Problems."

> **tip**
>
> Many commands have a keyboard shortcut. Instead of selecting the command, you can press the keyboard shortcut. For instance, the shortcut for printing is **Ctrl+P** (press and hold the Ctrl key and then press the P key). These shortcuts are listed next to the command name on the menu.

Using the Keyboard to Select Commands

If you are a fast typist, you might prefer to keep your hands on the keyboard and use the keys to open and select a menu command. You can use the keyboard shortcuts, or you can select menu commands with the keyboard. Follow these steps to use the keyboard for opening menus:

1. Press the **Alt** key. Notice that the program's menus now have an underlined letter. This is the letter you press to open the menu and select the command. For instance, press **Alt** and then look at File. To open this menu, press the **F** key.

2. Press the key letter for the menu. You see a drop-down list of commands. Notice again that each command has one key letter underlined (see Figure 3.8).

FIGURE 3.8

You can use the
keyboard to
select
commands.

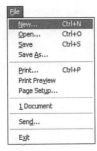

3. Press the key letter for the command.

Selecting Dialog Box Options

As mentioned, when you select some commands,
a dialog box appears prompting you for additional information. Like menus, dialog boxes
work the same across most Windows programs.
(This also includes commands in Windows itself.)

Dialog boxes vary from command to command
and from program to program. But they do
include like features that you select in the same
way:

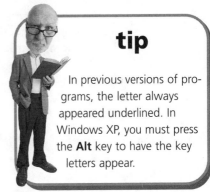

tip

In previous versions of programs, the letter always
appeared underlined. In
Windows XP, you must press
the **Alt** key to have the key
letters appear.

■ Tabs—If the dialog box has many options, they may be divided into tabs or
pages. Click the tab you want to view from the page of options. For example,
if you select **View**, **Options** in WordPad, you see the Options dialog box
with several tabs (see Figure 3.9). Click the tab you want.

FIGURE 3.9

Click the tab for
the options you
want to select.

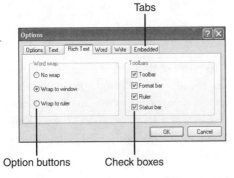

Tabs

Option buttons   Check boxes

■ Check boxes—Some options can be turned on or off, and these are controlled with check boxes (refer to Figure 3.9). If a box is checked, the option is on. If the box is unchecked, the option is off. You can click within the box to toggle between on and off. With check boxes, you can select as many options in a group as you want.

■ Option buttons—When you can select just one option in a group of options, you see radio or option buttons rather than check boxes. The button that is darkened is the one that is selected. You can select another option by clicking its option button (refer to Figure 3.9).

■ List boxes—For some options, you can select from a list. Sometimes the list is displayed, and you can click the item in the list that you want to select. You can also scroll through the list to view other options. For instance, in Figure 3.10, the Font list enables you to select a font. (To follow along, click **Format**, **Font** in WordPad.)

List box

FIGURE 3.10

You can select items from a list.

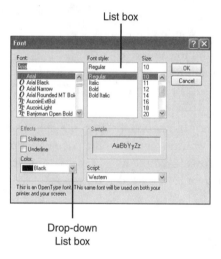

Drop-down
List box

■ Drop-down list boxes—To conserve space, some list boxes are condensed and only the current option is displayed. You can display and select from other options by clicking the down arrow next to the option and then clicking the new option you want to select. For instance, you can click **Color** in the Font dialog box and then select from a palette of colors (see Figure 3.11).

FIGURE 3.11

Click the down arrow next to a drop-down list to view the complete list of options.

■ Text boxes—For some items, you can enter text. For instance, you can enter the name of a file when you save a document. (Saving your work is the focus of the next chapter.) To enter something in a text box, click in the box and select the current entry. Then type your new entry. In Figure 3.12, for instance, you can type the page range to print.

FIGURE 3.12

This dialog box includes spin boxes, a text box, and command buttons.

■ Spin boxes—For values (numbers), programs commonly use a spin box. In this type of box, you can type the value or use the arrows to increase or decrease the value. The **Number of copies** option in Figure 3.12 is one example of a spin box.

■ Command buttons—Most dialog boxes include a confirm and cancel button. The confirm button is usually OK, but it may vary. For instance, when printing a document, you click the **Print** button to carry out the command. To cancel the options and command, click the **Cancel** button.

Using Right-Click Shortcut Menus

Because each person prefers a different style for performing certain tasks, Windows programs provide many ways to perform these common tasks. For instance, I like to use the keyboard because I am a fast typist and don't like to take my hands away from the keyboard to use the mouse. Beginners often use the menu commands because they are easier to figure out than toolbar buttons (covered next). Long-time computer users often use keyboard shortcuts because originally (wayyyyy back) programs were not menu-driven.

So yet another method for selecting commands is using the shortcut menu. To display this menu, right-click on the area you want to modify. For instance, right-click on some text to display a text shortcut menu in a word processing program. Right-click on a picture to display picture commands. You can even use the right-click within Windows: right-click the desktop to display desktop commands (see Figure 3.13); right-click the taskbar to display taskbar commands.

tip

Some dialog boxes provide access to still more options. For instance, you can click the Preferences button in the Print dialog box to display the Printing Preferences options for the printer. If you click one of these buttons, select the options and then click **OK** to return to the primary dialog box.

FIGURE 3.13

Another method for selecting commands is using a shortcut menu.

The commands you see vary depending on what you right-click. To select a command from a shortcut menu, click its name. To close the shortcut menu without making a selection, press **Esc** or click with the left mouse button outside of the menu area.

Using the Toolbar

In addition to using the menus and keyboard shortcuts, you can also use toolbar buttons to select commands. Most Windows programs include toolbar(s), which are displayed right under the menu bar. The buttons vary depending on the program, but most of them are similar. Figure 3.14 shows the toolbar buttons in WordPad.

FIGURE 3.14

Look for a tool-
bar for fast
access to com-
mon commands.

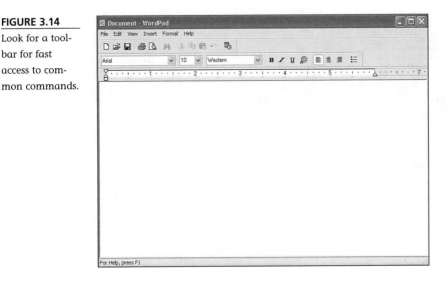

The following list gives you some insight on how to work with toolbars:

■ Toolbar buttons are shortcuts to commands. You can click the button instead
of selecting the command. For instance, click the **Save** button to save a document (same as selecting File, Save).

■ If you aren't sure what a toolbar does, hover the mouse pointer over the edge
of the toolbar. A **ScreenTip** (the button name) should appear.

■ Some programs have more than one toolbar. Usually the standard toolbar
includes buttons for common commands (**Save**, **Open**, **New**, and so on). The
program may also include a toolbar with formatting options (usually called
the Formatting toolbar or the Format bar). This toolbar includes buttons that
let you quickly make formatting changes
such as making text bold, changing the
font, and so on.

■ If you see a down arrow next to a command, you can click this arrow to display
a drop-down list of choices (see Figure
3.15). Then click the option you want to
select. For instance, you can click the
down arrow next to the **Font** button to
display a list of available fonts. From the
list, click the one you want to use.

tip

You can learn the basics of
entering, formatting, and
editing text by practicing
with WordPad. See Chapter
25, "Using Windows
Accessory Programs," for
more information.

FIGURE 3.15

If you see an
arrow next to a
button, click it to
display all your
button options.

If you don't use the toolbar and want more
room for the document to be displayed, turn
off the toolbar. You can also select to display
more than one toolbar in some programs
such as Word for Windows. Look in the
View menu for a Toolbar or **Toolbars** command. Any toolbars that are checked are
displayed (see Figure 3.16). The command is
a toggle: select the command to uncheck
and hide the toolbar. To display the toolbar,
select it again so that there is a check next
to it.

Another common fea-
ture in program windows is
the window control buttons. These
are located in the upper-right corner, and you can use these buttons
to change the size and shape of
the window. Chapter 2, "Getting
Started with Windows XP," covers
these buttons in detail.

FIGURE 3.16

Turn on or off
toolbars using
the **View** menu.

Exiting a Program

When you finish working in a program, close it to free system memory. (Your system memory is the working area of the computer where data and programs are stored temporarily while you are working within the program and on a document.) Too many open programs can tax your system's memory and slow the computer's processes. You can use one of several methods to close a program:

■ Click File and then click the Exit command. The program closes.

■ Click the **Close** button for the program window.

■ Press **Alt+F4**.

The program is closed.

If you created a document in the program, be sure to save before you exit. If you have not saved a file and you close the program, you are prompted to save. To save the document, click **Yes.** To close the document without saving, click **No**. To return to the document without exiting the program, click **Cancel**. See Chapter 4, "Saving Your Work," for the important details on saving files.

The Absolute Minimum

This chapter explains not only how to start programs but also how to work with common program features such as menu bars and toolbars. In summary, keep these points in mind:

■ You can start a program using the **Start** menu or a shortcut icon.

■ The menu bar enables you to select commands. Click the menu name to display the menu and then click the command you want. You may be prompted to select additional options for the command in a dialog box. Make your selections and click the command button (usually OK).

■ Other methods for selecting commands include keyboard shortcuts, shortcut menus, and toolbars.

■ When you are finished working in a program, save your work (covered in the next chapter) and then exit the program. You can exit using the File, Exit command or by clicking the program window's **Close** button.

4

SAVING YOUR WORK

Saving a Document

The most important computer skill you can learn is saving your work. Whether you are creating a budget, typing a resume, or entering checks in a checkbook program, saving your work is key. This chapter covers the basics of not only saving a document but also opening a saved document, creating a new document, and more. Like the previous two chapters, the skills you learn in this chapter are skills you can use throughout your computing experience. That's one of the great things about Windows XP: Basic skills such as saving or opening a document work the same in most Windows programs.

When you work in most programs, you save your work as some type of document—a word processing file such as a memo, a worksheet file such as a budget, a database file such as a list of clients, and so on. One of the most important things you should remember about using a computer is that you need to save your work and save often.

When you save your work, the program saves the file in an appropriate file format or type. For instance, if you save a document created in Word, that program saves the file as a DOC or Word file. Excel saves your spreadsheets (formally known as *worksheets* and *workbooks*) as XLS files.

The first time you save a file, you must assign that file a name and location. You can include up to 255 characters for the name, including spaces. Sometimes the program suggests a name, but it's better to replace the suggested name with a more descriptive name that you can remember.

For the location, you can select any of the drives and folders on your computer. The dialog box for saving a document has tools for navigating to and selecting another drive or folder for the file.

Follow these steps to save a document:

1. Click **File** and then click the **Save As** command. You see the Save As dialog box (see Figure 4.1).

2. Type a name—for example, **Christmas Shopping List**, or something you can readily relate to as discussed previously.

3. Select the location for the file:

   To save the document in another folder, double-click that folder if it is listed.

   To select one of the common folders, click the icon in the Places Bar. For instance, click the **My Computer** icon to open that folder.

   If the folder is not listed, you can move up through the folder structure by clicking the **Up One Level** button.

   To select another drive or folder, display the Save in drop-down list and then select the drive or folder.

tip

This chapter covers all the key document tasks except for printing. See Chapter 5, "Printing," for more information on this topic.

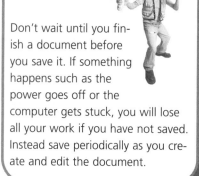

Don't wait until you finish a document before you save it. If something happens such as the power goes off or the computer gets stuck, you will lose all your work if you have not saved. Instead save periodically as you create and edit the document.

Places bar

Up One Level button

Create New Folder button

Dialog box for
saving in
WordPad. The
dialog box
options may
vary from
program to
program.

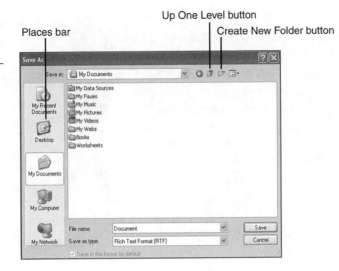

4. Click **Save**.

The document is saved, and the title bar displays the name of the document (see
Figure 4.2).

FIGURE 4.2

The name of
your document
appears in the
title bar after
you save. In this
example, the
document is
saved as
"Outline."

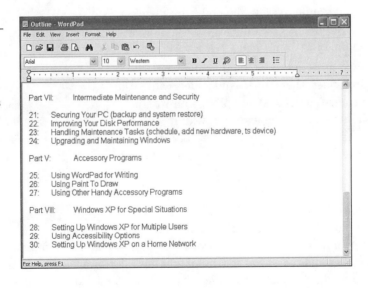

Switching Folders

The dialog box for saving a document provides tools for selecting another folder and for creating a new folder. To save a document in another folder, you open that folder. As mentioned, you have several options for navigating to that folder. Navigating through your folders is important for saving a document and also opening a document (covered later in this chapter).

Most computers have one or more hard drives where documents and programs are permanently stored. The default drive is named drive C:, but you may also have additional hard drives (lettered D:, E:, and so on).

Windows XP sets up one main folder for documents called My Documents. To keep files organized, folders are created (either by Windows, by a program, or by you) and like files are stored together. You can easily and quickly select this folder from the **Start** menu and from most Save dialog boxes; therefore, the My Documents folder makes a good choice as your main folder

But you don't want to lump all your documents into one folder. Therefore, create folders within that folder (called subfolders) and place your work in one of these folders. For example, within My Documents, you might have folders for reports, worksheets, memos, and so on. Or you might create folders for each project. (As an example, I create a new folder for each book that I write.)

You basically have a path, then, starting at the top (your hard drive) it burrows down into folders and folders within folders. If you think of yourself as a groundhog tunneling through to a particular folder, you can see that if you have burrowed down one path and want to go to another branch, you have to backtrack up through the tunnels to a fork and then down to access other paths in the tunnel.

tip

The steps for saving a document are basically the same from program to program. Some programs offer additional options for saving. Be sure to check your program's manual for information about any additional ways to save your files.

note

You learn more about file management basics in Chapter 6, "Understanding File Management Basics." But this section gives you a quick summary of how documents are stored on your computer.

For instance, suppose that you have this folder structure:

My Documents

Books

Absolute Beginners Guide to Windows XP

Easy Windows XP

Worksheets

Budgets

Project Tracking

If you open My Documents, you see these folders: Books and Worksheets. (You also will see any other subfolders, including some additional folders such as My Pictures and My Music that Windows XP has set up.) You can double-click either of these folders to open that folder (refer to Figure 4.1).

If you open Books, you again have two folders that you can open: Absolute Beginners Guide to Windows XP and Easy Windows XP. Again, you can double-click either of these folders to open that folder.

This process of tunneling down is straightforward because you can see listed what your options are. Where it can get confusing is when you want to move to another branch of the folder structure.

If you want to open Budgets, for instance, you need to backtrack. You need to move back two levels to My Documents and then tunnel down through Worksheets and then Budgets. In a dialog box, you use the **Up One Level** button to jump back a level. You can also go to the top level or to another drive using the Save in drop-down list (see Figure 4.3).

note

Your computer also most likely has a floppy drive (usually drive A:) and another media drive. Your media drive may be a CD drive, a CD-R or RW drive, or a DVD drive. You can insert a disk into one of these drives to open it. You can also save documents to a floppy drive and to a rewritable media drive. See Chapter 19, "Organizing Files," for more information on using other drives.

At first, navigating to folders may be confusing, but you will quickly get the hang of it. You use the same techniques for saving a document and for opening a document. It's also important to use good organization for your work, a topic covered in Chapter 6, "Understanding File Management Basics," to make it easy to navigate among folders and find documents.

FIGURE 4.3

Use the **Up One Level** button to jump up a level. Use the Look in drop-down list as another way to move up through a folder and drive organization.

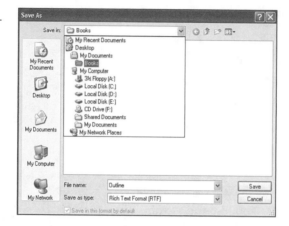

Creating a New Folder

You can set up folders before you save your document and then navigate to them when you're ready to save. You also can create a new folder on-the-fly—that is, when you are saving the document. To create a new folder on-the-fly, follow these steps:

1. Click the **Create New Folder** button. You see a new folder icon with the default name New Folder (see Figure 4.4).

FIGURE 4.4

You can create a new folder when you save a document.

2. Type the new folder name and press **Enter**. The folder is added.

3. Open the new folder and then follow the steps for saving (type a filename and click **Save**). The document is saved to this new folder.

Tips for Saving a Document

Because saving is critical, most programs provide
many shortcuts and safeguards for saving.
Review the following list of tips for saving:

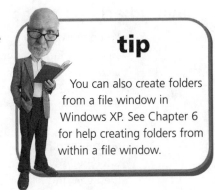

tip

You can also create folders
from a file window in
Windows XP. See Chapter 6
for help creating folders from
within a file window.

■ The first time you save a document, you
see the Save As dialog box even if you do
not select the **Save As** command. This
dialog box is displayed automatically to
remind you to type a filename and select
a location for the file.

■ After you've saved and named a file, you
can click **File** and select **Save** to resave that file to the same location with
the same name. When you save again, the disk file is updated to include any
changes or additions you made to the file.

■ Instead of the **Save** command, you can also use the toolbar shortcut (look for
a **Save** button) or a keyboard shortcut (most often **Ctrl+S**).

■ If you close a document or exit a program without saving, that program
prompts you to save (see Figure 4.5). You can click **Cancel** to return to the
document, click **No** to close the document without saving, or click **Yes** to save
the document. If you have saved previously, the program saves the document
with the same filename and in the same location. If you have not yet saved,
you see the Save As dialog box for entering a name and location.

FIGURE 4.5

Most programs
remind you to
save if you close
the document or
exit the program
without saving.

■ Just because the program reminds you to save doesn't mean that you should
rely on this reminder. Get in the habit of saving before you exit. It is easy to
whiz past the reminder prompt and possibly lose your work.

■ Some programs save your work automatically. For instance, a database is
saved each time you add a new record. You do not have to select a particular
command to save the data. The same is also true of check-writing programs
such as Quicken or Microsoft Money. Again, think "save" first and then check
out any automatic save features to be careful.

Saving Backup Copies

You often want to have more than one copy of a document. For instance, you might save a backup copy to another drive or disk. You also might use one document to create a new, similar document. You learn more about backing up files in Chapter 21, "Securing Your PC." You can also use the File, Save As command to create a duplicate document.

For instance, you might have a cover letter that you want to reuse, changing the address or other information. Instead of retyping the letter, you can open the original letter, save it with a different name (and therefore create a new document), and then edit and resave this copy. To use the **Save As** command to create a new document, follow these steps:

1. Click **File** and then click the **Save As** command. You see the Save As dialog box (refer to Figure 4.1).

2. Type a new name.

3. Select a different location for the file if you want to store the new file in another location.

4. Click **Save**.

A new document is created and saved. This document remains open so that you can continue working. The original document remains on disk, intact or unchanged.

Saving in a Different File Format

Another common saving task is to save a document in a different format. Sometimes you share your work with someone who doesn't have the same version of a particular program that you have or perhaps uses a different program entirely. Because sharing data is common, most programs enable you to select from several basic file formats. For instance, in most word processing programs, you can save a document in a plain vanilla format (as a text file), as a document with some formatting changes (rich text format—RTF), as other popular program file types, or as previous versions of the same program.

To save a document in a different file format, follow these steps:

1. Click **File** and then click the **Save As** command. You see the Save As dialog box (refer to Figure 4.1).

2. Type a new name, if necessary.

3. Select a different location for the file, if needed.

4. Display the Save as type drop-down list (see Figure 4.6).

FIGURE 4.6

You can select different file formats in which to save a document.

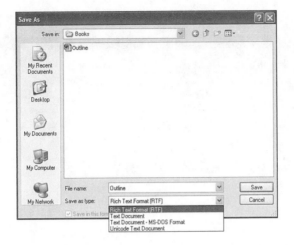

5. Click **Save**.

A new document is created and saved using the filename, location, and type you selected. This document remains open so that you can continue working. The original document remains on disk, unchanged.

Closing a Document

When you are finished working with a document, close it to free up system resources. Most programs, with the exception of WordPad and Paint, include a **Close** command and a **Close** button for the document window. To close the document, select **File**, **Close** or click the **Close** button for the document window. In WordPad, Notepad, and Paint, you must open another document, create a new document, or exit the program to close the document.

Note that closing a document is not the same as exiting the program. To close the document and exit the program, select **File**, **Exit** or click the **Close** button for the program window (see Figure 4.7).

Program Close button

FIGURE 4.7

Use the document window's Close button to close the document; use the program window's **Close** button to close the document and exit the program.

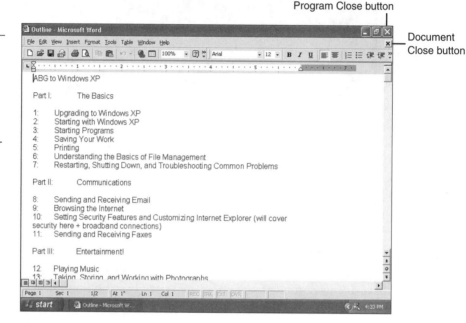

Document Close button

Opening a Document

When you save a document, the information is saved in a file at the location (folder and drive) you selected. When you want to work on that file again—to make changes, to print the file, and so on—you open the file.

Follow these steps to open a document:

1. Start the program you used to create the file.

2. Click **File** and then click the **Open** command. You see the Open dialog box (see Figure 4.8). If you see the file you want to open, skip to step 4.

3. If necessary, change to the location where the file was stored by doing any of the following:

   Double-click the folder that contains the file. For instance, in Figure 4.8, double-click the Books folder icon to view files within that folder.

tip

In addition to the File, Open command, look for shortcuts for opening files. You can click the **Open** button in the toolbar or use the keyboard shortcut (usually **Ctrl+O**). Some programs also list the last few files that were opened at the bottom of the File menu. You can click the filename to open that document.

Places bar   Up One Level button

FIGURE 4.8

Use the Open dialog box to display and then open the document you want to work with.

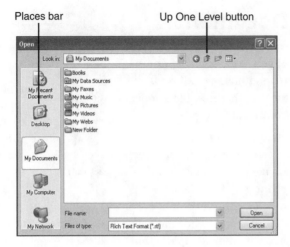

If you don't see the folder listed, click the **Up One Level** button to move up through the folders and display other folders.

To display another drive or folder, display the Look in drop-down list and select the drive or folder.

To display one of the common folders, click its name in the Places Bar. For instance, to open the My Documents folder, click the **My Documents** button in the Places Bar.

tip

See the section "Switching Folders" for more information about how to move among the folders and drives on your computer.

4. When you see the file you want to open, double-click its name to open the file. For example, in Figure 4.9, you can double-click the Outline file to open that document. The document is displayed onscreen.

FIGURE 4.9

Navigate to the folder that contains the file and then double-click the file icon to open the document.

Creating a New Document

When you start most programs, a blank document is displayed. If you want to create another new document, you don't have to exit and restart. You can create another new blank document at any time from within the program.

In addition to a blank document, many programs enable you to select a template on which to base the new document. A *template* is a predesigned document that may include text and formatting. To get a head start on content or formatting, you can select a template for the new document—if the program has a template that matches your needs.

To create a new document, follow these steps:

1. In the program, click **File** and then click the **New** command.

2. If you see a New dialog box, click the type of document you want to create and then click the **OK** button. For instance, in WordPad, you can select from several document types (see Figure 4.10). When you click **OK**, a new document is displayed. You can use any of the program tools to create and save this new document.

tip

If you can't find the file you want, it could be because you did not save it where you thought you did. Try looking in a different drive or folder. If you still can't find it, try searching for the file. For more information about searching for files, see Chapter 20, "Viewing and Finding Files."

tip

In addition to the **File**, **New** command, look for a **New** icon in the toolbar or a shortcut key (usually **Ctrl+N**).

FIGURE 4.10

If the program includes templates, you are prompted to select the template or document type from the New dialog box.

After the blank document is displayed, you can start entering data. Entering data in most programs is pretty straightforward. For example, in a word processing program, you just start typing. In a worksheet, you select the *cell* (intersection of a row and column) and type the entry. Instructions for more complex programs—for example, a database program—may require more upfront work. For exact instructions on how to use a program to create a document, check the program's documentation.

The Absolute Minimum

This chapter covers the main skills you need to save, open, and close documents. In summary, keep these points in mind:

- You should save and save often the work that you create. The first time you save, you enter a filename and select a location for the document.
- You can save a copy of a document or save a document in a different file format as needed.
- When you want to work on a document that you have previously saved, use the **File**, **Open** command.
- When you are finished working in a document, close the document. If you are finished with that program, close the document and exit the program.
- To create a new document, use the **File**, **New** command.

5

PRINTING

Adding a Printer

In the preceding chapter you learned about saving and opening documents. These are basic skills to get you started in all programs. Another common task that you will use often is printing your work. Printing is usually the end result of working on a document. You might print a document to include in a report or to share with others. You might print a document to edit the content from a hard copy rather than onscreen.

Even though you print from within a program, Windows XP manages the print job behind the scenes. The program uses the printer you have set up in Windows along with any special settings for that printer. Windows XP also manages all the print jobs, letting you pause or cancel a print job if needed. In addition to managing the printer and features of the printer, Windows XP also handles the available fonts.

This chapter focuses on the key printer tasks. With the information in this chapter, you will be able to print documents, handle print jobs, and deal with any printer problems.

In many cases, Windows can automatically set up your printer after you attach it to your computer. Automatic setup is the easiest way to set up a printer. But if that doesn't work, you have several other options.

If you have a newer printer that is not yet added to Windows XP's Plug and Play (a feature that automatically recognizes and installs hardware) list or an older printer, Windows XP might be unable to automatically install it. If this happens, you can add a new printer to your Windows setup using a step-by-step guide called a *wizard*. You can use one of Windows XP's drivers, or you can use a driver supplied with the printer. This section covers both of these manual setup options.

Automatic Setup

When you connect your printer, Windows XP queries the printer and then pulls key technical details about the printer, using that information to set up the printer. All you have to do is plug in the printer and wait.

Windows XP initiates the process and alerts you that the printer has been found and installed with messages that pop up from the system tray. If this happens, you are set. You can use your printer and skip the rest of this section!

Manual Setup Using Windows's Drivers

If the automatic setup doesn't work, you can add a printer using the Add Printer Wizard. You might need to do this if you have a printer that isn't on Windows' Plug and Play list. Cutting edge printers,

note
A *driver* is a file that tells Windows the specific details of your hardware component, such as how it works and what features it has. The driver enables Windows to communicate with the hardware component and put the component to use. Printers, for instance, have drivers as do other hardware components, such as modems. You learn more about other hardware drivers in Chapter 24, "Upgrading Windows."

note
This feature is called *Plug and Play* and works with other components you add to your computer. For information on adding other hardware components, see Chapter 24.

older printers, or budget printers, for instance, may require a little push to get started on the installation.

You can see whether Windows XP has a driver that works with this printer. Or you can use the disk that came with your printer. If you are upgrading to Windows XP and have had your printer for a while, you may not be able to find the printer disk. In that case, use this method.

Follow these steps to add a new printer:

tip

If you want to customize the printer—change the default settings that affect how the printer works—you can do so. This topic is covered later in this chapter.

1. Click **Start** and then click **Control Panel**.

2. In the Control Panel window, click the link for **Printers and Other Hardware**. You see a task for adding a printer as well as Control Panel icons for printers and faxes, gaming options, keyboard, scanners and cameras, and the mouse (see Figure 5.1).

FIGURE 5.1

You often use the Control Panel to add new hardware, including printers.

3. Click the **Add a printer** link to start the Add Printer Wizard.

4. Click **Next** to move from the welcome screen to the first step of the wizard. For the first step, select to set up a local printer or network printer (see Figure 5.2).

FIGURE 5.2
Select to install a
local printer
(one connected
to the computer)
or a printer con-
nection (basi-
cally a network
printer).

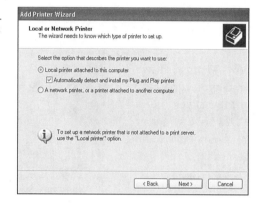

5. Select **Local printer**. If you want to install
   the printer manually, uncheck Automatically
   detect and install my Plug and Play printer.
   Click **Next**.

   If you selected to detect your printer and it is
   found and installed, you can skip the
   remaining steps. If the printer is not found
   or if you did not select automatic detection,
   you are prompted to select the printer port
   (see Figure 5.3). Printers are most often
   attached via the LPT1 or parallel port.

6. Select the port and click **Next**. You see a list
   of printer manufacturers and printers.

note

If you are installing a
printer that you want to
share on a network, check out
Chapter 28, "Setting Up Windows
XP on a Home Network," to see
what you need to do differently
for printer setup.

FIGURE 5.3
The port is the
plug that con-
nects the printer
cable to the
computer.

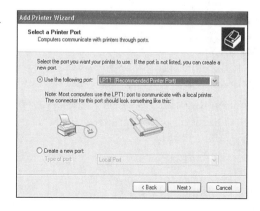

7. Select your printer manufacturer in the list on the left. Then select your particular printer from the list on the right (see Figure 5.4). Click **Next**.

FIGURE 5.4

Windows XP lists the printer models for which it has drivers.

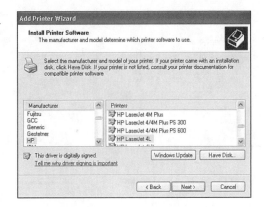

You are next prompted to type a name for the printer. This name is used to identify the printer icon for this printer.

8. Type or accept the suggested name and also select whether you want to make this the default printer by clicking Yes or No. Click **Next**.

You are asked whether you want to share this printer. Sharing a printer usually involves a home networked PC. If you are connecting a network PC, see Chapter 28.

9. Select **Do not share this printer** and then click **Next**. You are asked whether you want to print a test page.

10. Select **Yes** or **No** for the test page question and then click **Next**. The final step of the wizard lists all your selections (see Figure 5.5).

11. Click **Finish** to install the printer driver.

note

When you select a printer and it is recognized by Windows, you see a note in the dialog box that says the driver is digitally signed. This means that, according to the help information, "hardware products that display the Designed for Windows logo have been tested to verify compatibility with Windows." You can install printers even if they aren't digitally signed.

FIGURE 5.5

The final screen of the wizard lists all your choices for confirmation. You can finish up or go back and make changes.

Manual Setup Using the Printer's Drivers

Most printers come with a disk that contains a driver for using the printer. If your printer is not listed in the Add Printer wizard and you have this printer disk, you can install the appropriate driver from the disk. You can also find drivers at different Internet sites (for instance, www.WinDrivers.com). You can find the printer driver from the site of the printer maker, from a Windows or Microsoft site, or from a general hardware help site (www.pcguide.com). Check your printer documentation to see what online resources you have. Try searching the Microsoft site www.microsoft.com) for printer drivers. Or look for sites in computer articles for general help (www.pcworld.com).

tip

Click the Back button in a wizard dialog box to return to the previous dialog box and review or modify your selections.

If you have the disk, follow these steps to install the driver from the disk:

1. Follow the preceding steps to start the wizard.

2. When prompted to select the printer software, click **Have Disk**. You are prompted to select the disk that contains the driver file (see Figure 5.6).

tip

See Chapter 10, "Browsing the Internet," for more help on visiting Web sites.

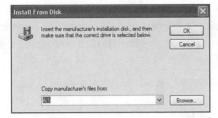

3. Insert the floppy or CD disk and then select the appropriate drive from the
   drop-down list.

4. Click **OK** to install the file from the disk.
   The driver is installed, and the printer is
   set up.

Printing a Document

After your printer is set up, printing is straightforward. The options for printing vary from program to program, but the basic steps are the
same.

To print a document, follow these steps:

1. Click **File** and then click the **Print** command. As a shortcut, look for a **Print** button in the program's toolbar or use the
   shortcut key combination (usually
   Ctrl+P). You see the Print dialog box
   shown in Figure 5.7.

> **tip**
>
> Most programs enable you
> to preview a document to
> check the margins, heads,
> graphics placement, and so
> on before you print.
> Previewing can save time
> and paper because you
> can make any needed adjustments
> before you print. Click **File** and
> select the **Print Preview** com-
> mand. After you finish viewing the
> preview, click the **Close** button.

FIGURE 5.7

The Print dialog
box for
WordPad.

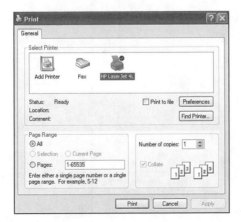

2. Make any changes to the print options. Most programs enable you to select a printer, select what is printed (for instance, a particular page range), and select the number of copies to print. Note that the available options vary from program to program.

3. Click the **Print** button. The document is printed.

Viewing and Canceling Print Jobs

The print queue lists the documents that have been sent to a printer, and it shows how far along the printing is. Using the print queue, you can pause, restart, or cancel print jobs. For instance, you might need to pause a print job to change paper. You may cancel a print job that you started by mistake.

Follow these steps to make changes to a print job in progress:

1. Click the **Start** button and then choose **Control Panel**.

2. Click the **Printers and Other Hardware** category.

3. Click the **Printers and Faxes Control Panel** icon. You see a list of all the installed printers and faxes (see Figure 5.8).

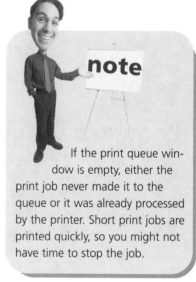

note

If the print queue window is empty, either the print job never made it to the queue or it was already processed by the printer. Short print jobs are printed quickly, so you might not have time to stop the job.

FIGURE 5.8

You can view the installed printers when you want to view the print queue.

4. Select the printer you want to view and click **See what's printing** in the Task pane. You see the print queue (see Figure 5.9). You can also display the print queue by double-clicking the Printer icon in the system tray of the taskbar (on the far left side). The Printer icon appears whenever you are printing a document.

FIGURE 5.9

Use the print queue to pause, restart, or cancel a print job.

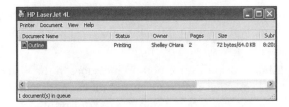

5. Do any of the following:

To cancel all print jobs, click **Printer** and then click the **Cancel All Documents** command. Click **Yes** to confirm the cancellation.

To pause printing, click **Printer** and then click **Pause Printing**. To restart after pausing, click **Printer** and then click **Pause Printing** again.

To cancel, pause, resume, or restart a particular print job, click the print job in the list. Then click **Document** and select the appropriate command (**Pause**, **Resume**, **Restart**, or **Cancel**).

6. Click the **Close** button to close the queue.

Printing Tips

When you are printing, keep in mind the following tips:

■ To print a document within a program, use the **File**, **Print** command. You can also look for a **Print toolbar** button or press **Ctrl+P** (the shortcut key for printing in most programs).

■ Before you print in a program, preview the document. Most programs have a **Print Preview** command (or something similar). Look for this command in the **File** or **View** menu. You can also often find a toolbar button for **Print Preview**.

■ You are not limited to printing from just within a program. You can also print from a file window. To do so, select the file and then click the **Print this file** link in the Tasks list.

■ As another option for printing, if you have added a printer shortcut icon to your desktop, you can drag a file to this printer icon to print the document.

■ To create a printer shortcut icon, open the Printers and Faxes window and then drag the icon from the printer window to your desktop. Windows XP creates a shortcut printer icon.

Common Printer Problems (and Their Cures)

Printing is supposed to be straightforward, but there can be times when the printer just won't give you what you want. In this case, you can fix common problems by reviewing this list:

■ Windows XP should display error pop-up messages in the system tray (far right of the taskbar) when the printer is not functioning correctly. If the printer isn't connected or is out of paper, check for printer messages from Windows to locate the problem.

■ If you missed the error message, start with the basics if a document won't print. Make sure that the printer is plugged in and turned on. Also, check the printer cable: is it solidly connected to the printer and the computer? A loose cable is easy to fix and overlook.

■ Check the printer for error messages. Usually these are displayed as flashing lights. More sophisticated printers may display a message. On my particular printer, I have error lights for paper and error. Paper means a paper jam. Error means something else, usually something simple like the paper drawer isn't all the way pushed in, or I didn't clear the paper jam correctly. If you get an error message from the printer and don't know what it means, check your printer manual.

■ You can tell whether the printer and computer are communicating because the printer should display some type of indication when it is receiving data. (Mine flashes the data light.) If you see this light, you know the data is getting to the printer, but the printer just isn't printing.

■ Some printers can "choke" on documents that are too complex. The computer may not have sufficient memory to print this complex of a document. If you are trying to print a complicated layout or complex graphic and the print job never comes out of the printer, you might not be able to print that document. Try printing a single page. If that works, print the pages in batches. If it doesn't, you might need to make some modifications to the layout and formatting (or get a better printer).

■ For additional troubleshooting advice on printers, click **Start**, select **Control Panel**, click **Printers and Other Hardware**. Then from this window, under Troubleshooters, click **Printing**. Select your problem from the list of problems and then click **Next** to use the Troubleshooter to check out the problem and recommended solutions. Chapter 7, "Troubleshooting Common Problems," provides more information on using the Windows Troubleshooter.

THE ABSOLUTE MINIMUM

This chapter covers all the details of printing including the basic information (how to install a printer and how to print) as well as more detailed information (how to change printer properties and how to install new fonts). With the information in this chapter, you should understand how to get the most from your printer. In particular, keep these points in mind:

- The first step in printing is to set up your printer. The easiest way is automatic setup, which works for common printers. You can also set up the printer manually using a printer driver from Windows XP or a driver from your printer maker.

- Printing works the same in most programs: Select **File** and then **Print**. The Print dialog box enables you to make selections such as what to print and which printer to use.

- You can view the print queue to modify any print jobs in progress. For instance, you can cancel a print job you didn't intend. Or if you need to change paper, you can pause a print job.

6

UNDERSTANDING FILE MANAGEMENT BASICS

As you work with a computer creating more and more documents, you need to find a way to keep this information organized. Without a good organizational method, all your files are lumped together in one place. This would be the equivalent of shoving all your files into one filing cabinet.

Good file management does not take that long and involves just a few key ideas. This chapter covers these ideas as well as explains the important tasks for working with files.

Understanding Why File Organization Is Important

Good file management is important for beginners so that they get off on the right foot as well as intermediate users who might need to adjust their file organization. In general, if you follow a few guidelines, you will make working with your computer much easier. This section covers these guidelines.

Set Up Folders

Before you create many files, set up a folder structure. As covered in Chapter 4, "Saving Your Work," you can place all your data files in the My Documents folder but create subfolders within this folder to store like documents together. You might, for instance, create folders for each document type (memos, worksheets, publications, and so on). Or you might set up folders for projects. Any organization scheme is acceptable as long as it makes finding the files you need simpler.

To set up new folders, see the section "Creating a New Folder," later in this chapter. If you have been using your computer for some time and your files are scattered, you can still rearrange them, creating new folders and then moving files as needed. Creating folders is covered here. For information on moving and copying files, see Chapter 19, "Organizing Files."

Use Descriptive Names

When you save a document for the first time, you are prompted to type a filename. If you start out using descriptive names, you are set. You should be able to tell at a glance what a file contains by its name.

If, on the other hand, you did not use a descriptive name, you can rename a file. You can also rename folders as needed. Renaming files is covered in "Renaming a File," later in this chapter.

Make Backup Files

To safeguard your data, save a copy of your work to a location other than your primary hard drive. You might save it to another drive or to a disk (floppy or CD). For business, you might have a special tape drive for backing up data. Chapter 21, "Securing Your PC," covers the basics of backing up data. You can also use the **File**, **Save As** command (covered in Chapter 4) or the **Copy** command (covered in Chapter 19). Use this quick method when you want to save copies of a couple of files.

Clear Out Unneeded Files

You'll be surprised at how quickly your disk fills up with files. You should periodically delete files you don't need. This chapter covers deleting files to free up disk space as well as undeleting files (if you delete them by mistake).

In addition to manually deleting files, Windows XP offers other methods for keeping your disk in tip-top shape; these are covered in Chapter 22, "Improving Your Disk Performance."

Opening My Computer

Now that you have an understanding of what you need to do to keep your files organized, you are ready to explore the tools Windows XP includes for file management. The most commonly used tool is My Computer. My Computer is an icon that represents all the drives on your system. After you open this window, you can then open any of your drives to see the folders and files contained on that drive.

Follow these steps to open My Computer:

1. Click **Start** and then click **My Computer**. You see icons for each of the drives on your computer as well as system folders (see Figure 6.1).

FIGURE 6.1

When you want to work with the folders or files on your computer, you can start with My Computer.

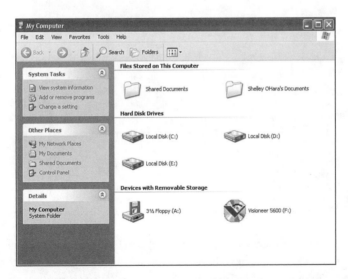

To help you keep your documents organized, Windows sets up several special folders in addition to My Computer. These include My Documents, My Pictures, and My Music. You can view the contents of any of these folders by clicking Start and then clicking the folder you want to open.

Opening Drives and Folders

Most computers have at least one floppy drive (drive A:) and a hard drive (drive C:). Your computer may also have additional drives including other hard drives or additional media drives (such as a CD or DVD drive). If you have more than one drive, they are named D:, E:, and so on. If you have a CD drive or a DVD drive, it also is named with a letter.

By default, Windows XP groups the drives by type, as shown in Figure 6.1. Opening a drive is easy: double-click the icon representing the drive you want to open (see Figure 6.2).

tip

If you have added the shortcut icon for My Computer to your desktop, you can double-click this icon to open My Computer. See Chapter 2, "Getting Started with Windows XP," for information on adding this icon to your desktop.

FIGURE 6.2

The contents of the hard drive D:. Note the different icons for folders and files.

Back   Forward   Up   Search   Folders   Views

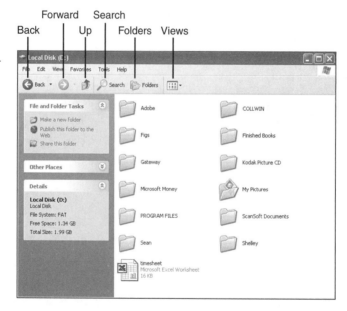

Each page icon represents a document (file). Each folder icon represents a folder on your hard drive. You can nest folders within folders to organize the contents of your hard drive. To open a folder, double-click its icon. You can continue opening folders until you see the file or folder you want to work with. To close a window, click the **Close** button.

Navigating Folders

Each folder window includes a toolbar that you can use to navigate from folder to folder. You can go back and forth among previously viewed content windows. You can also move up one level in the folder structure to the containing folder. For instance, you might move up to the desktop level and then open drives and folders to move to another branch of the folder structure. Table 6.1 identifies each toolbar button and its purpose.

Table 6.1 Folder Window Toolbar Buttons

Button	Click to...
Back	Go back to a previously viewed folder.
⊙	Return to a previously viewed folder. You can go forward only if you have clicked Back to go back a step.
↥	Display the next level up in the folder structure.
Search	Display the Search bar to search for a folder or file. See Chapter 20, "Viewing and Finding Files," for more information.
Folders	Display a hierarchical folder list (similar to Windows Explorer in previous versions of Windows). See the next section "Using the Folders Bar."
⊞ ▾	Change how the contents of the folder are displayed.

Using the Folders Bar

If you want to see a hierarchical listing of all the folders on your system, you can display the Folders Bar. You might prefer this view when working with folders and files because you can see the contents of the selected folder as well as all the other drives and folders on your computer. The Folders Bar makes it easier to move and copy by dragging, for instance. Click the **Folders** button to display the Folders Bar (see Figure 6.3).

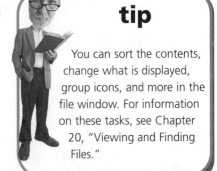

tip

You can sort the contents, change what is displayed, group icons, and more in the file window. For information on these tasks, see Chapter 20, "Viewing and Finding Files."

FIGURE 6.3

Displaying the Folders Bar lets you view all the drives and folders on your computer.

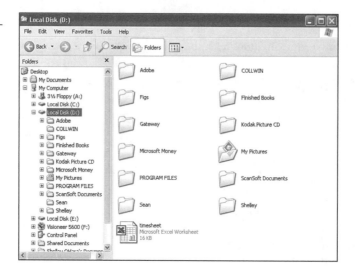

The top level is the desktop; beneath that you see the drives and folders on the desktop. You can expand or collapse any of the folders and drives in the list by clicking the plus sign next to the drive or folder. For instance, click the plus sign next to My Computer. When you click a plus sign to expand the folder or drive, the icon changes to a minus sign. You can click the minus sign to hide the contents of that item. For instance, you might hide content that isn't relevant to the task you are performing.

To close the Folders Bar, click the **Folders** button again or click the **Close** button for the bar.

Using the Task Pane

Windows XP also displays a task pane with common tasks as well as Other Places and a Details area. When you click an icon, you can see information about the icon in the Details area. For instance, in Figure 6.4, you can see the information about the selected file. You also see commands relating to working with the selected item. This chapter covers using these commands for common tasks.

note

If you are upgrading from a previous version of Windows, one where you used Windows Explorer to work with files, you'll find that the Folders Bar serves the same purpose. It displays a hierarchical view of the drives and folders.

FIGURE 6.4

Check the Task pane for common tasks as well as information about the selected item.

Creating a New Folder

Finding, saving, and opening documents are easier if you group related files into folders. For example, you might want to create a folder for all your word processing documents. Or you might create folders for each person who uses your computer. Creating a folder enables you to keep your documents separated from the program's files so that you can easily find your document files.

You can create a folder within any of the existing folders on your computer. Follow these steps:

1. Open the folder in which you want to create the new folder.

2. In the Task pane, click **Make a new folder**. The new folder appears in the window, and the name is highlighted (see Figure 6.5).

3. Type a new name and press **Enter**. The folder is added.

tip

Windows XP includes several shortcuts to the My Documents folder. Therefore, you might want to set up all your document folders within this one key system folder.

If you do not see the Make a new folder option listed, you probably have a file or folder selected in the window. Click in a blank part of the window.

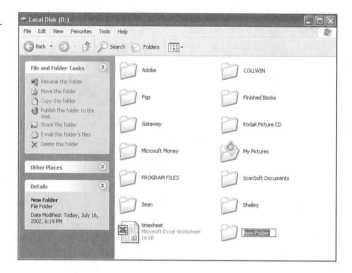

Displaying and Selecting Files

When you want to perform some file- or folder-related task, you start by selecting that file or folder. You can select a single file or multiple files. For instance, if you wanted to delete a group of files, you could select the ones to delete and then give the command to delete them.

For any task, the first step is to open the drive and folder where the file is stored. After you display the files you want to work with, you then select the file or files by doing any of the following:

- To select a single file, click it.

- To select several files next to each other, click the first file of the group that you want to select, and then hold down the Shift key and click the last file. The first and last files and all files in between are selected. Figure 6.6 shows multiple files selected.

- To select several files that are not next to each other, hold down the **Ctrl** key and click each file you want to select.

tip

When you select a single file, you can view details about the file in the Task pane. If the Details area is not displayed, click the down arrow next to the heading. If multiple files are selected, this area displays the number of files selected as well as the total file size.

FIGURE 6.6

FIGURE 6.6

Note that when several files are selected, Windows XP displays the number of items selected as well as the approximate size of all the selected files.

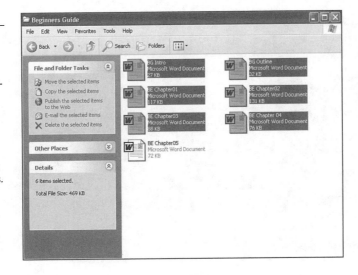

- To select all files, click the **Edit** menu and then click the **Select All** command. Or press **Ctrl+A**.
- To deselect a file, click outside the file list.

Deleting and Undeleting Files

Eventually, your computer will become full of files, and you'll have a hard time organizing and storing them all. You can delete any files you no longer need.

Windows XP doesn't really delete a file; instead, it moves the file to the Recycle Bin. If needed, you can retrieve the file from the Recycle Bin. This common task is also covered in this section.

Deleting a File

Follow these steps to delete a file:

1. Select the file(s) you want to delete.

2. Click **Delete this file**. You are prompted to confirm the deletion (see Figure 6.7).

3. Click **Yes** to confirm the deletion. Windows removes the file(s), placing it in the Recycle Bin.

tip

You can have Windows clean up files as part of your maintenance routine. See Chapter 22 for information on using the Disk Cleanup wizard.

FIGURE 6.7

Before deleting a file, Windows XP prompts you for confirmation.

Undeleting a File

Sometimes you will delete a file or folder by mistake. If you make a mistake, you can retrieve the file or folder from the Recycle Bin (as long as the Recycle Bin has not been emptied) and return the file to its original location. Usually Murphy's Law goes into effect: the minute you delete an old file is a minute before you determine you need it. Don't fret, though, you can undelete a file.

To do so, follow these steps:

1. Double-click the **Recycle Bin** icon on your desktop. You see the contents of the Recycle Bin, including any folders, icons, or files you have deleted (see Figure 6.8).

2. Select the file(s) you want to undelete.

3. Click **Restore this item** in the Task pane. The file is moved from the Recycle Bin back to its original location.

4 Click the **Close** button to close the Recycle Bin.

tip

You can also press the Delete key to delete selected files. Or as another option, right-click the selected files and then select **Delete** from the shortcut menu.

tip

Follow these same steps to undelete a folder. Select the folder and then click **Restore this item**.

FIGURE 6.8

The Recycle Bin
includes any
files and folders
you have
deleted.

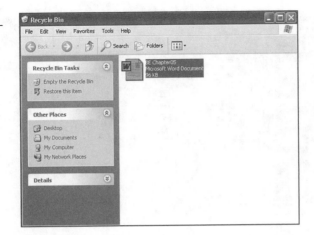

Emptying the Recycle Bin

The contents of the Recycle Bin take up disk space, so periodically you should empty
it. You can permanently delete the contents by emptying the Recycle Bin. Be sure
that it doesn't contain any items you need.

Follow these steps:

1. Double-click the **Recycle Bin** icon.

2. Check the contents of the Recycle Bin and
   undelete any files or folders you need.

3. Click **Empty Recycle Bin** in the Task
   pane. Windows displays the Confirm
   Multiple File Delete dialog box, prompting you to confirm this action.

4. Click **Yes** to empty the Recycle Bin.

> **tip**
>
> You can also right-click the
> Recycle Bin icon and then
> select the Empty Recycle Bin
> command from the shortcut
> menu.

Renaming a File

If you did not use a descriptive name when you saved the file or if the current name
doesn't accurately describe the file contents, you can rename it. You can rename
only a single file at a time.

Follow these steps:

1. Select the file you want to rename.

2. Click **Rename this file** in the Task pane. The current name is highlighted
   (see Figure 6.9).

FIGURE 6.9

Type a new
name for the
highlighted file.

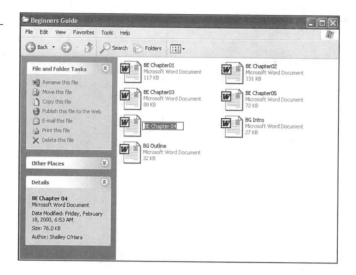

3. Type the new name and press **Enter**. The
   file is renamed.

You can use this same technique to rename a
folder. Select a folder for step 1 and then follow
the same steps.

tip

For all file tasks, you have
the option of using the
shortcut menu. Right-click
the selected file and then
select the command from the
shortcut menu. For
instance, you can select a
file, right-click to display the shortcut menu, and select the **Rename**
command.

ABSOLUTE MINIMUM

This chapter provides a crash course in file management. Later chapters build on these key tasks, but for the most part, you should learn all the basics of managing files here, including the following concepts:

- You have at least one hard drive on your system, and this is drive C:. You might have additional drives, lettered consecutively.

- To view the drives, folders, and files on your computer, open the My Computer icon. You can then navigate and open any of the drives and folders on your system.

- To keep your files organized, you can create folders. Windows XP starts with a system folder called My Documents. Consider storing all your work within subfolders within this one main folder. You can create new folders as needed.

- When you want to perform an action on a file (such as delete it), you select it. You can select a single file, multiple files, or all files within a window.

- Delete files you no longer need. If you delete a file by accident or find that you really do need it, you can undo the deletion by retrieving the item from the Recycle Bin.

- If you did not use a descriptive name for a file or a folder, you can rename it.

7

TROUBLESHOOTING COMMON PROBLEMS

Closing Stuck Programs

Problems are part of working with any sophisticated piece of equipment, especially one as complex as a computer. But Windows XP makes it easier than previous versions to pinpoint and deal with problems.

This chapter covers some common, simple-to-fix problems as well as explains how to restart your computer (when it gets stuck) and how to get help. You should have a good understanding of these common troubleshooting techniques in your "toolkit" of computer skills.

When you are finished working in a program, save your work and exit that program. The basics of starting and exiting are covered in Chapter 3, "Starting Programs." You might find that a program gets stuck (or as Windows XP says "is not responding"). If this happens, you might have to try some other methods for unjamming the stuck program, as covered in this section.

Is the Program Busy?

If you think a program is not responding, make sure that it is not busy with another task. Is the disk light active? Can you hear the drives moving? Does the keyboard respond? If the computer is active, you might just have to wait a few seconds to get the program to respond.

Also, make sure that the program is the active window. It is an easy mistake to have more than one window displayed and *think* you are working in one window (but it's not responding), but actually another program or window is active. Click in the program window or use the taskbar to switch to the program.

Also make sure that the menu bar is not active. If you press **Alt**, the menus are activated. If you try to type, nothing will happen (or a menu will open). Press **Esc** a few times to make sure that you are actually in the working area (not in the menu bar).

tip

Your **Esc** key is just that— an escape. If you think you are stuck, try pressing **Esc**. You might get out of the jam, and even if you don't, pressing **Esc** doesn't hurt anything.

Closing a Program from the Taskbar

If the computer is not busy and you still can't get a program to respond, try closing it from the taskbar. Follow these steps:

1. Right-click the taskbar button for the program. You see a shortcut menu for that window (see Figure 7.1).

FIGURE 7.1

Use the taskbar button to try to close a program.

2. Select the **Close** command. The program may be closed. Or if it's not closed, Windows XP displays an error message saying that the program is not responding. You can choose to wait or to close the program now.

3. Click **End Now** if prompted.

Closing a Program from the Task Manager

If the taskbar method doesn't work (or if you are not sure what's running on your computer), you can display the Task Manager. The Task Manager displays all the open programs (as well as any behind-the-scenes Windows programs that are running). From the Task Manager, you can exit a program.

Follow these steps:

1. Right-click a blank area of the taskbar.

2. Select **Task Manager**. The Windows Task Manager appears (see Figure 7.2), listing all the programs that are running.

3. Select the program you want to close.

4. Click **End Task**.

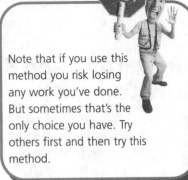

Note that if you use this method you risk losing any work you've done. But sometimes that's the only choice you have. Try others first and then try this method.

tip

These exit methods work for stuck programs. You can also use them as another way to exit regular programs (those that aren't stuck).

FIGURE 7.2

The Task Manager displays what programs are running.

The program is closed. If the program is "stuck," you see a message that the program is not responding. You can click **End Now** to close down the stuck program.

Restarting and Shutting Down the Computer

If your computer gets stuck, your first task is to close any open programs using one of the previous methods. If you get them all closed, you can then restart. If you can't get a program to close, you can restart using the menu command or by turning off the computer (last resort).

tip

Sometimes you can't even click the mouse. That's when you are really stuck. So are you out of luck? Not yet. Try pressing **Ctrl+Alt+Del** (all three keys together) and see whether that pops up the Task Manager. You can then try closing a stuck program.

Restarting with a Command

To try restarting to clear up problems, you can use the **Turn Off Computer** button on the taskbar. You might also need to restart if you make system changes; restarting puts the changes into effect. If you need to restart, try using the **Start** menu first:

1. Click the **Start** button.

2. Click the **Turn off Computer** button. You see the various shutdown options (see Figure 7.3).

tip

The **Log Off** button is used when multiple people use the computer and each has his or her own settings. See Chapter 26, "Setting Up Windows XP for Multiple Users," for more information on using the **Log Off** button.

Also, from the Turn Off dialog box, you can select to hibernate the computer to conserve power. Select the Hibernate button. This is most commonly used for laptops.

FIGURE 7.3
You can select to restart or turn off the computer.

3. Select **Restart** to restart the computer. The computer is restarted. This usually clears up your problem.

Restarting by Turning Off the Computer

Sometimes everything freezes: you can't use your mouse or the keyboard. In this case, you need to do what is sometimes called a *hard reboot*. If your computer has a reset button, you can press this button to force the computer to restart. If you do not have a reset button, you need to turn off the computer by pressing the power button.

Turn off the computer, wait a few seconds, and then turn the computer back on. Doing so is a last resort, but it does clear out any programs that are not running.

When you turn off and on the computer, Windows XP usually runs a disk check program to check for errors. For more information on this procedure, see Chapter 22, "Improving Your Disk Performance."

tip

The power button is located in different places on different computers. You might have a reset and power button on the front of the computer. You might have only a power button. Or the power button might be located on the back of the system unit.

Shutting Down the Computer

To avoid problems, you need to shut down properly before you turn off your computer. Doing so allows Windows XP to perform behind-the-scenes tasks before shutting down. Normally when you want to turn off your computer, follow this procedure:

1. Click the **Start** button.
2. Click the **Turn off Computer** button.
3. Select **Turn Off**. The computer is shut down.

Getting Help

Another useful feature for handling problems or just getting information is Windows online help. You can select from a list of help topics, browsing through a table of contents of help. You can also use the index to look up a topic or search for a topic.

tip

Should you turn off your computer each time you are finished? Different people have different opinions. Some think it's best to always turn off the computer. Doing so conserves power and provides some measure of security for power surges. Others leave the computer running. This camp thinks that powering on and off the computer repeatedly degrades the power supply. And the computer is protected (or should be) from power surges with a surge protector. You should do what is most comfortable for you.

The online help also includes troubleshooters that help you pinpoint problems and offer suggested fixes. These troubleshooters are most often used to pinpoint problems with hardware components or "devices." See Chapter 23, "Handling PC Maintenance," for information on these hardware-related troubleshooters.

Browsing Help Topics

Follow these steps to get help:

1. Click the **Start** button.

2. Click **Help and Support**. You see the Help and Support Center window (see Figure 7.4).

FIGURE 7.4

You can get extensive help from the Windows XP help guide as well as online sources.

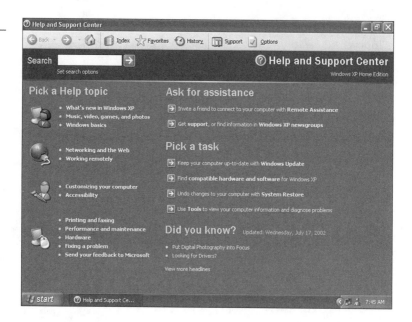

3. Click the topic you want help on. For instance, select **Windows basics**. You see the related topics.

4. Click the subtopic you want. The right pane lists relevant help topics. Figure 7.5, for instance, shows the topics for protecting your computer.

FIGURE 7.5

Use Windows help to get detailed information about features.

5. Click the topic you want in the pane on the right. Windows displays the relevant help information (see Figure 7.6).

FIGURE 7.6

You can display step-by-step information on using Windows XP features.

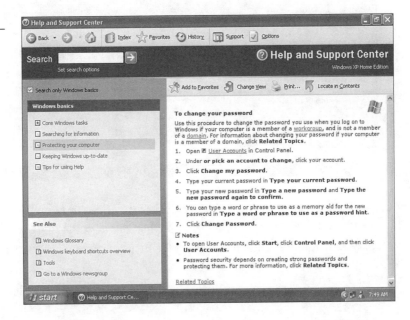

6. When you are finished reviewing the help information, click the help window's **Close** button.

Searching for Help

Rather than browse for help, you can go directly to a related help topic by searching for it. To do so, follow these steps:

1. Click the **Start** button.

2. Click **Help and Support**. You see the Help and Support Center window (refer to Figure 7.4).

3. In the Search text box, type your question or topic and click the search button (the green arrow). Windows XP displays related help topics (see Figure 7.7).

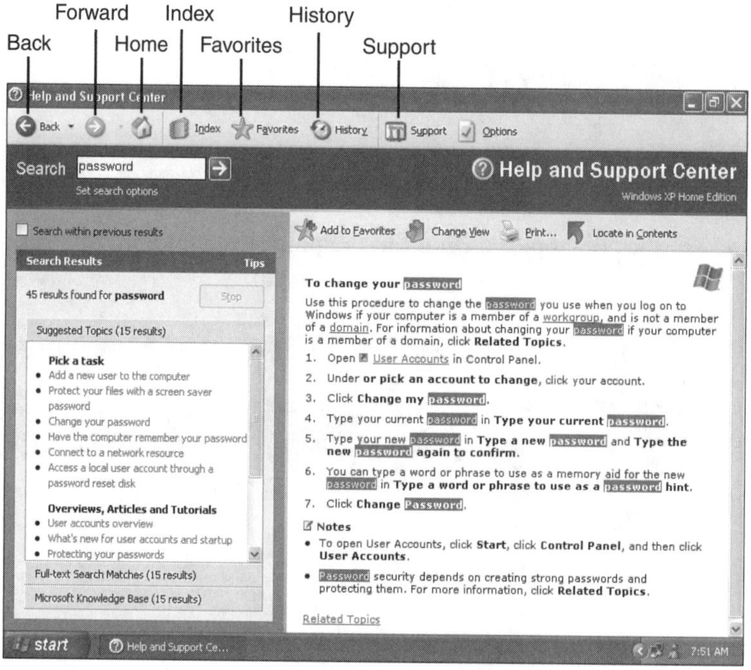

FIGURE 7.7

You can go quickly to a certain topic by searching for it.

4. Select the task you want from the list of suggested topics. Windows XP displays the related information in the help pane on the right.

5. When you are finished reviewing the help information, click the help window's **Close** button.

Using the Help Window Toolbar

In addition to browsing and searching, you can also use the toolbar buttons to get help in other ways:

- If you have looked up several pages during your browsing or searching, you can return to previous pages or go forward by using the Back and Forward buttons.

- To return to the opening help page, click the **Home** button.

- To display an index of topics, click the **Index** button. Then type the keyword in the pane on the left. Windows XP displays matching topics. Click the topic you want to display help information in the pane on the right.

- If you frequently refer to the same help pages, you can set up a list of favorite pages. Use the **Favorites** button to go to favorite pages.

- If you recently used help and want to return to a topic you know you looked up, use the History list to display a list of recently viewed help pages. You can then select the relevant page from this list.

- To access online support, click the **Support** button. Your options are displayed in the left pane and include sending an email to a friend for help, getting help from Microsoft, or visiting a Windows Web site forum. For more information about online browsing (including help options), see Chapter 10, "Browsing the Internet."

- To customize the help options, use the **Options** button. You can change such options as the font size and what appears in the navigation bar (also known as the toolbar).

THE ABSOLUTE MINIMUM

Most computer problems are easily solved, and you will be surprised how disaster-proof your PC is. Common problems can be fixed usually by restarting. If not, you can use Windows XP help's system. Keep these "tools" in mind:

- If you are having problems, try exiting all your programs. (Save your work first.) You can exit using the program's **File**, **Exit** command. If that doesn't work, try exiting from the taskbar button. Still no luck? Try using the Task Manager to exit.

- You might have to restart your computer. You might do this if the computer gets stuck or if you make changes to your computer (such as add a new hardware component or a new software program). To restart, use the **Turn Off**

Computer button on the **Start** menu. If that doesn't work, you can turn off the computer by pressing its reset button or power button.

- Make it a habit of shutting down the computer properly. To do so, use the **Turn Off Computer** button and select the **Shut Down** option.

- Windows provides extensive help in its help system. You can look up topics by browsing, searching, or using one of several other tools including Web support and an index.

PART

COMMUNICATIONS

8

GETTING WIRED FOR COMMUNICATION

Understanding the Internet

One of the most exciting things you can do with a computer is connect to the Internet. The Internet provides a vast source of information, communication, entertainment, and more. This chapter covers the equipment you need to get connected, as well as provides an understanding of the basics of setting up that equipment. You also get a quick overview of some of the many things you can do once connected. Other chapters in this part provide more how-to information on Internet topics.

The Internet is a network of networks all loosely connected through the phone lines or network hookups. You can connect to one network (your service provider) and then gain access to the entire network via a connection (usually a phone line or a cable connection). When connected, you can navigate from one network system to another network; this process is called *browsing* or *surfing*.

You don't need to know a lot about the details of how the Internet works or is organized. All you need to worry about is how to set up your connection the first time and then how to get connected thereafter. If you are curious about how the Internet was developed or want more technical details on the Internet, consider *How to Use the Internet, Eighth Edition* (ISBN# 0-7897-2813-3) by Que Publishing.

When connected, you can do any of the following:

- Send and receive email—You can send email messages to anyone with an email address. You can also receive email. Email is covered in Chapter 9, "Sending and Receiving Email."

- Communicate live online by typing messages—You can type instant messages to others who are online at the same time you are, having a live conversation through these typed words. You can also participate in *chats*. Again, in a chat, you type your messages, but the conversation involves a group of people, everyone within a particular *chat room*. Anyone can see and respond to your typed messages. You can find informal chats as well as scheduled and monitored chats with famous people, such as authors, actors, and other individuals.

- Post messages and review responses in a newsgroup—Another way to connect with other users is through a *newsgroup*. (Newsgroups have little to do with news, even though they are called *news*groups.) Rather than a live conversation, you post messages to an electronic bulletin board. Then anyone who visits that newsgroup can read and respond to your message. You can find newsgroups on topics as diverse as Elvis sightings to molecular biology.

note

Often the Internet is called the World Wide Web or the Web for short. The World Wide Web is not a physical part of the Internet; instead, it is a way of presenting information. Initially, the Internet was all text based, but someone came along and developed a new method that allowed for graphics and other media elements (sounds, animation, and so on). Sites that were set up in this multimedia format were part of the World Wide Web. As more sites became graphical, the Internet and the World Wide Web became pretty much synonymous.

■ Browse Web sites—You can go to other sites on the Internet (see Figure 8.1). You can go directly to a site by typing its address, search for sites, or browse from site to site by using links. For more information on browsing, see Chapter 10, "Browsing the Internet."

FIGURE 8.1

The first site you see is your home site. From this site, you can go to other Web sites.

Getting the Right Equipment

To access the Internet, you need certain hardware components. You also need some additional items such as an Internet provider and a way to get connected. Basically, you need the following items:

■ A modem

■ An Internet service provider (often abbreviated to ISP)

■ A connection

■ A program for browsing the Internet

■ A program for handling mail

This section describes each of these items.

Describing Modems

A *modem* is a device used with a telephone line or cable wiring and your computer. The modem enables your computer to connect to and communicate with other computers via the phone line or a cable line. Regular phone-connection modems are often referred to as *dial-up modems*. Faster connections, including cable modems, are often called *broadband connections*.

Most new computers come with a modem that is most often stored inside the computer. You can also purchase external modems that connect to your computer with a cable and sit on your desk. One of the newer ways to get connected is through a cable connection (usually provided by your cable TV company). To use a cable connection, you need a cable modem; you can purchase one, or sometimes the cable company provides one when you subscribe to its service. (More on connection types later.)

You plug in the phone line or cable line to the modem. Now you can connect to your Internet provider, which allows you to access email and browse the Web.

Finding an Internet Service Provider

An Internet service provider (ISP) has one or more high-powered networks that your computer calls to get connected. Your connection type (covered next) determines how you get connected and also which provider you use. For instance, if you decide to use a cable modem, you need to select a cable provider.

In addition to providing online browsing, your provider also serves as your mailbox. When someone sends you an email message, it is sent to your provider's network and stored there. When you get connected, you can then *download* or transfer any messages from your ISP to your computer.

You pay a monthly fee for this service; the amount of fees and services varies from company to company. Usually you can shop around for an ISP that meets your needs.

Windows XP provides links and even free trials for popular Internet providers including America Online (AOL) and Microsoft Network (MSN). Some providers are nationwide; some are local. Picking a local provider does not limit your connection to local sites; it just means that the company that provides the service is local.

tip

You can search for a provider using the New Connection Wizard. See "Getting Connected" later in this chapter for information on this wizard. Another great site for finding ISP is a site called The List at www.thelist.com.

If you do not have a provider or you are thinking of upgrading or changing your provider, do some research first by asking the following questions:

- Does the company provide service for your type of connection? That is, if you want to use a cable connection, does that company have cable hookups?

- What is the cost? Expect a monthly fee around $20 for basic service and up to $50 or more for high-speed access. Fees also vary from one area of the country to another.

- What other services are provided? As you become more proficient, you might want to expand your Internet skills. If you think that down the road you might want to create your own Web site, see whether your provider has Web hosting services. If so, what is the fee? Also, if more than one person uses your computer, consider multiple email addresses, one for each person. Check to see whether your ISP provides for (and what they charge) multiple addresses.

- What is the top connection speed? Speed is measured in bits per second (bps) or kilobytes per second (Kbps). Regular modems max out at about a speed of 56,000 bps or 56K. Cable and DSL lines are much, much faster. DSL lines and cable connections include speeds ranging from 128K to 768K on up to 1500K. Check out the various speeds for providers in your area. A great Web site for reviewing broadband speeds is BroadbandReports.com.

Selecting a Connection Type

Most users connect to the Internet through a phone line, but it is becoming more popular to hook up through your cable provider or through a special phone line such as DSL. (Again, these connections are called broadband connections.) This method often costs more but provides a faster connection. Common connection types include

- Cable—You can connect to the Internet through the same company that provides your cable television. Usually, the cable company provides the modem and runs the cable line for you for a setup fee. You then pay a monthly fee for the service. (Prices vary. Comparison shop among the various high-speed or broadband connections to get the best speed *and* price.)

Cable modems are usually connected 24/7 (24 hours a day, 7 days a week). To protect your computer, you need to turn on a safety device called a *firewall*. You can find more on this topic in Chapter 17, "Customizing Email and Internet Explorer."

Initially, not all cities and neighborhoods were wired for cable Internet, but that is becoming less of an issue. Check with your local cable company for availability in your area.

■ Special phone line—You can get connected through a high-speed phone line such as a DSL line. Again, this provides a faster connection but requires a special phone line and a higher service fee. Check with your local phone company for information about this connection option.

■ Network connection—Businesses often use a network connection as their access to the Internet. The network is often directly connected to the Internet through a networking line.

Selecting Browser and Email Programs

In addition to the service provider and hardware equipment, you also need programs for browsing the Internet and for sending and receiving mail.

> **note**
>
> Many DSL providers (for instance, Verizon) can now use your regular phone line rather than a special phone line. You have to put filters on the jacks you don't want to use for DSL but the filters are easy to install. They plug into the jack and you plug your phone into the filter. If you are looking into DSL as your connection type, check into all your options.

Windows XP includes a mail program called Outlook Express. This program suits the needs of most users. (Sending and receiving email is the topic of Chapter 9.) Figure 8.2 shows the Outlook Express window.

FIGURE 8.2

You can check your email with Outlook Express.

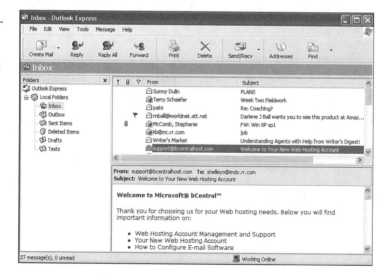

Some users may prefer a different mail program. For instance, your company may use a different mail program for interoffice email. Or you may prefer a full-featured mail program. For instance, if you use Microsoft Office, you can use Outlook, a personal information manager program that includes mail, calendar, and contact features.

Windows XP also includes a browser program called Internet Explorer. Browsing the Internet is covered in Chapter 10 and in Chapter 11, "Searching the Internet." Figure 8.3 shows the Internet Explorer. Again, different users may prefer to use different programs. Initially, Netscape Navigator was the most commonly used browser program. Some users still use this program; you can get more information and download this browser from www.netscape.com. Picking a browser is simply a matter of preference (and sometimes price given that Internet Explorer is included with Windows XP, and you might have to pay for software for other browser programs).

FIGURE 8.3

The most popular Internet browser program is Internet Explorer, included with Windows XP.

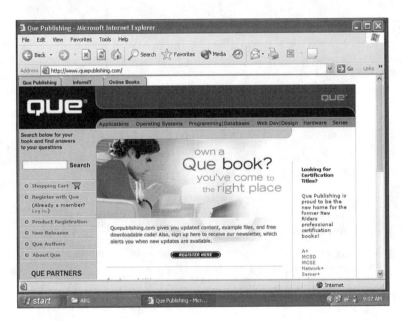

Getting Connected

To summarize so far, you need certain hardware components, software, and a provider to access the Internet. After you have these lined up, your first task is to set up Windows for your new connection. You only have to do this once. After that, starting your email program or going to a Web site is as simple as clicking an icon. But for the first time, you need to enter some technical information about your connection and provider.

Stepping Through the New Connection Wizard

Windows XP provides the New Connection Wizard, which leads you step-by-step through the process of getting connected. Using information supplied by your provider, this setup wizard gets you up and running in no time. If you have any problems or questions, contact your Internet provider.

Follow these steps to start the New Connection Wizard and get connected:

1. Click the **Start** button and then click **All Programs**.

2. Click **Accessories** and then Communications and then New Connection Wizard.

3. Complete each step of the wizard, clicking Next to advance to the next step. Click **Back** if you need to change one of your selections. Keep in mind that the steps vary depending on the type of connection. You can get a rough idea of setting up a dial-up account from the following:

   Select the connection type (dial-up modem), broadband connection (DSL or cable), and network broadband (DSL or LAN).

   Enter the name of your ISP.

   Enter the connection information. For instance, for a dial-up account, you type the phone number your computer dials to connect with the service provider.

   Type your account information (username and password). Use the information provided to you by your ISP.

4. When you have completed all your steps, click the **Finish** button. You are set!

The other chapters in this part of the book assume that you have set up your Internet connection and email account. Because the process varies from provider to provider, this book cannot list the exact steps. Use the New Connection Wizard to help you get set up. If you have problems, try Windows help.

note

You can also use this wizard to set up a home network. See Chapter 28, "Setting Up Windows XP on a Home Network."

Starting Your Connection

After you finish with the wizard, you connect to the Internet or email by clicking Start and then clicking Internet or E-mail from the **Start** menu. You see your connection prompt (see Figure 8.4). For dial-up accounts, you normally type your username and password. Then Windows XP dials your provider and connects you to the Internet.

tip

You also need to set up your mail accounts. The first time you start Outlook Express you are prompted to do so. You learn more about mail programs in Chapter 9, "Sending and Receiving Mail."

FIGURE 8.4

Follow the steps to log on to your provider.

You are now ready to start your Internet journey.

Exiting and Disconnecting

When you are not working online, you should exit your mail and browser program and log off (if you have a dial-up account). To do so, click the **Close** button for the program window. You are prompted to log off the connection if you have a dial-up connection. If you are prompted to log off, select **Yes** or **Disconnect**.

If you are not prompted, right-click the connection icon in the taskbar and select **Disconnect** (see Figure 8.5).

tip

You can set up your connection so that Windows XP remembers the phone number to dial as well as your username and password.

FIGURE 8.5

FIGURE 8.5

Use the status icon in the system tray to log off or display connection information.

THE ABSOLUTE MINIMUM

This chapter explains what you need to access the Internet either for mail, Web browsing, or both. In particular, this chapter covered these key points:

- To get connected, you need a modem, an Internet service provider, a connection (usually a phone line or cable line), and software for email and Web browsing. You can use two programs included with Windows XP for email and browsing: Outlook Express and Internet Explorer.

- To set up a new connection, use Windows XP's New Connection Wizard, completing each of the required steps by entering specific information about your provider and connection.

- After you have set up your Internet account, you can log on to the Internet and check and send email as well as browse the Internet.

9

SENDING AND RECEIVING EMAIL

Electronic mail (or *email*) is a fast, convenient, and inexpensive way to stay connected. You can send a message to anyone with an email address, and it is sent immediately. You can send a message to a friend down the street or a colleague across the world! The recipient can then, at his or her convenience, respond to your message.

In addition to typing messages, you can send pictures or other documents. For instance, you may want to submit an expense report to your home office. Or you may send pictures of your new puppy to your family.

Windows XP includes a mail program called Outlook Express. You can use this program to create new mail as well as handle mail you have received. This chapter covers the basics of sending and receiving email with Outlook Express.

Setting Up Your Email Account

Before you can use Outlook Express, you need to set up your Internet connection and email account information. Setting up an Internet connection is covered in Chapter 8, "Getting Wired for Communication." You also need to set up information about your particular email account.

The first time you start Outlook Express you are prompted to set up your email account. You should have handy all the connection information from your Internet service provider (ISP), including your username, email address, password, and technical information, such as the incoming mail server name (called the POP3, IMAP, or HTTP server) and the outgoing mail server (called the SMTP server). If you have problems or questions about this information, contact your Internet service provider.

Checking Your Email

After your email account is set up, you can start Outlook Express and check your mail. Follow these steps:

1. Click **Start** and then click **E-mail** (Outlook Express).

2. If prompted, connect to your Internet service provider. Outlook Express starts and checks your email server for any messages. Messages are then downloaded to Outlook Express. The number of new messages appears in parentheses next to the Inbox in the Folders list. The message header pane lists all messages. Messages in bold have not yet been read. You can open and read any message in the message list (see Figure 9.1).

3. If necessary, in the Folders list of the Outlook Express window, select **Inbox**.

4. Double-click the message you want to read. The message you selected is displayed in its own window (see Figure 9.2). You can display the previous or next message in the list with the Previous and Next buttons in the toolbar. To close the message, click the **Close** button.

Folders list

FIGURE 9.1

Start Outlook
Express and then
check your
Inbox for new
messages.

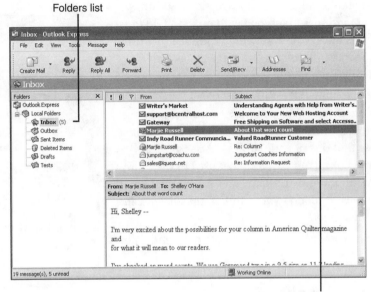

Message header pane

FIGURE 9.2

You can open
and review any
of the messages
you receive. Use
the toolbar but-
tons to display
other messages.

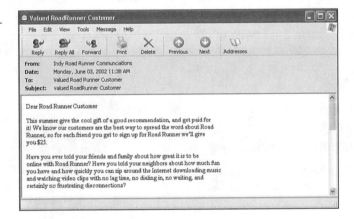

Sending Messages

In addition to reading messages you have received, you can also send your own messages. You have several options for creating new mail. You can reply to an existing
message. For instance, suppose that your sister emails you some dates for the upcoming family reunion. You can reply to her message. Replying is convenient because
you don't have to type the email address. Also, the text of the original message is
included in the reply so that the recipient understands the context of the reply.

You aren't limited to simply replies. You can send messages to anyone with an email address. For instance, you may send a message to a family member that lives out of town, keeping in touch via email. Or you may email a company asking about a product or service.

As another option, you may forward a message you received to someone else. For instance, suppose that one of your co-workers sends you a funny joke. (You'll quickly get used to the many jokes that are swirling around the Internet.) You can pass it along to your father, the joke master of the family.

This section covers how to create and send email messages.

tip

Many Web pages include email links. You can click this email link to send a message to someone at that site. You also can use Internet Explorer's toolbar buttons to send a link to a particular Web page or a copy of the Web page itself. See Chapter 10, "Browsing the Internet," for more information on these types of messages.

Responding to Email

You can easily respond to a message you've received. Outlook Express completes the address and subject lines for you and also includes the text of the original message; you can then type your response. You can reply to just the original sender or to the sender and any other recipients (anyone cc'd in the message). You can also forward the message to someone else.

To reply to a message you have received, follow these steps:

1. Display the message to which you want to reply.

2. Do any of the following:

   To reply to just the sender, click the **Reply** button in the toolbar.

   To reply to the sender and any other recipients, click **Reply All**.

   To forward the message to another recipient, click **Forward**. Then type the email address for that person.

   The address and subject lines are completed, and the text of the original message is appended to the bottom of the reply message (see Figure 9.3).

note

The subject line is modified, including prefixes. Replies start with Re: in the subject line; forwarded messages start with Fw: in the subject line.

FIGURE 9.3

You can respond to a message, typing a reply and then sending the message.

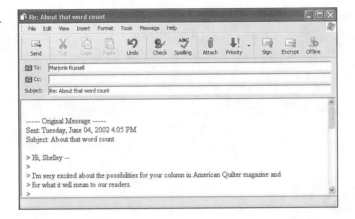

3. Type your message.

4. Click the **Send** button. The message is placed in your Outbox and then sent.

Depending on your email preferences, the message may be sent immediately or may be placed in the Outbox and sent when you click the **Send/Recv** button. Also, by default, Outlook Express saves a copy of all sent messages in the Sent Items folder. You can view this folder by clicking Sent Items in the Folders bar.

Creating New Mail

You aren't limited to replying to existing messages. You can send a message to anyone with an Internet email address. To do so, you must know that person's email address. You can type it or select it from your Outlook Express address book. In addition to the address, you can type a subject and the message.

Follow these steps to create and send a new email message:

1. In the Outlook Express window, click the **Create Mail** button. You see a blank email message (see Figure 9.4).

tip

The easiest way to reply to and create new messages is using the toolbar buttons. You can also use Message menu commands. You can select to create a new message, reply to sender, forward, and other options.

tip

You can customize your email setup. To change your email preferences, such as saving copies, use the Tools, Options command. See Chapter 17, "Customizing Email and Internet Explorer."

FIGURE 9.4

Create a new email message and then complete the To and Subject fields and type the message.

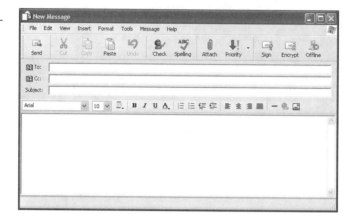

2. Type the recipient's address. Addresses are in the format *username@domainname.ext* (for example, sohara@msn.com). Press **Tab**.

3. To send a carbon copy (cc) to another recipient, type an address for that person and press **Tab**. To skip the Cc field, simply press **Tab** again.

4. Type a subject in the Subject text box, and then press **Tab**.

5. Type your message.

6. Click the **Send** button. Like replying to a message, the message is either sent immediately or placed in your Outbox and sent when you click **Send/Recv**, as determined by your email preferences.

Sending New Messages

Depending on how Outlook Express is set up, your messages may be sent immediately when you click the **Send** button. Or they may be placed in your Outbox, waiting to be sent. You might save up all your messages and send them at once. Using the Outbox also enables you to compose messages offline (when you are not connected). You can then get connected and send the messages.

tip

Rather than type the email address, you can set up an address book and select recipients by name (rather than chance a mistyped address). See Chapter 17 for more information.

tip

You can use a special pre-designed format for messages (called stationery) as well as format the text. Because some mail programs may be unable to display your formatting choices, I usually recommend keeping the message plain and simple. You do have options for changing the appearance, though, and they are covered briefly in Chapter 17.

Keep in mind these tips when sending messages:

- The Folders list displays the mail folders as well as information about the contents. For instance, if you have messages in your Outbox, the Outbox folder appears in bold, and the number of messages to be sent is listed in parentheses after the folder name. You can view these messages by clicking Outbox in the Folders list.

- If you have not yet sent a message, you can cancel it by opening the Outbox and deleting the message. (See "Deleting and Undeleting Messages" later in this chapter.) After you send a message, you cannot retrieve it.

- You can control what is included with a reply and a forward, whether copies of your sent messages are saved, and when messages are sent. To do so, click **Tools** and then **Options**. Use the tabs in the Options dialog box. For more information on mail options, see Chapter 17.

- If your messages are stored in the Outbox, you can click the **Send/Recv** button in Outlook Express to send the messages. To send messages, you must be connected. If you are not connected, you are prompted to do so. Follow the logon procedure for your particular ISP. The messages are then sent.

If you enter an incorrect address and the message is not delivered, you usually receive a Failure to Deliver notice. You can then check and correct the address and resend the message.

If you are angry or upset and fire off a message, it's usually best to let the message sit for some time before sending. Wait overnight or at least a few hours. Then read your message and make any edits. Because you cannot convey tone of voice, facial expressions, or body language through typed comments, your message might not have the intent you wanted. Double-check any sensitive messages before sending them.

Sending and Handling Attachments

In addition to the text of a message, you can also attach a file. As mentioned, you might email an expense report to your home office. Or perhaps you have pictures you want to share with your family and friends. (You learn more about pictures in Chapter 14, "Working with Photographs and Movies.")

This section covers how to attach and send files as well as how to handle files sent to your email address.

Attaching a File to a Message

To attach a file, follow these steps:

1. Click the **Attach** button in the email message window. You see the Insert Attachment dialog box.

2. Open the folder that contains the file you want to attach. The dialog box includes tools similar to those you use for opening a document (covered in Chapter 4, "Saving Your Work"). You can use the Look in drop-down list to select another drive or folder. You can click the **Up One Level** button to navigate up through the folder structure. You can double-click any listed folder to display its contents.

3. Select the file to attach (see Figure 9.5).

FIGURE 9.5

Browse through the folders on your computer and then select the file(s) you want to attach.

4. Click the **Attach** button. The file attachment is listed in the Attach text box of the message (see Figure 9.6).

FIGURE 9.6

Your attachment is listed in the message header.

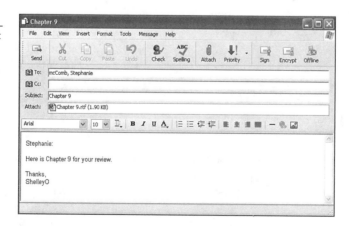

5. Click the **Send** button to send the message and file attachment.

When sending attachments, keep a few pointers in mind:

- For the recipient to open and work with a file, he must have a program compatible with the file type. For instance, if you send a Word document, that person must have Word to view and open the file. (You can save documents as other file types if you share work with someone who uses a different program. See Chapter 4 for more information on saving documents as other file types.)

- You can attach more than one file, but keep in mind that downloading attachments takes time. Also some ISPs have a limit to the size of file attachments. You can send files individually to get around the limit. Or consider compressing the files. This topic is covered in Chapter 19, "Organizing Files."

- If you need to send a large file or several files, create a compressed folder and then send the folder. You learn more about compressing files in Chapter 19.

Opening a File Attachment

If someone sends you a file attachment, you can either open it or save it to disk. Messages with file attachments are indicated with a paper clip icon. Note that to open the attachment, you must have a program that can open and display that particular file type.

Follow these steps to open an attachment:

1. Double-click the message. The file attachment(s) is listed in the Attach text box (see Figure 9.7).

FIGURE 9.7

You can receive messages with attachments.

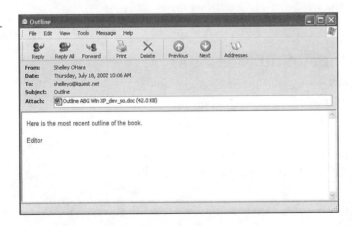

2. Double-click the attachment icon. You see the Open Attachment Warning dialog box (see Figure 9.8).

FIGURE 9.8

Select how to
handle any
email
attachments.

3. Select **Open it** or **Save it to disk**.

If you open it, the file is displayed in the associated program (usually the program used to create
the file). If you save the attachment, you see the
Save Attachment As dialog box. Type a filename,
select a folder, and click **OK** to save the attachment. (See Chapter 4 for more information on
saving files.)

Handling Messages

Your inbox will quickly fill up with messages. To
keep Outlook Express streamlined, get in the
habit of handling messages and then deleting
them or saving them, as needed. Delete old,
unneeded messages. Move messages you want to
save to a special folder. This section includes some
of the options you have for dealing with messages, including deleting messages, moving or
copying messages, printing, and more.

Deleting and Undeleting Messages

As part of keeping your Inbox uncluttered, you
can delete messages. In the Outlook Express window, select the message you want to delete, or
open the message you want to delete, and click
the **Delete** button. When you delete a message, it
is not deleted, but moved to the Deleted Items
folder.

If needed, you can undelete a message. Follow
these steps:

One way computer
viruses spread is through
email attachments.
Before you open any
file—from strangers or
people you know—scan the file for
viruses. You learn more about
viruses and security precautions in
Chapter 17.

You may set up some
file types to open auto-
matically. For instance,
some forwarded email
messages come with
attachments that contain the forwarded message. If you have told
Windows XP to go ahead and
open this file type automatically,
you may open the file when you
double-click. To select a different
option (save, for instance), right-
click the attachment and then
select **Open** or **Save**.

1. In the Folders list, click the **Deleted Items** folder. You see the messages that have been deleted.

2. Click the message you want to undelete.

3. Drag the message from the message header pane to one of the folders in the Folders list. For instance, drag the message from Deleted Items to Inbox. For more information on moving and copying messages, see "Organizing Messages" later in this section.

To permanently delete a message, open the Deleted Items folder, select the message, and click the **Delete** button or press the **Delete** key. You are prompted to confirm the deletion (see Figure 9.9). Click **Yes** to permanently delete the message.

FIGURE 9.9

Permanently delete messages by confirming their deletion from the Deleted Items folder.

Electronic junk mail is called *spam*, and you can easily get unwanted messages from people and companies. You can use some of Outlook Express's customization features to block spam (see Chapter 17). But it's virtually impossible to get rid of all the unwanted mail. One thing you can do to keep spam at a minimum is to carefully check any information you agree to when you visit a site or purchase an item online. For instance, some sites include a check box (which is usually checked) that says in effect "go ahead and send me information about new services and products." After you are on one mailing list, your name pops up in many other lists. Uncheck any invitations for free newsletters or product information. Also, be careful when submitting personal information such as your address. See Chapter 17 for more information.

Printing Messages

On occasion, you might want to print a hard copy of a message. For instance, suppose that someone sends you directions to a party. You can print the directions and take them with you. You also might want to print and save a hard copy of messages with important information such as an online order confirmation.

To print an open message, follow these steps:

1. Select the message from the Outlook Express window or open the message.

2. Click the **Print** button. You see the Print dialog box (see Figure 9.10).

FIGURE 9.10
Select the print-
ing options for
the message.

3. Click **OK** to print the message.

Organizing Messages

If you think you need to keep some of your messages, consider creating a mail folder and storing
the messages in that folder. Doing so keeps your
Inbox uncluttered. You can just keep messages
that you need to handle in the Inbox and either
delete, print, or move other messages out of the
Inbox folder to another folder. For instance, suppose that you have several business messages
that you need to keep. You can set up a folder for
these messages and then move them from the
Inbox (or other folder) to the business folder. As
another example, you might want to keep copies of the funny jokes you receive. You
can set up a joke folder and move joke messages to this folder. You can use Outlook
Express to both create a new folder as well as move or copy items to different folders.

To create a folder, follow these steps:

1. Click **Local Folders** in the Folders list. Doing so ensures that the new folder
   will be placed at the same level of existing folders.

2. Click **File**, **New**, and then **Folder**. You see the Create Folder dialog box (see
   Figure 9.11).

tip

If you want to delete all
messages in this folder, click
Edit and then select **Empty
'Deleted Items' Folder**.
Confirm the deletion by clicking **Yes**. Be sure that this is
what you want to do.
When deleted messages are
deleted this way, you cannot
retrieve them.

FIGURE 9.11

Type the folder name here to create a new mail folder.

3. Type the folder name and click **OK** to create the folder.

After the folder is created, you can move or copy messages to this (or any other folder). To do so, follow these steps:

1. Select the message you want to copy or move.

2. Click the **Edit** menu and then select **Move to Folder** or **Copy to Folder**. You see either the Move or Copy dialog box (see Figure 9.12). The dialog box is identical except for the name; both list the mail folders.

tip

Outlook Express sets up several mail folders for you including Inbox, Outbox, Deleted Items, Sent Items, and Drafts. Some messages are automatically moved or saved to these folders. For instance, when you delete a message from your Inbox, it is simply moved to the Deleted Items folder.

FIGURE 9.12

Select the folder to which you want to move or copy the selected message.

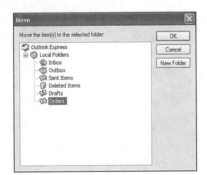

3. Expand the Folders list by clicking the plus sign next to Local Folders. Then click the folder in which you want to place the selected message.

4. Click **OK** to move or copy the message.

Finding Messages

If you don't (and sometimes even when you do!) organize your messages, you may find it difficult to find a message you received. For instance, suppose that you placed an order for a product via the Internet and kept the order confirmation message. Because the product has not arrived, you want to review the confirmation. Rather then sift through the various folders and messages, you can search for a message.

To help you find a message, Outlook Express includes a **Find** command. You can use this command to search for messages, matching the sender, the recipient, the subject, or a word or phrase in the content of the message. Follow these steps to search for a message:

1. Select the folder to search in the Folders list. If you don't know which folder contains the message, click **Local Folders** to search all the folders.

2. Click **Edit**, then **Find**, and then **Message**. You see the Find Message dialog box (see Figure 9.13).

tip

You can also nest mail folders within existing folders. For instance, you could create business and personal folders within the Inbox. To do so, click the Inbox for the first step or expand the Folders list in the dialog box by clicking the plus sign next to Local Folders and then clicking the folder you want.

tip

You can also drag a message from the message header pane to the appropriate folder in the Folders list of the main Outlook Express window to move a message.

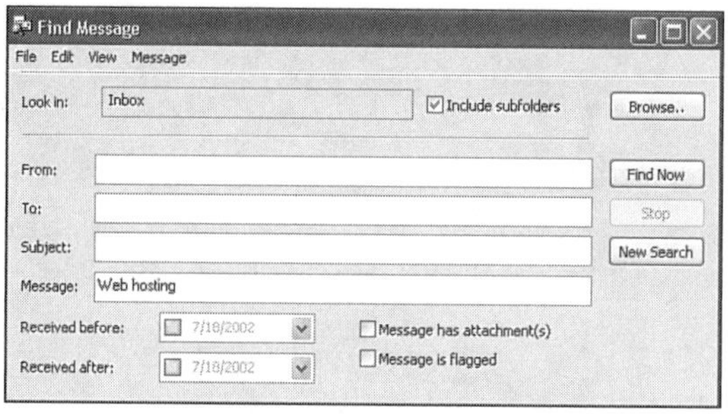

FIGURE 9.13

Enter your search requirements in this dialog box.

3. Click in the text box next to the item you want to search and then type or select a value. You can do any of the following:

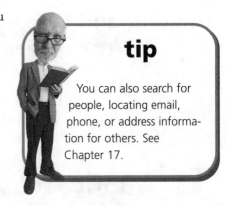

To search for a message based on the sender, click in the From text box and type all or part of the sender's name.

To search for a message based on who it was sent to, click in the To text box and type all or part of the recipient's name.

To match the subject of a message, click in the Subject text box and type all or part of the message subject.

If you don't know the exact sender or subject, click in the Message text box and type a unique word or phrase from the message content. (Typing a unique word or phrase helps limit the matches to those of interest.)

If you don't know the contents or details of the message but know when it was sent, select a date. You can select to view messages received before or after a certain date.

To search for messages that have an attachment or that were flagged for attention, check these check boxes.

4. If you selected Local Folders for step 1, make sure that the Include subfolders text box is checked to search all the folders.

5. Click **Find Now**. Outlook Express searches the messages and displays any matches in the lower half of the dialog box (see Figure 9.14). You can double-click any message to open it.

FIGURE 9.14

You can search for messages in any of your mail folders.

Find Message
File Edit View Message
Look in: Inbox — ☑ Include subfolders — Browse..
From: — Find Now
To: — Stop
Subject: — New Search
Message: Web hosting
Received before: ☐ 7/18/2002 — ☐ Message has attachment(s)
Received after: ☐ 7/18/2002 — ☐ Message is flagged
! 0 ▽ From — Subject — Receive
🖅 support@bcentralhost.com Welcome to Your New Web Hosting Account 6/4/2002
1 message(s), 0 unread, monitoring for new items.

Exiting and Disconnecting

When you are not working online, you should exit your mail program and log off (if you have a dial-up account). To do so, click the **Close** button for the Outlook Express window.

You are prompted to log off the connection if you have a dial-up connection. If you are prompted to log off, select **Yes** or **Disconnect**. If you are not prompted, right-click the connection icon in the taskbar and select **Disconnect**.

THE ABSOLUTE MINIMUM

This chapter covered the basics of using Outlook Express, the mail program included with Windows XP. With this program (and an Internet provider), you can send and receive email messages from all over the world. Email is quick and free! Keep in mind the following key points about Outlook Express and email features:

- The first step to using Outlook Express is to set up a mail account. Use the information from your ISP to set up your mail account. The steps vary depending on the provider and type of provider.

- To check your mail, start Outlook Express. New mail messages are listed in your Inbox. You can open any messages by double-clicking them.

- You have several choices for creating new mail: you can respond to messages you received, you can forward messages, and you can create new messages. The fastest way to do so is using the toolbar buttons in the Outlook Express program window.

- In addition to typing messages, you can also attach files to send, such as pictures. You may also receive email messages with attachments, which you can open or save to your computer.

- Try to keep your Inbox uncluttered. You can do so by deleting messages you no longer need, setting up folders and moving messages that you want to save to these folders, and printing and saving hard copies if needed.

- If you cannot find a message you received by looking through the various mail folders, you can search for a message using the **Edit**, **Find**, **Message** command. You can search by sender, recipient, subject, or content.

Browsing the Internet

The Internet is a huge resource of information and entertainment. You can find sites with current news, financial data, online stores, music, computer articles and help information, and much, much more. You simply cannot sum up all the content that you can find on the Internet. You have to experience it yourself.

This chapter covers how to log on to the Internet and then navigate from site to site using several methods.

Getting Started with Internet Explorer

To access the Internet, you need a program called a *Web browser*. And luckily enough, Windows XP includes Internet Explorer, a Web browser. You can use Internet Explorer to go to and view Web pages.

To start Internet Explorer, follow these steps:

1. Click **Start** and then click **Internet**.

2. If prompted, enter your username and password (some information might have been completed for you), and then click the **Connect** button. Depending on the type of connection, you may not need to complete this step.

   Windows connects to your ISP and displays the Internet Explorer window. You see your start page, usually the MSN home page, in the program window (see Figure 10.1).

tip

You can select a different start page as covered in Chapter 17, "Customizing Email and Internet Explorer."

FIGURE 10.1

Take a look the various tools in the Internet Explorer program window.

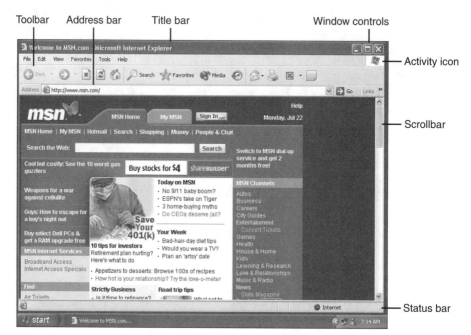

Understanding the Internet Explorer Window

Like most programs, the Internet Explorer window has a toolbar with various buttons to help you navigate from page to page. Before you start on your Internet journey, take a few minutes to look closely at the program window, including the following key items:

■ Title bar—Like other program windows, Internet Explorer displays a title bar at the top. This title bar lists the page title for the current page.

■ Window controls—In the upper-right corner you see window control buttons for changing the size of the window. You can close the window (and exit Internet Explorer). You can minimize the window, as another option. For information on changing the size of the window, see Chapter 2, "Getting Started with Windows XP."

■ Activity icon—Right beneath the window controls, you see an icon with the Microsoft Windows XP logo. This icon moves when Internet Explorer is busy. For example, displaying some pages (especially pages with many graphics) can take a while. You may think that the program is stuck. A good way to see whether the program is stuck or just simply busy is to take a look at this icon. If the flag is moving, the program is still busy trying to display the page.

■ Toolbar—Underneath the title bar and menu bar, you see a row of buttons. Again, like many other programs, Internet Explorer includes a toolbar with buttons for frequently used commands. See the next section, "Using the Toolbar," for a description of each of the toolbar buttons.

tip

Before you can take advantage of all the benefits of the Internet, you must set up your Internet connection. The specifics of setting up depend on your type of connection and your provider. Therefore, follow the specific instructions you received from your Internet provider. You can learn more about getting connected in Chapter 8, "Getting Wired for Communication."

If you have problems connecting—the line is busy, for example—try again. If you continue to have problems, check with your ISP.

■ Address bar—The address bar lists the address of the current page. You can type another address to go to a particular site. Using the address bar is covered later in "Typing a Web Address."

■ Scrollbar—If the page contains more than one screen of information (and most do), you see scrollbars along the right side of the window. You can scroll down the page by clicking the down arrow or by dragging the scroll box (the colored part of the scrollbar) up or down. To scroll up through a page, click the up scroll arrow.

■ Status bar—The status bar appears along the bottom of the program window. This displays link information. For instance, if you place your mouse pointer over a link (more on links later), you see the address of the linked page or site. If Internet Explorer is busy downloading data for the page, you see the status of this activity in the status bar.

Using the Toolbar

The most common way to navigate from page to page is to use the toolbar buttons. To use most buttons, you simply click the button. Other buttons have a down arrow next to them. For these buttons, you can click the down arrow and then select your choice from the button menu. For instance, if you click the down arrow next to the Mail button, you see commands for mailing pages (see Figure 10.2).

FIGURE 10.2
Some buttons have a drop-down menu for making a selection.

Some buttons open a bar on the left part of the program window. You then use the options in this bar to display other pages. For instance, you can click the **Media** button to display a list of media sites. You can click the **Search** button to display a list of search tools (more on searching in the next chapter). As well as using any of the links within the bar, you can scroll through the bar (click the scroll arrows or drag the scroll box), resize the bar (drag the bar border), and close the bar (click the **Close** button).

Table 10.1 lists each of the buttons as well as provides a description of each one.

Table 10.1   Internet Explorer Buttons

Button	Name	Click To...
	Back	Go to the last page you visited. You can click the button several times to go back several pages. And you can click the down arrow next to the button and select a page from the drop-down list. The same is true for the **Forward** button.
	Forward	Go forward a page. This button is available only if you have clicked Back to go back a page.
	Stop	Stop the display of a page. Use this button if the page is taking too long to display or if you change your mind.
	Refresh	Redisplay the page, refreshing the data on that page.
	Home	Return to your home page.
	Search	Display the Search bar to search for a site. See Chapter 11, "Searching the Internet" for more information.
	Favorites	Display a list of favorite sites. See Chapter 17.
	Media	Display a Media guide with access to music, videos, and other media features.
	History	Display a list of recently visited sites. See "Using the History List" later in this chapter.
	Mail	Email a page or link to a page. See "Emailing Web Pages" in this chapter. For more information on all email messages, see Chapter 9, "Sending and Receiving Email."
	Print	Print the current Web page.
	Edit	Open the page in a Web editing program. If you are interested in Web publishing, try one of Que's many guides to this topic including *10 Minute Guide to Microsoft FrontPage 2002*.
	Discuss	Join a discussion server for sharing comments about different topics.

Viewing the Page Content

Now that you are familiar with the program window, you can take a look at the page itself.

The first page you see when you log on to the Internet is your *start* or *home page*. (Both names are commonly used to refer to that first page.) Your home page will vary. Your ISP may display its opening page as your home page. For instance, if you have a cable connection, you may see your Internet cable provider page (such as Road Runner for Time Warner's cable connections). You may see MSN, the home page for Microsoft's online service. Or you may see a page you have selected yourself. You can customize the home page, selecting the page you want (see Chapter 17).

Regardless of what page you see, all home pages (and most every page you visit on the Internet) have the same basic elements. Here's what you can expect to find in the content area of the Internet Explorer window:

> **tip**
>
> If you are unsure what a button does, you can display its ScreenTip name. Place the mouse button on the border of a button. The button name should pop up.

- Links—The great thing about the Internet is how information is linked. You can click a link to view other information. For instance, you may see a headline on a page. By clicking the headline, you can view the complete story. You learn more about using links in the next section.

- Information—You also see articles about various topics, similar to the front page of a newspaper. You can review any of the articles posted on the page.

- Advertisements—Nearly all Web content is provided free of charge. To finance this free information, most sites sell advertising. You may see ads at the top, bottom, or sides of the page.

- Table of contents—Many sites provide a quick table of contents to the site. You can jump to other pages at the site using this table. These may also be named *channels* or *categories*. For instance, in Figure 10.1, you see the MSN Channels. Information is organized into topics such as Business, News, and so on. You can find these table of contents links along the top, side, or bottom of the page. Sometimes they appear on the page in more than one place.

- Search button—Because a site may include a lot of information, you may find a **Search** button on the page. Use this

> Don't be surprised if you see pop-up windows with advertisements when you log on. Usually these are displayed in their own window. You can click the Close button for that window to close the ad. Some have pop-behind ads, ads that appear behind the program window and show up when you close the program window. Again, you can click the Close button to close any advertisement windows.

Search button to search for particular content at that site (see Figure 10.3). You may also see a **Search** button for searching the Internet—that is, not limited to just content at the site. Chapter 11 is devoted to the topic of searching.

- Resource features—Many sites include useful resource features. For instance, maps are a common resource tool. You can click the link for maps to get directions to a place. Business and other listings (such as the Yellow Pages) are another common resource. You can use these directories, for instance, to find the address or phone number of a company.

- Entertainment—Many sites have multimedia elements. You can listen to music, view a short video, check out animations, and more.

- Custom information—Many home or start sites let you customize what appears on this opening page. For example, you might display local weather or news stories. You might display your horoscope for the day. The process for customizing your home page depends on that particular site. Look for links on your home page for specific information on customizing the contents.

Now that you know what to expect at your starting page, you are ready to jump from that page to other sites. Keep in mind that sites are constantly changing. Also, most sites follow a similar structure—that is, have articles, a table of contents (sometimes called a *site map*), advertisements, and so on. The next section covers how to navigate from page to page using links.

Using Links to Navigate

Information on the Internet is easy to browse because documents contain links to other pages, documents, and sites. A *link* is text or graphic reference to other sites. Links, also called *hyperlinks*, usually appear underlined and sometimes in a different color. Images can also be links.

Links are what makes the Internet so valuable; you can use the links to jump to related sites. For instance, if you see a link for Careers (refer to Figure 10.1, which contains a Careers link), you can click that link to view career-related pages. At the career page, you may see a link for resume tips or job postings (see Figure 10.4). You can click one of these links to go to that page. Jumping from link to link is called different things: navigating, searching, browsing. Using links is simple and the best way to become familiar with the wealth of information on the Internet.

tip

The preceding list gives you a quick overview of what you can expect. You'll find much more information and many more links at your site. And the content is frequently updated. The best way to get a sense of what's available is to explore and experiment with your own home page.

FIGURE 10.4

Use links to navigate from page to page.

You can click a link on the current page to view the page associated with that link. Sometimes the link takes you to another section in the current page. Sometimes the link takes you to another page at the current Web site. Other times, clicking a link takes you to an entirely different site. Half the fun of browsing is exploring all types of topics and levels of information using links.

To go to a link, simply click it. You can jump from link to link until you find the information you seek. If you get too far astray remember that you can use the **Back** button to return to the previous page. You can click the **Back** button as many times as needed to return several pages back. You can also click the down arrow next to the **Back** button and select the site from the list.

tip

You can tell when text or an image is a link because when you point to it, the pointer changes to a hand with a pointing finger, and the address to that link appears in the status bar.

If you have gone back to a page, you can also move forward again to pages you have viewed. Use the **Forward** button to do so.

Finally, if you get lost or want to start over from the home page, you can click the **Home** button to go back to your start page.

Typing a Web Address

Browsing is a great way to explore the Internet, especially if you are not exactly sure what you are looking for. You can browse around to see what information or resources you can find. Think of browsing as flipping through the pages in a book to get a sense of content or looking through the table of contents. Browsing is like an expedition, and you are not always sure where you'll end up!

If you don't want to browse, you can go directly to a site. Typing a site's address is the fastest way to get to that site. Keeping the book metaphor, typing an address would be similar to looking up the page number in the index and then going directly to that page. When you know where you want to go—that is, when you know the site's address—you can use this method for accessing content on the Internet.

Every page on the Internet has an address (sometimes called a *URL* or *uniform resource locator*), and this address follows a certain naming method. For instance, the address to Que's Web site is `http://www.quepublishing.com`. The URL breaks down like this:

- The first part is the protocol (usually `http://`, *hypertext transfer protocol*) and indicates that the site is a graphical, multimedia page. This designation indicates a file site. You do not have to type that part (`http://`) of the address. Internet Explorer assumes that you want to go to an HTTP site.

■ The next part of the address is the host name (usually www for Web servers). When you type this part, you usually can leave off the www.

■ The important part of the address is the domain name (which also includes the extension). The domain name is the name of the site and is usually the name or abbreviation of the company or individual. For instance, Que's domain name is quepublishing.

■ The extension indicates the site type. Common extensions include .com, .net, .gov, .edu, or .mil (commercial, network resources, government, educational, or military, respectively).

■ The address (or URL) might also include a path (a list of folders) to the document.

You can find Web site addresses in advertisements, newspaper or magazine articles, and other media sources.

To go to an address, follow these steps:

1. Click in the **Address** bar.

2. Type the address of the site you want to visit, and then press **Enter**. Internet Explorer displays the page for that address.

note

The other common protocol is ftp:// (*file transfer protocol*). This type of site is commonly used for sharing files.

tip

Most Web site names are some form of the site or company name, so often you can simply guess. For instance, to go to the NFL site, type www.nfl.com. If the address is incorrect, you'll see a page explaining that the site is not available. You can try another version of the name or search for the site as covered in Chapter 11.

Using Shortcuts for Web Browsing

To help you quickly get to sites, Internet Explorer provides several shortcuts including using the Favorites list, the History list, and others.

Setting Up a Favorites List

If you find a site that you especially like, you might want a quick way to return to it without having to browse from link to link or having to remember the address.

Fortunately, Internet Explorer enables you to build a list of favorite sites and to access those sites by clicking them in the list.

To add a site to your favorite list, follow these steps:

1. Display the Web site that you want to add to your list.

2. Open the **Favorites** menu and click the **Add to Favorites** command.

3. In the Add Favorite dialog box, shown in Figure 10.5, type a name for the page (if you're not satisfied with the default name that is provided).

4. Click **OK**.

FIGURE 10.5

Add favorite sites to your Favorites list.

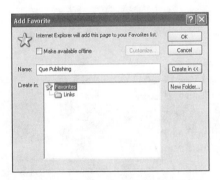

After you have added a site to your Favorites list, you can go to that site. Follow these steps:

1. Click the **Favorites** button.

2. In the Favorites bar that is displayed (see Figure 10.6), click the site you want to visit. The selected favorite site is displayed in the main window.

3. Click the **Close** button in the Favorites bar to close this pane of the window.

FIGURE 10.6
Use the Favorites
list to go quickly
to your most vis-
ited sites.

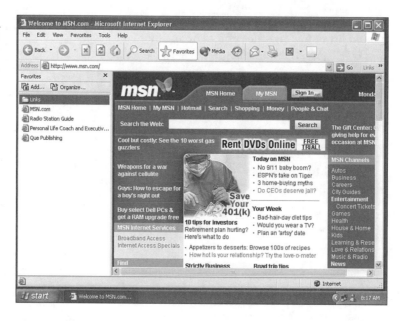

Using the History List

In addition to using the Favorites list, you can
also use the History list to go to a site. If you
have recently visited a site that you liked, but
can't remember its address, you can view the
History list, which lists the sites and pages you
have visited in the last several weeks. From this
list, you can find the site you want and click the
link to go to that site.

Follow these steps to view and go to a site in the
History list:

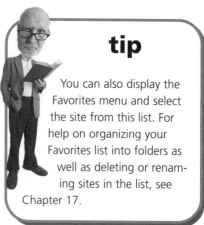

tip

You can also display the
Favorites menu and select
the site from this list. For
help on organizing your
Favorites list into folders as
well as deleting or renaming sites in the list, see
Chapter 17.

1. Click the **History** button. The History bar
   is displayed.

2. Click **Today** to view sites visited today. Or click one of the weeks you want
   (last week, two weeks ago, three weeks ago). The list expands to show sites for
   the time period you selected (see Figure 10.7).

FIGURE 10.7

Use the History list to go to a site you have visited recently.

3. Click the site you want to visit. The list expands again to display pages (if applicable) that you have visited at that particular site.

4. Click the specific page at that site. That page is displayed.

5. Click the **Close** button to close the History bar.

tip

As another shortcut, you can click the down arrow at the far right of the address bar to display a list of sites you have gone to by typing the address. You can click any listed site to go to that site.

Emailing Web Pages

Often in your Web browsing, you come across sites that might be of interest to others. Internet Explorer makes it convenient to send a link or the actual page to others.

To view the mail commands, click the down arrow next to the **Mail** button. Using these commands, you can read your mail (open your Inbox) or create a new, blank message. (Chapter 9 is devoted to email messages.) You can also select **Send a Link** or **Send Page**. When you select either of these commands, Internet Explorer displays a new mail message. You can complete the address and click **Send** to send the message (see Figure 10.8).

FIGURE 10.8

You can email a page or a link to a page.

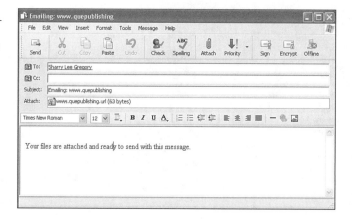

If you send the page, the recipient can view the contents of the page but usually cannot use any of the links. (This is like taking a snapshot of the page.) If you send a link, the link is included as an attachment or as a link within the message text. The recipient can open the attachment or click the link to go to that page. The recipient can then access any of the information and links at this site.

tip

To print a Web page, click the Print button. In the Print dialog box, make any changes to the print options and then click OK to print.

Exiting and Logging Off the Internet

When you are finished browsing the Internet, you should not only exit Internet Explorer but also log off your dial-up account. (If you have a broadband connection that is always connected, you do not need to log off.)

To exit Internet Explorer, click its **Close** button or click **File**, **Close**. When you exit Internet Explorer, you may be prompted to log off your Internet provider. Click **Yes** or **Disconnect Now**. If you are not prompted, be sure to log off. Right-click the connection icon in the system tray and select **Disconnect**.

The Absolute Minimum

This chapter covered the basics of using Internet Explorer, the Web browser program included with Windows XP. With this program (and an Internet provider), you can access the many resources of the Internet. Keep in mind the following key points:

- The first step to using Internet Explorer is to set up an Internet account. Use the information from your ISP to set up this account. The steps vary depending on the provider and type of provider.

- To start Internet Explorer, click **Start** and then **Internet Explorer**. If prompted to get connected, follow your logon procedure (usually type your username and password). The first page that is displayed is called your home page.

- You have two basic methods for displaying Web pages: you can browse from page to page using links, or you can type the page address to go directly to a page.

- Use the toolbar buttons to navigate among pages. Click **Back** to go back a page, **Forward** to go forward a page, and **Home** to return to your starting page.

- If you frequently visit a site, add it to your Favorites list. You can then display this list and go to any of the sites by clicking its name.

- You can display pages you have viewed on the current day as well as several weeks ago by displaying the History bar.

11

SEARCHING THE INTERNET

The Internet includes many different sites. Looking for the site you want by browsing can be like looking for the proverbial needle in the haystack. Instead, you can search for a topic and find all sites related to that topic.

You can use Internet Explorer's search tool. Or you can visit and use the search features at any number of Internet search sites.

Searching with Internet Explorer

To help you get where you want to go quickly, Internet Explorer provides a Search bar. You can use the features in this pane to search for sites relating to a particular topic or interest.

To search for sites using Internet Explorer, follow these steps:

1. Click the **Search** button in the toolbar. You see the Search bar in the left pane of the Internet Explorer window.

2. Type what you want to find (see Figure 11.1). Type a unique word or phrase, as specific as possible. For instance, if you type "beads," you will find too many matches to make the search worthwhile. If you type "Mardi Gras beads," your results will more closely match what you want to find.

FIGURE 11.1

Type the topic that you want to match.

3. Click the **Search** button. You see the results of the search in the window on the right (see Figure 11.2). Sponsored links appear in the search bar on the right. Usually a sponsored site in a search engine is one that has paid to get itself listed higher in the search results.

4. Scroll through the list to see information about the first set of matches.

5. To go to any of the found sites, click the link in the search results window. The page you selected appears in the right pane.

FIGURE 11.2

You can review all the matches found for your topic. You can also refine the search using suggestions in the Search bar.

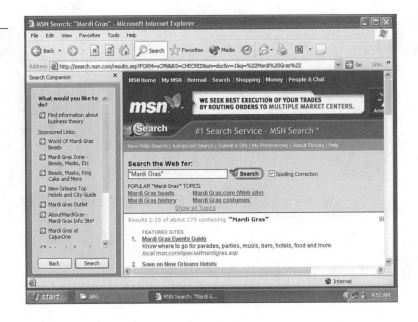

Getting the Most from the Search Results

If you use the **Search** button, MSN (Microsoft Network) is the search engine that is used. (You can also use other search tools, covered later in this chapter, and you can change the engine used by Internet Explorer.) MSN's search results page includes several useful features for finding the most closely matching site. Review these tips:

- To see as much of the search results as possible, close the Search bar by clicking its **Close** button. Also, the header as well as the left side of the search page has other MSN links (and ads). Scroll further down the page to view the actual matches.

- Different search engines use different matching formulas that determine which sites are listed first. MSN tries to place the most common sites related to your search topic. These are listed at the top.

- To get an idea of the scope of your search, check out the number of found matches. For instance, in Figure 11.3, sites 1–15 are displayed out of 2469 matches.

- If more than one set of results is found, MSN lists the most popular. You can view other matches by clicking the **Next** button (refer to Figure 11.3).

FIGURE 11.3

Review the
search results
and search-
related informa-
tion to fine-tune
your search.

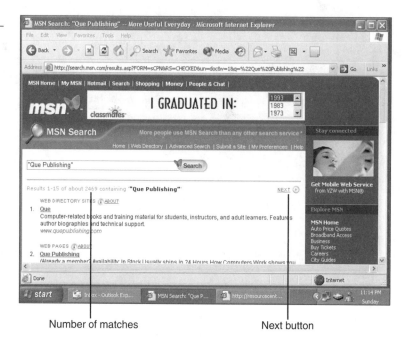

Number of matches

Next button

- The site name is listed as well as a
  short description and the address for
  the site. Use this data to determine
  whether a particular listed site has the
  information you want.

- To go to any matching site, click its
  link. Figure 11.4, for instance, shows
  the Que Publishing site, one of the
  matching links from the search.

- You'll find that in searching, you normally try one of the links and then go
  back to the results; try another link
  and go back to the results. You may
  need to go back and forth several times
  to find the information you need. Also,
  you may find valuable information
  at more than one site, so you can visit
  several.

tip

As mentioned in Chapter
10, "Browsing the Internet,"
many sites provide Search
tools on their pages. You can
use these to search for content at that site. Type the
word or phrase to locate
and click the Search button. You
can also use Internet Explorer's
Edit, Find (on This Page) command
to search for a word or phrase on
the current page.

FIGURE 11.4

The descriptions of the matches give you a general sense of the site content, but you usually need to go to the site to see what information it contains.

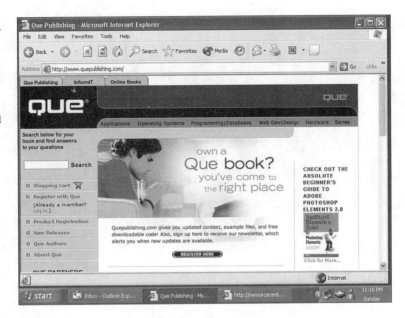

FIGURE 11.4

The descriptions of the matches give you a general sense of the site content, but you usually need to go to the site to see what information it contains.

Fine-Tuning the Search

If you don't find an appropriate match, you can refine your search. The Search bar provides some suggestions for fine-tuning the search. You can also use more complex search criteria. For instance, if you are searching for the White House, most sites start with listings of sites that include both words. But the listing also includes sites that have "White" or "House." You can limit the search to only those that contain both "White House."

To use MSN's additional search features, click the **Advanced Search** link on the MSN Search page. You see the various options for refining your search criteria (see Figure 11.5). Here you can pick and choose from among several search options including how matches are made: all of the words, any of the words, words in the title, the exact phrase, and others. You can limit the search to particular domains (only government or .gov sites, for instance). You also can specify that the matching sites contain certain elements (such as audio or images). Make your choices and then start the search.

tip

If you are unsure about the various help options, click the help link next to each for an explanation.

FIGURE 11.5

If you get too many matches (or none!), try using some of the advanced search options.

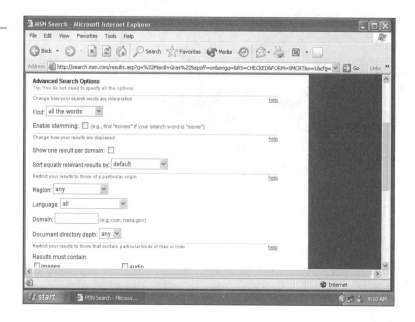

Using Other Search Sites

In addition to MSN's search tool, you can also go to other sites dedicated to searching. New search sites are popping up all the time, adding to the several already established and popular search sites. The search site is often called by various names including *search tool*, *search directory*, or *search engine*. Each search site uses its own method for categorizing and cataloging the sites. They also usually provide various other research tools (such as access to maps or email searches), and the options for searching vary. But the basics of using the services remain the same.

Follow these steps to use another search site:

1. Go to the site by typing the address and pressing **Enter**.

Once at the site, follow these general steps:

2. Type the word or phrase you want to find. Be as specific as possible.

3. Click the search button. (The name of the button varies.) You see the results of the search.

tip

Is one search engine better than another? Not definitively so. You'll find that you just prefer one site over another, usually when you get the most success on your searches from a site. I prefer, for instance, Google because the start page is streamlined and doesn't include an overwhelming set of options.

Some popular search sites include

- Google—www.google.com
- Yahoo!—www.yahoo.com
- Excite—www.excite.com
- Alta Vista—www.altavista.com
- Lycos—www.lycos.com
- IXQuick—www.ixquick.com
- Kartoo—www.kartoo.com

tip

If you don't find the information you need, try using another search site. The results you get vary from site to site.

Refining Your Search

Most search sites provide many options for fine-tuning the search. Common search features may be listed on the home page. Also, look for a link named something like Advanced Search or More Search Options.

Browsing Through Directories or Channels

In addition to search tools, many sites provide channels or directories of content. You can browse through these categories to find information.

THE ABSOLUTE MINIMUM

When you don't know an address or don't know what content is available, the best way to find out is to search. You can search using MSN's search feature (built into Internet Explorer), or you can use any of the other search sites. Keep the following guidelines in mind:

- You can use Internet Explorer's Search button to open a search pane. Internet Explorer, by default, uses MSN Search as its search tool.

- When the results are displayed, you can go to any listed site by clicking its link.

- In addition to MSN's search tool, you can use any of the many Internet sites devoted to searching. Type the address to that site and then follow the specific instructions for searching from that site. Basically, you type the topic or question and click the search button.

- To fine-tune your search, look for a link to advanced or more search options. Then limit your search with these features.

- Many search sites include directories (or channels) that you can browse through to find sites related to that category.

12

SENDING AND RECEIVING FAXES

In addition to communicating via email, you can also use Windows XP to send and receive faxes. Windows XP includes a program, called Fax Console, that organizes your incoming faxes and enables you to create new faxes.

To fax from Windows XP, you must have a fax modem. (Most dial-up modems also function as a fax.) If you have a broadband connection (such as a cable modem), you cannot use this modem to send a fax.

This chapter covers the basics of sending and receiving faxes.

Setting Up the Fax Console

Before you can use your fax modem to send and receive faxes, you must set it up in Windows, entering information about the fax phone number and fax device. To help you with this process, Windows XP includes the Fax Configuration Wizard. This program starts the first time you open the Fax Console. To start Fax Console, click **Start**, **All Programs**, **Accessories**, **Communications**, **Fax**, and finally **Fax Console**. You see the welcome screen of the wizard.

To start the Fax Configuration Wizard manually (if it does not start when you open Fax Console), click **Tools** from within Fax Console and then click the **Configure Fax** command.

To set up your fax, complete each step in the wizard, entering information and clicking **Next** to move to the next step. You can expect to complete the following:

If the Fax component is not installed, you can install it through the Add/Remove Programs Control Panel. See Chapter 24, "Upgrading Windows." You can also find information by searching for this topic at support.micrsoft.com.

■ Enter your contact information (name, fax number, email address, company, and other phone information). Figure 12.1 shows the first screen you see after the welcome wizard screen.

FIGURE 12.1

To use your fax, you need to set it up, entering information about your setup.

■ Select the fax device for sending and receiving. To do so, select the fax device from the drop-down list. You can also enable send and receive by checking the respective check box. Finally, you can select to manually answer a fax call or to automatically answer the call after the number of rings you designate. Figure 12.2 shows this step of the Fax Configuration Wizard.

FIGURE 12.2

Set up your send and receive options for this step of the Fax Configuration Wizard.

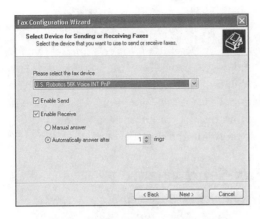

- Enter the TSID. A TSID is a line that identifies your fax when it sends a fax. You can type your business name or fax number.

- Enter your CSID. CSID is a text line that identifies your fax machine when it receives a fax.

- Select how received faxes are handled (printed directly to the printer or stored in a folder). If you choose to print the faxes on receipt, you can select the printer from the drop-down list. If you select to store the faxes in a folder (which you can then open and view the faxes in that folder), select this option and then select the folder to use. Figure 12.3 shows these options.

tip

Be sure to check Enable Receive in this wizard step. A common problem is being unable to receive faxes, and this occurs if this option is not checked. (You can make this change later if you forget here.)

FIGURE 12.3

When you receive a fax, you can choose to print it on a printer or store it within a folder.

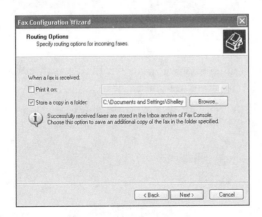

The fax is set up and ready for use.

Sending a Fax

After the Fax Console is set up, you can use it to send and receive faxes. To help you create and send a fax, Windows XP provides a Fax Send Wizard. This wizard leads you through the steps for creating and sending a fax cover page. You can also send a fax from within a program. For instance, you may want to fax a document you created in Word. To fax within another program, you "print" to the fax. This section covers both these methods for sending a fax.

Sending a Fax with the Fax Send Wizard

To send a fax using the wizard, follow these steps:

1. If the Fax Console is not open, click **Start**, **All Programs**, **Accessories**, **Communications**, **Fax**, and finally **Fax Send Wizard**.

   If the Fax Console is open, click **File** and then click the **Send a Fax** command. Both start the Send Fax Wizard.

2. Click **Next** to move from the welcome screen to the first step.

3. Enter the name and fax number of the recipient (see Figure 12.4). Click **Next**.

FIGURE 12.4

Enter the recipient name and fax number.

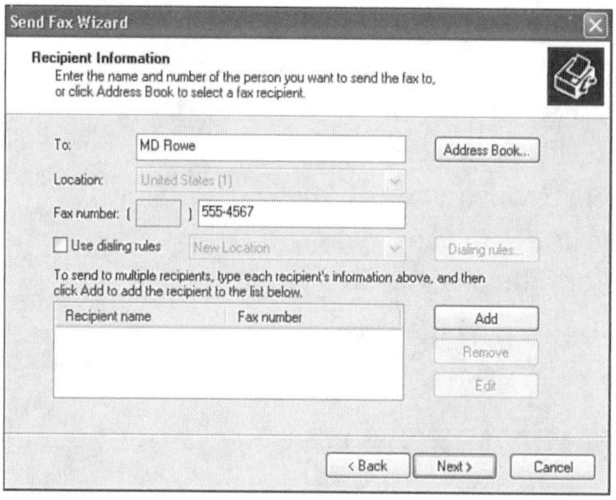

4. If you want to use a different cover page template, display the template drop-down list and select the template you want.

5. Type a subject and the note for the fax cover sheet (see Figure 12.5). Click **Next**.

FIGURE 12.5

Type the con-
tents for the fax
in this dialog
box, including
the subject and
note.

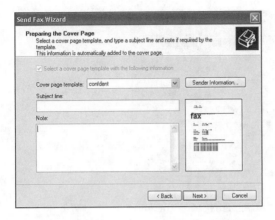

6. Select when to send the fax (see Figure 12.6). Click **Next**.

FIGURE 12.6

You can send the
fax immediately
or schedule it for
delivery at
another time.

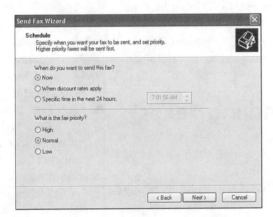

7. Click **Finish**. The fax is sent at the time you selected in step 6.

Faxing from a Program

You can also fax documents created in Windows programs by "printing" to the fax;
the program uses the fax modem you have set up with the configuration wizard.
This method starts the Fax Send Wizard but faxes all the pages in the document.

To fax a document from a program, follow these steps:

1. Open the document you want to fax.

2. Click **File** and then click the **Print** command. You see the Print dialog box.

3. Display the printer drop-down list and select **Fax** (see Figure 12.7).

FIGURE 12.7

To fax a document from within a program, print it, selecting **Fax** as the printer.

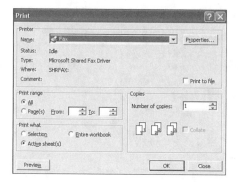

4. Click the **OK** button. This starts the Send Fax Wizard. Follow the same steps as covered in the preceding section. That is, complete the recipient and other information for the fax, clicking **Next** to complete each step in the fax wizard. The document is then faxed to that recipient.

Receiving and Handling Faxes

Depending on what options you selected when you used the Fax Configuration Wizard to set up your fax modem, receiving faxes can vary. For instance, if you set up your fax to automatically answer a fax call, all fax calls are answered. If you set up your fax to manually answer the call, you are notified when a fax is being sent. You can then choose to answer the call.

tip

You can also access and send a fax using the Send Fax Wizard from the Printers and Faxes Control Panel. Click **Start**, **Control Panel**. Then click **Printers and Other Hardware**. Under Pick a task, click **View** installed printers or fax printers. Then under Printer Tasks, click **Send a fax** and follow the steps to complete and send the fax.

If you set up your fax to automatically answer your call, the modem receives any incoming faxes and handles them according to the option you selected. If you selected to print the faxes on receipt, they are printed on the printer you selected. If you selected to store them in a folder, they are placed in that folder. You can open that folder and then view the faxes. You can also view faxes from the Fax Console by selecting **Inbox** in the Fax list.

Opening Faxes

To open the Fax Console and view any stored faxes (either new faxes or faxes you have received previously), follow these steps:

1. Click **Start**, **All Programs**, **Accessories**, **Communications**, **Fax**, and finally **Fax Console**. You see the Fax Console window (see Figure 12.8). Notice that the Fax Console is similar to Outlook Express. Both include a list of folders on the left side of the program window. In Outlook Express, you see mail folders. In Fax Console, you see fax folders. You can click any of the folders to view the faxes in that particular folder.

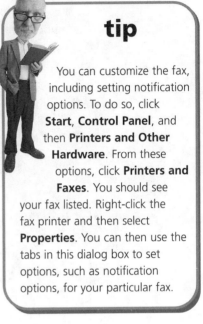

tip

You can customize the fax, including setting notification options. To do so, click **Start**, **Control Panel**, and then **Printers and Other Hardware**. From these options, click **Printers and Faxes**. You should see your fax listed. Right-click the fax printer and then select **Properties**. You can then use the tabs in this dialog box to set options, such as notification options, for your particular fax.

FIGURE 12.8

Use the Fax Console to send and receive faxes.

2. To open a fax you have received, click **Inbox** in the Fax folder list. You see a list of the faxes you have received. The fax list also includes identifying information about each fax including when the fax was received, the number of pages, and so on.

3. To open a fax, double-click it (see Figure 12.9).

FIGURE 12.9

You can open faxes in your Inbox.

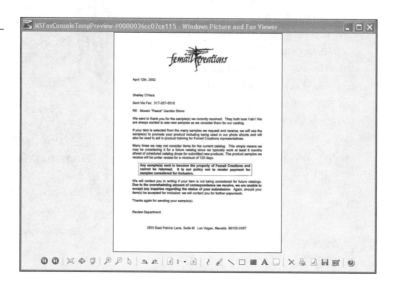

Handling Faxes

You also have other options besides viewing. You can't do much from the preview window, but from the Fax Console, you can print, delete, or email any of the received faxes. To do so, follow these steps:

1. Click the fax in the fax list.

2. Do any of the following:

   To print the fax, click the **Print** button or click **File** and then click the **Print** command. Select print options in the Print dialog box and then click **OK**.

   To save a fax to another folder, click the **Save As** button. Select a folder, type a name, and select a file type. The default is .tif (a popular graphic file format). Click **Save**.

If you have problems receiving faxes, your fax device might not be set up to receive faxes. You can enable send and receive. To do so, click **Start**, **Control Panel**, **Printers and Other Hardware**, and finally, **Printers and Faxes**. Right-click the fax device, right-click **Receive**, and then click **Auto**.

To email a fax, click the **Mail To** button. You see a New Message window with the fax attached. Complete the recipient, subject, and message and click **Send**. For more information on sending email messages, see Chapter 9, "Sending and Receiving Email."

To delete a fax, click the **Delete** button. Then confirm the delete by clicking **Yes**.

THE ABSOLUTE MINIMUM

This chapter covered the basics of using your computer to both send and receive faxes. Windows XP includes the Fax Console for these tasks. The important fax points to keep in mind include the following:

- Before you can use your computer to fax, you must set up the fax. Do so using the Fax Configuration Wizard. This starts automatically the first time you open the Fax Console.

- You can send simple faxes, typing a subject line and a note using the Send Fax Wizard. Or you can fax a document from within a program.

- You can set up Fax Console to handle faxes the way you want. You can choose to answer a fax call manually or automatically. You can choose to print any received faxes or to store them in a fax folder.

- To view and work with received faxes, open the Fax Console. You can then view, print, save, or delete any of the faxes.

PART III

ENTERTAINMENT!

13

PLAYING MUSIC AND VIDEOS

Windows XP includes a wealth of entertainment features, including turning your PC into a boom box, music mixer, radio, video player, and even a movie-editing program. This chapter covers the basics of each of these entertainment elements.

Playing Audio CDs with Windows Media Player

If you like to listen to music while you work or if you just plain want to play some music, you can play audio CDs using Windows Media Player. In addition to playing music, you have many more options. You can adjust the volume, view visualization, download track information for the CD, and more.

Playing a CD

To play an audio CD, simply insert it into your CD drive. Doing so starts Windows Media Player automatically, and the CD begins to play. If the CD does not play (your drive may not be set up for Autoplay), click **Start**, **All Programs**, and then **Windows Media Player**. Then click the **Play** button. The music is played, and you see the default visualization.

If the CD has the title information on it or if you have downloaded the CD information from the Internet, you see the name of the album and each of the tracks (see Figure 13.1). You also see the time of each track as well as the total CD play time. The current song is highlighted in the playlist.

Keep in mind that this is a beginner's book, and some of the programs—in particular Movie Maker—could easily be the subject of an entire book.

FIGURE 13.1

When you play a CD, you see track information in the playlist. You also see a visual representation of each song.

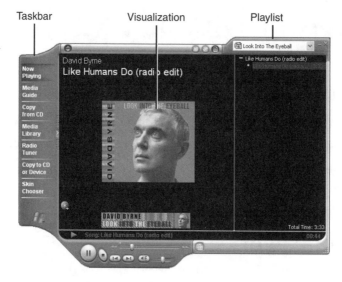

If you see generic names (Track 1, Track 2, and so on), you can download the track information from the Internet. To do so, connect to the Internet while the CD is playing. A quick way to connect is using the Media Guide. See "Playing Music from the Internet" later in this chapter.

The taskbar appears to the left of the Media Player window and includes buttons for performing other music-related tasks. You learn more about these options later in this chapter.

Working with Windows Media Player Controls

The Media Player window provides several buttons for controlling the playback of the CD. These controls let you adjust the volume, play another track, and start and stop the playback. Figure 13.2 identifies the basic controls. With these controls, you can do any of the following:

Note that the quality of the playback is determined by the quality of your speakers. Don't expect stereo quality!

FIGURE 13.2

You can use the controls in the Windows Media Player window to play a different track, change the volume, and more.

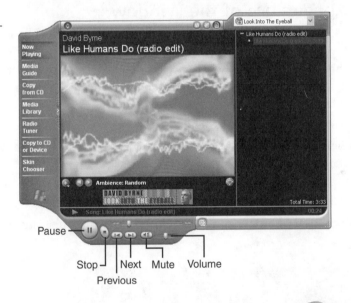

Pause

Stop | Next Mute Volume

Previous

- To play a different track, double-click it in the track list.

- To play the next track, click **Next**. To play the previous track, click **Previous.**

- To change the volume, drag the volume control. You may also need to adjust the volume button on your speakers.

- To mute the music (say when you get a phone call), click the **Mute** button.

tip

To hide the taskbar, click the little red arrow on the bar that divides the taskbar from the media play area.

■ To stop the playback, click **Stop**. If you stop and want to restart, click the **Play** button again.

■ To pause the playback, click **Pause**. To restart, click the **Play** button. (The **Pause** button becomes the Play button.)

■ To keep the music playing, but hide the Media Player window, click its **Minimize** button.

■ To stop the music and close Media Player, click the **Close** button.

tip

If you are not sure what a particular button does, point to it: the name of the button pops up.

Changing the Appearance of the Window

You can change the appearance of the Media Player window using one of two methods. First, you can choose a different *skin*. A skin is a layer over an application that changes how it looks. Second, you can select different visualizations that appear when the music is playing. Both are purely personal choices. You can experiment and pick the style you like.

To change the skin, follow these steps:

1. Click the **Skin Chooser** button in the taskbar. You see the different skin choices.

2. Click any of the listed skins. You see a preview of the selected skin. Figure 13.3, for instance, shows Optik selected.

3. Click **Apply Skin**. Your newly designed player appears, playing the CD.

FIGURE 13.3

You can change the look of the Windows Media Player window.

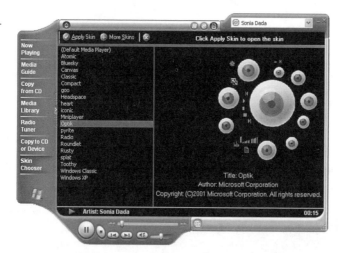

To return to the main playback window, click the **Now Playing** button in the taskbar.

In addition to changing the appearance of the player, you can choose from several visualizations. A *visualization* is a moving graphic image displayed during a song, making the music a more multimedia experience. Again, pick the one you like best. You may want to vary them according to your mood.

To select a visualization, do any of the following:

- Click **Next** visualization to display the next visualization or click **Previous visualization**. When you use these buttons, you select different options within the visualization. For instance, if Ambience is selected (usually the default), you can select **Warp**, **Falloff**, **Water**, and others.

- To display another category of visualizations, click the **Select visualization** button to display a list. Then select the item you want. You can select **Album art**, **Bars and Waves**, **Battery**, **Particle**, **Spikes**, as well as several others. You can also further fine-tune your selection by viewing and selecting the various visualizations within this category. Figure 13.4 shows spikes.

tip

You can click More Skins to go online and select from other Windows Media Player skins.

With some of the skins, the control buttons are not easy to figure out. If you use a new skin, you may need to experiment to figure out which button does what. Also, remember you can display a button's name by placing the mouse pointer on the edge of the button.

FIGURE 13.4

You can select from several visualizations, including album art.

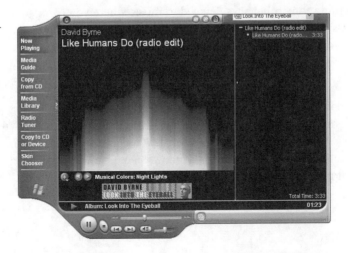

Playing Music from the Internet

In addition to audio CDs, you can also go online and play music tracks. You can find many sites devoted to music. Windows Media Player conveniently provides access to its music site. Click **Media Guide** in the taskbar to access WindowsMedia.com. From here you can find not only music but also videos and other links (see Figure 13.5).

tip

If you are not connected, you will be prompted to log on to your Internet provider so that you can access the online site.

FIGURE 13.5

Use the Media Guide to get entertainment news.

You can find many other sites devoted to music where you can get information about CDs and artists, hear sound clips of tracks, purchase albums, and download music to your computer.

Viewing Videos

The Windows Media Player is not just for playing music. You can also view video clips and animations. These might be files sent to you (such as a video clip of a friend's wedding) or files you have created. You can also access online sites and view clips from these sites. For instance, WindowsMedia.com provides links to video clips of current movies.

Tuning the Radio

In addition to listening to music, playing music online, and viewing videos, you can also tune into your favorite radio station and listen to taped or live radio broadcasts right from your computer. You can select from several preset radio stations, including BBC World, NPR (National Public Radio), Billboard, and others. To use this feature, you must be connected to the Internet.

Click the **Radio Tuner** button in the Media Player window's taskbar to find and listen to radio stations (see Figure 13.6).

note

Downloading music from the Internet is beyond the scope of this book. You'll find several sites and programs for this task. Try mp3.com or realplayer.com as some music sites.

FIGURE 13.6

Tune into the radio tuner from the Radio Tuner tab in Windows Media Player.

Using Other Windows Media Player Features

In addition to simple playback, you can also use Windows Media Player for several other music tasks. You can do any of the following:

tip

In addition to being able to play video clips within Media Player, you can also play video clips from Internet Explorer.

- Copy tracks from a CD to your computer. You can then play back the song from the computer rather than the audio CD. You can also then copy the song track from your computer to a CD disk if you have a recordable CD drive or to a portable music player such as an MP3 player. Use the **Copy from CD** and **Copy to CD or Device** buttons in the Media Player window taskbar for these features.

■ Use the Media Library to access all the audio, video, and radio stations set up on your computer. You can set up playlists on this page as well as organize contents by category. For instance, you can arrange music files by album, artist, or genre.

Playing and Recording Sounds with Sound Recorder

For simple audio needs, you can use the Sound Recorder accessory program to play back and record sounds. You can record your own sounds and insert the sound files into your documents or attach to an email. To use Sound Recorder, you need a sound card and speakers, which are standard on most computers.

Playing Sounds

Follow these steps to play a sound file:

1. Click **Start**, **All Programs**, **Accessories**, **Entertainment**, and select **Sound Recorder**. You see the Sound Recorder window.

2. Click **File** and then click the **Open** command.

3. Change to the drive and folder that contains the sound file you want to play.

note

MP3 is a popular format for music files. You can find MP3 files on various Internet sites. With an MP3 player, you can copy tunes to your player and take the music with you, much like a Sony Walkman. In addition to MP3 files, you can find other standard music file types.

When copying audio files, be sure that you understand the legal ramifications of copyright protection. Recently there's been a big brouhaha over certain sites, such as napster.com, that provide free music for downloading. That site has been shut down. You can find other free sites as well as music sites that enable you to purchase songs.

4. Double-click the sound file to open it in Sound Recorder (see Figure 13.7). Then click the **Play** button to hear the file.

FIGURE 13.7

You can play sound files in Sound Recorder.

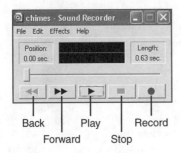

Back | Forward | Play | Stop | Record

5. Click the **Close** button to close the Sound Recorder window.

Recording Sounds

You can also record sounds using Sound Recorder. For instance, you might want to attach a recording of you signing happy birthday to an email message. You might record notes about a particular project to send along to a co-worker.

To record sounds, follow these steps:

1. Start Sound Recorder.

2. Click **File** and then click the **New** command.

3. Click the **Record** button.

4. Speak into the microphone to record your sound. When you are finished recording, click the **Stop** button.

5. To save your sound, click **File** and then click the **Save As** command. Select a folder, type a filename, and click **Save**. See Chapter 4, "Saving Your Work," for more information on saving files.

6. Click the **Close** button to close the Sound Recorder window.

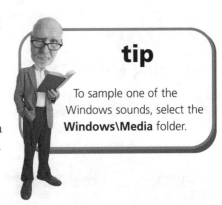

tip

To sample one of the Windows sounds, select the **Windows\Media** folder.

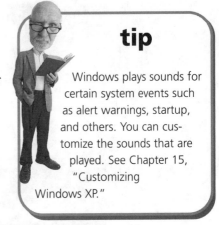

tip

Windows plays sounds for certain system events such as alert warnings, startup, and others. You can customize the sounds that are played. See Chapter 15, "Customizing Windows XP."

Using Windows Movie Maker

New with Windows XP is Windows Movie Maker. You can use this accessory program to view and edit movies. You can become a filmmaker creating your own home movies or even business training materials or other presentations.

To create your own movies, you need a camera capable of recording digital videos. You can then download the video from your camera to your computer and use Windows Movie Maker to view and edit it. You can also import other videos or music to use in Windows Movie Maker. Keep in mind that movie-making is a complete topic itself.

note

To record sounds, you must have a microphone or other sound input device connected. Check with your particular sound system for instructions on connecting and testing this device.

Starting Movie Maker

To start Movie Maker, click **Start**, **All Programs**, **Accessories**, and then **Windows Movie Maker**. You see the Windows Movie Maker window. Figure 13.8 shows one of Windows' sample movie files displayed in Windows Movie Maker.

FIGURE 13.8

You can create, edit, and play back movie files with Windows Movie Maker.

From this window, you can then do any of the following:

- To import a movie clip, click **File**, **Import** and then select the media file you want to import. Click **Open**. Use this method if you have existing media files already on your computer.

- To copy material from a video recorder to Windows Movie Maker, use the **File**, **Record** command. You can then use the Record dialog box to record the video from the player to Windows. Basically, Windows Movie Maker converts and then saves the video file into a format Movie Maker can work with.

- The video source is divided into clips, and these are displayed in the pane along the bottom of the window. You also see the clips listed in the Collections bar along the left of the window.

- After the video source is opened in Movie Maker, you can make editing changes. You can rearrange the clips into the order you prefer. You can delete or trim clips if they are too long or not appropriate. You can also split clips or combine clips. Finally, you can select transitions between clips.

- In addition to ordering the visual elements, you can also record narration to go along with the clips.

- As you edit the clips, you need to save your work. Windows Movie Maker stores a group of clips as a project. You can use the **File**, **Save Project** command to save the project. To open a previously saved project, click **File**, **Open Project**.

- As you work on your project, you can preview them or play them back. You can use the timeline along the bottom to play back just certain segments of the project.

tip

For detailed information on all the features of Windows Movie Maker and any accessory program, use commands in the program's Help menu.

note

Note that this list includes just a sampling of the many things you can do with Windows Movie Maker.

The steps for using all these features vary depending on your type of equipment. Probably the most difficult step is getting the hardware (the video recorder) set up to work with Windows XP. You can use the Add Hardware Wizard (covered in Chapter 24, "Upgrading Windows"). Then you can experiment with the many features in Windows Movie Maker. For step-by-step advice, use the help system for Windows Movie Maker.

THE ABSOLUTE MINIMUM

This chapter explored some of the ways you can use Windows XP as an entertainment system. You can play audio CDs, go online and view video clips or play music tracks, and more. When working with entertainment media, keep these key points in mind:

- To use the media features, you must have the proper hardware, and you must have the hardware set up. To play back music, you need speakers and a sound card (standard on most computers). For video recording, you need a digital video recorder (compatible with a PC). Or you need access to video files (recorded videos saved in a file format that you can work with in Windows XP).

- You can play any audio CDs. The quality of the playback is determined by your speaker quality. When playing a CD, you can select a different track, adjust the volume, view visualizations, and stop the music.

- If you want to personalize your Media Player, you can do so by selecting a skin. A skin is like an "outfit" that the program puts on to change how it looks. The program works the same and has the same features; it simply looks different.

- One place that's convenient to access for online music and videos is WindowsMedia.com. You can access this from the Windows Media Player window.

- You can listen to radio broadcasts from your computer. To do so, you must have an Internet connection. Use the **Radio Tuner** button in the Media Player window to tune in.

- If you are a video buff, you can use your video recorder to record videos. Then download the video to Windows XP and edit it using Windows Movie Maker.

14

WORKING WITH PHOTOGRAPHS AND MOVIES

One of the newest additions to a computer is a digital camera. Like most new digital devices, initially the item was pricey. But as digital cameras became more popular, the price decreased, and now they are affordable and provide some additional benefits over traditional cameras.

This chapter covers the basics of setting up a digital camera and then working with the picture files. You can print or email the pictures or order prints of the pictures from online photo services.

Using a Digital Camera

A digital camera works basically the same way as a regular camera, and the features available on a particular camera are the same. That is, to take a picture with a digital camera, you point and shoot. Instead of film, though, the digital camera saves the image in its internal memory or on a special memory card. You can then copy the pictures from the camera's memory or this card to your computer for editing, printing, emailing, and so on.

You can find a wide range of cameras. High-end cameras provide higher quality pictures and have extra features such as additional lenses, zoom features, and so on. With some cameras, you can even shoot and store a short video.

The exact steps for using your particular camera vary depending on the model you have. Consult the documentation that came with the hardware to learn how to take pictures. Taking pictures isn't difficult, but you need to learn about the special features of the camera including the following:

note

Cameras range in price from a couple hundred dollars all the way up to several hundred. You can find reviews of cameras in several computer publications and Web sites including www.pcworld.com. Before shopping, read the reviews so that you know what key features you need and what the price range is for those features.

- Some cameras let you shoot pictures at different resolutions (quality or sharpness of the image). You usually select the resolution from the camera's menu system or with a dial on the camera. Quality affects not only how well the pictures look but also how big the file is (how much memory is used to store the image). The higher the quality, the more memory it takes and the fewer pictures you can store at one time on your camera.

- Most cameras enable you to preview the picture immediately after you take it. Don't like it? Delete it and reshoot the picture. This is one of the great benefits. You no longer waste film on "bad" pictures. Your camera will have some method for scrolling through the pictures stored in memory as well as deleting any images you choose not to keep.

- Digital cameras don't use film. As mentioned, the images are stored in the camera's internal memory or on a memory card (called a SmartMedia or CompactFlash card). When the memory is full, you can download the pictures to your computer via a cable and then delete the images from the camera's memory. You can then take your next batch of pictures. Your camera most likely came with a cable used to attach the camera to your computer.

Also, you usually receive a photo program for transferring, viewing, and even editing the pictures with the camera. Again, these vary from camera to camera. For Kodak cameras, for instance, you use the Kodak Transfer program (see Figure 14.1).

note

■ You can print your pictures on a regular printer (the quality will be so-so) or on a special photo printer with special photo paper. As other options, you can order prints online from printing services. Also, you can take your camera storage media (the memory card) to regular film service sites and have them developed. You learn more about this in the section "Printing Pictures" later in this chapter.

Some newer cameras can save pictures to a floppy disk or CD directly. For instance, Sony's Mavica line offers these capabilities.

FIGURE 14.1

You can transfer pictures from your camera to your computer.

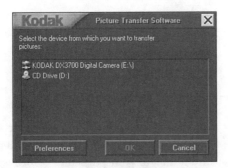

Setting Up Your Digital Camera

Windows XP recognizes common cameras and scanners, so often you need only attach the device to your computer and Windows XP recognizes the new hardware and sets it up automatically. You'll know this is happening because Windows XP alerts you with messages that pop up from the system tray.

If you have a camera that Windows XP does not recognize, you can set it up manually using the Scanner and Camera Installation Wizard. Follow these steps:

tip

If your camera did not come with a photo software transfer program, you can use Windows XP's Photo Wizard. See "Setting Up Your Digital Camera" later in the chapter for more information.

1. Click **Start** and then click **Control Panel**.

2. Click **Printers and Other Hardware**.

3. Click the **Scanners and Cameras Control Panel** icon.

4. In the task pane, click the **Add an imaging device** link (see Figure 14.2) to start the Scanner and Camera Installation Wizard.

FIGURE 14.2

You can start Windows' Scanner and Camera Installation Wizard from the Control Panel.

5. Follow the steps in the wizard, entering or selecting the correct settings and clicking **Next** to move from one step to the next. The basic steps ask you to select the manufacturer and model of your particular device (see Figure 14.3). You also select the port to which the device is attached as well as type an identifying name for the device. When you've entered all the information, click **Finish** to complete the setup.

FIGURE 14.3

You can select your particular camera from the list.

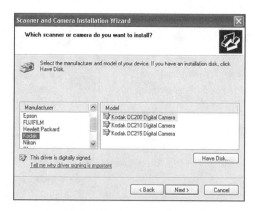

Transferring and Working with Pictures

The basic mechanics of using a digital camera is that you take the pictures and then download them to your computer. When downloaded, you have several options for working with the pictures as covered in this section.

Transferring the Pictures

The steps vary depending on your camera setup, but the general process for transferring pictures is as follows:

1. Connect the camera to your computer via a cable.

2. Using Windows XP's Transfer Wizard or your camera's Transfer Wizard, transfer the images from the camera's memory (or media card) to your hard disk.

3. Select any options for the download. For instance, you may choose to delete the pictures from the camera's memory after downloading. As another option, you may select to download only some of the images or all the images. Figure 14.4 shows the download options for Kodak's transfer program.

FIGURE 14.4

You can download pictures from your camera to Windows XP.

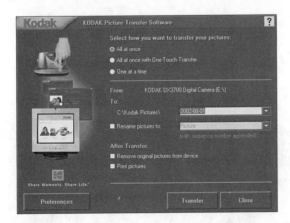

Check your particular camera and its transfer program for the specifics.

Working with Picture Files

After the images are transferred, you have several options for working with the files. This section covers basic file management tasks. See "Printing Pictures," "Emailing Pictures," and "Ordering Photo Prints from the Internet " later in this chapter for task-based options.

Here are some of the common things you do with pictures to finalize them for printing or emailing:

- To organize pictures, Windows XP includes a special folder named My Pictures. Consider placing all pictures within this folder. You can create subfolders within the main My Pictures folder to store similar pictures together.

- When you open a folder that contains pictures and then select picture files, the task pane displays picture-related tasks. For instance, Figure 14.5 shows some pictures from a digital camera.

- Most cameras come with software for working with the images. You can use this software to get rid of red eye, crop images, combine images, and make other changes. This is yet another benefit of digital cameras; you have many options for improving the shot.

note

Windows XP prefers that you store these images in the My Pictures folder and contains handy links within this folder for working with images. Your particular camera software, though, may automatically transfer the images to another folder. For instance, with my Kodak camera, the transfer program places all the images in the Kodak Picture folder and names each folder by the date the images where transferred. You can always move and rename the files.

FIGURE 14.5

New with Windows XP are content-specific commands in the task pane. For instance, in the My Picture folder, you see commands for working with pictures.

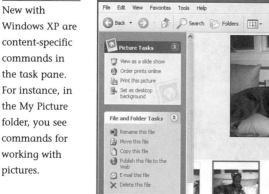

■ The default names used for the images are not descriptive. To effectively store your pictures, you should rename them. Right-click the image, select **Rename**, type a new name, and press **Enter**. Doing so can be tedious, but you will be glad when you are looking for a photo. The folder names are usually the dates of transfer (2001_05_24, for example). Again, rename these to something more descriptive (such as Michael's Birthday).

■ Picture files can be large. You usually don't want to permanently store them on your hard disk. Instead, you can work with them and then print or email them. After that task is done, you can consider a more efficient storage media. For instance, if you have a CD-R disk drive (the R indicates *recordable*), you can store pictures on a CD disk. To copy pictures to a CD-R disk, right-click the folder or picture(s) you want to copy. Then select **Send To**. From the **Send To** menu, select **CD drive** and follow the instructions in the wizard.

■ You might also simply want to delete the picture files. (If you keep all your picture negatives from a traditional camera, you'll want to save them to another media. If you throw out the negatives after receiving your prints, you might want to delete some if not all of the picture files.)

> **tip**
>
> If you don't have software or if you want a more sophisticated program, you can purchase a picture-editing program. These range from simple—Adobe's $99 Photoshop Elements—to complex—the complete Adobe Photoshop. You can find other programs besides those created by Adobe, although Adobe is the most popular.

Printing Pictures

After your pictures are organized, renamed, and touched up (as needed), you can print them on a regular printer, on a special photo printer, or on a regular printer that has special photo printing features.

Follow these steps to print pictures:

1. Open the folder that contains the pictures you want to print.

2. Click **Print** pictures in the task pane. This starts the Photo Printing Wizard.

3. Follow the steps in the wizard, clicking **Next** to move from step to step. You can select which pictures are printed (see Figure 14.6). You can check or uncheck individual pictures to make your selections. You can clear all selected pictures by clicking **Clear All**. Or you can select all pictures by clicking **Select All**.

FIGURE 14.6

As one option in the Photo Printing Wizard, you can select which pictures are printed.

As the next steps, you select the printer to use and then the layout for the pictures (full page, 8×10, 5×7, and other common photo sizes). When the pictures are printed, you see the final step of the wizard, telling you the pictures have been printed. Click **Finish** to close the Photo Printing Wizard.

Emailing Pictures

It's fun to share pictures with friends and family. In addition to printing, you can also email pictures using the **E-mail picture** command in the task pane. You might, for instance, email a picture of your new puppy to your friends. You might email pictures from a family reunion to your family members that live out of town. Follow these steps:

1. Open the folder that contains the pictures you want to email.

2. Select the picture(s) you want to send. Pictures are like regular files. You can change how they are displayed using the **View** menu, and you can select them just like you select regular files. (See Chapter 6, "Understanding File

tip

You won't get photo quality pictures with a regular computer printer. You can, though, purchase special photo printers and photo paper. Expect to pay from $200 to $800 or more for a special photo printer. Some new printers are good for both document, color, and photo printing. Visit computer retail stores to see the various options. The best way to pick a printer? Check the actual printouts from various printers to find one with an acceptable print quality.

Management Basics," and Chapter 20, "Viewing and Finding Files," for more information.)

3. In the File and Folder Tasks area of the task pane, click **E-mail this file**. You are prompted to optimize the image (which speeds sending and opening the picture).

4. Make your selection and click **OK**. Windows opens an Outlook Express email window with the picture attached (see Figure 14.7).

5. Complete the email address and any message you want to send with the picture attachment. Then click the **Send** button. See Chapter 9, "Sending and Receiving Email" for more information on sending messages.

> **tip**
>
> You can also include pictures within documents. The exact steps vary depending on the program. In Word for Windows, for instance, you use the **Insert**, **Picture**, **From File** command.
>
> Check your program documentation for exact instructions on inserting pictures in your particular program(s).

FIGURE 14.7

Complete the email address, type a message, and click **Send** to send the picture.

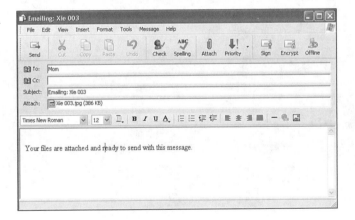

Ordering Photo Prints from the Internet

In addition to printing and emailing pictures, you can also select to order photo shop quality prints from the Internet. Windows XP includes a wizard that leads you step-by-step through the process of ordering prints from popular print services. You can get pricing information when you order the prints. Also, expect to pay a small shipping charge. For payment, you must supply a credit card number and shipping information. Pictures usually arrive in a couple of days. Some services offer several free prints as a trial run.

To order copies from the Internet, you must be connected to the it. If you are not connected, you are prompted to do so. When connected, follow these steps to order prints:

1. Open the folder that contains the pictures you want to print.

2. Click **Order prints online**.

3. Complete the steps in the wizard to order your copies, clicking **Next** to move from step to step. The steps vary depending on the service you select, but you can expect to select which pictures you want to order (much like selecting which pictures to print), the size of the pictures (costs for print size are listed), and the shipping and payment information. Figure 14.8, for instance, shows some of the available options for Shutterfly.

FIGURE 14.8

You can select the size and other options for ordering prints online.

4. For the final step, click **Finish** to submit your pictures.

Using a Scanner

Another way to work with not only photos but also other illustrations is with a scanner. With a scanner, you can take any image—photographs, drawings, documents, and so on—and scan the image, saving it as a file on your computer. Like pictures, you can then modify, print, and email the image. You can even include the image within a document. For instance, you can scan a picture of your family and insert it in your annual Christmas letter.

The exact steps for using your particular camera and scanner vary depending on the model you have. Therefore, you'll need to consult the documentation that came with the hardware to learn how to scan images.

Setting Up a Scanner

As with printers, Windows should recognize your scanner after it is hooked up, query it for information, and if it is a Plug and Play device, install it automatically. If this doesn't happen, you can use the Camera and Scanner Wizard (see "Setting Up Your Digital Camera" earlier in this chapter). The steps are the same, only you select your scanner. You can use a Windows XP driver or the driver supplied with your scanner.

Scanning an Image

If you have a flatbed scanner, you insert the picture or document you want to scan and then use the buttons on the scanner or the commands in the scanner program window to start the scan. The available program options will vary, so you need to check your own particular program for specific instructions.

After the document is scanned into the scan program, you have options for modifying, saving, and working with the image. Figure 14.9 shows options in PaperPort. You can crop, rotate, add text, and more.

FIGURE 14.9

This figure shows the available options for editing a scanned image.

Inserting a Scanned Image into a Document

When the scanned image is fine-tuned, you can insert it into documents. For instance, you might insert images into a Web document if you want to display them as part of your Web site. Or you might include pictures or illustrations in a Word document. Check with the specific program documentation or online help for the specifics on inserting scanned images. In Word, for instance, you can use the **Insert**, **Picture**, **From File** or **From Scanner or Camera** command to insert an image from a camera or scanner.

THE ABSOLUTE MINIMUM

This chapter covered some of the fun and exciting things you can do with a digital camera. If you are thinking about buying a camera or already have one, keep these key points in mind:

- You can purchase a digital camera and use it with your computer. A digital camera offers many advantages. You can preview your images after you shoot them, deleting or reshooting as needed. You don't need to purchase film. You can edit the pictures before printing, and you can print, email, or order prints online.

- When you attach your camera, Windows XP should query it and set it up automatically. If not, you can run the Scanner and Camera Installation Wizard to set up the camera manually.

- Different cameras have different features and work differently. The basics of taking a picture are the same: point and shoot. But you need to look at your camera's documentation to find out how to change settings such as image quality as well as how to preview and handle images.

- You can copy the images from your camera's memory to your computer. You can then work with your pictures. You can make editing changes using a photo-editing program. You should also rename the files and folders because the default names are not very descriptive.

- You can print your pictures on a regular printer or a printer that supports picture printing. Usually you get the best quality when you use a photo printer and special photo paper.

- You have other printing options. For example, you can also order prints online or take your camera's media card to a regular print service bureau and have copies made. As another option, you can email photos.

- In addition to cameras, another common imaging device is a scanner. You can use this hardware component to scan in photos, illustrations, documents, and other types of visual or textual information.

PART IV

YOUR OWN PERSONAL WINDOWS

15

CUSTOMIZING WINDOWS XP

Windows XP provides many customization options so that you can personalize your computer. Some of these changes are practical. For instance, if you are left-handed, you can change the mouse buttons so that the buttons work for the left hand. If you have trouble seeing the display, you can alter the size (the resolution) of the desktop. If you prefer the taskbar on another part of the desktop, you can move it.

Other changes are purely personal. For instance, you may want to display a wallpaper image on your desktop. Or you may want to change the sounds that are played for system events (such as shutdown). This chapter covers the most common customization changes. The other chapters in this part of the book cover other customizing options, in particular for setting up programs and for customizing email and Internet Explorer.

Customizing the Taskbar

The taskbar, although small in size, actually tells you a lot. It lets you know which programs are running and which windows are open. It tells you the time, and shows icons when other activities are going on. For example, if you see a printer icon, you know that your computer is sending data to the printer. If you see a connection icon, you are connected to the Internet.

Windows XP enables you to customize the taskbar and system tray. To make any changes, display the Taskbar and Start Menu Properties dialog box by following these steps:

1. Right-click a blank part of the taskbar and select the **Properties** command from the pop-up menu. You see the Taskbar and Start Menu Properties dialog (see Figure 15.1).

FIGURE 15.1

Use this dialog box to customize the taskbar and system tray.

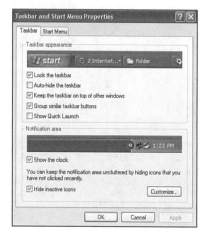

2. Make any changes:

   You can lock the taskbar so that it can't be moved, or unlock it so that it can be moved. Check or uncheck Lock the taskbar.

   You can hide the taskbar so that you have more desktop room. Check **Auto-hide** the taskbar. When the taskbar is hidden, you can always redisplay it by pointing to the bottom of the desktop.

   You can also select to show the clock, hide inactive icons, keep the taskbar on top of all windows, group similar taskbar buttons into one stacked button, and show a Quick Launch toolbar with buttons for sending email and logging on to the Internet. Check any options to turn them on. Uncheck them to turn an option off.

3. When you are finished making changes, click **OK**.

The Taskbar and Start Menu Properties dialog box also enables you to customize the **Start** menu, selecting which items are displayed. For information on these changes, see Chapter 16, "Setting Up Programs."

Customizing the Desktop

You have lots of choices for customizing the desktop. You can use a desktop theme, change the color scheme, use a screen saver, and more. All of these options are available in the Display Properties dialog box.

To get started making any of these changes, right-click an empty spot on your desktop, and select Properties from the pop-up menu that appears. The Display Properties dialog box appears, with the Themes tab displayed. The following sections describe the most common changes. You can pick and choose which you'd like to try.

To make one change, select the options and click **OK** to close the dialog box. To make several changes, select the option and then click **Apply**, leaving the dialog box open to make additional changes. When you are done customizing the display, click **OK**.

Using a Desktop Theme

Desktop themes consist a of background, sounds, icons, and other elements. Windows XP offers numerous color-coordinated themes to choose from; alternatively, you can create your own.

To use a desktop theme, display the Themes drop-down list and select a theme. If the theme you want to use does not appear in the Themes drop-down list, either select **More Themes Online** to download additional themes, or click **Browse** and then, in the Open Theme dialog box, open the

tip

You can also move the taskbar to another location on the desktop and change its size. To move the taskbar, put the mouse pointer on a blank part of the taskbar and drag it to the location you want. To resize the taskbar, put the mouse pointer on the border and drag to resize. To do so, the taskbar must be unlocked. (The Lock the Taskbar option should not be checked.)

tip

If the date and time are incorrect, you can correct them by right-clicking the time display in the taskbar and selecting **Adjust Date/Time**. Select the correct date and time. You can click on a date in the calendar or display other months or years from the drop-down list to change the date. You can type or edit the correct time in the text box or drag the hands on the clock. When the date and time are correct, click **OK**.

folder and select the theme you want to use. You can find Windows themes in the WINDOWS\RESOURCES\THEMES folder.

When you select a new theme, you see a preview in the Sample window. Figure 15.2 shows the Windows Classic theme.

FIGURE 15.2

You can apply a set of options, called a theme.

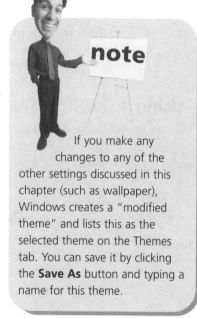

tip

If you don't have the other Windows XP themes installed, you can do so using the Add/Remove Windows Components Wizard. See Chapter 24, "Upgrading Windows."

Using a Background Image

If you want, you can use an image such as a favorite picture or pattern as your Windows desktop. To apply a background picture or pattern to your desktop, follow these steps:

1. From the Display Properties dialog box, click the **Desktop** tab.

2. Select the background you want to use from the Background list. Figure 15.3 shows a picture of Stonehenge selected as the background image.

note

If you make any changes to any of the other settings discussed in this chapter (such as wallpaper), Windows creates a "modified theme" and lists this as the selected theme on the Themes tab. You can save it by clicking the **Save As** button and typing a name for this theme.

FIGURE 15.3
Use a background image to jazz up your desktop.

Customizing Desktop Icons

By default, the Windows XP desktop does *not* contain the My Computer icon and the My Documents icon. If you are upgrading and prefer this setup, you can add the icons. Even if you are not upgrading, you may prefer fast access to these common folders from the desktop rather than the **Start** menu.

To select which desktop icons are displayed, follow these steps:

1. From the Display Properties dialog box, click the **Desktop** tab.

2. Click the **Customize Desktop** button. You see the Desktop Items dialog box (see Figure 15.4).

FIGURE 15.4
You can add icons to the desktop using this dialog box.

> **tip**
>
> If you'd rather display one of your own digital pictures, click the Browse button on the Desktop tab. In the Browse dialog box, navigate to the folder that contains the picture, select it, and then click **Open**. For more information on navigating through folders, see Chapter 6, "Understanding File Management Basics." The image is added to the list of Background choices; select it to use it as your background.

3. Check any desktop icons that you want displayed. If an item is checked and you want to hide or remove it from the desktop, click the checkbox to remove the check.

4. Click **OK**.

You'll also find these other options in the Desktop Items dialog box:

- You can also select a different icon style using the **Change Icon** button. You can experiment by clicking the icon you want to change and then clicking the **Change Icon** button. Select the new icon and click **OK**.

- If you have made changes and want to go back to the original icons, click the **Restore Defaults** button.

- You can clean up the desktop, removing icons that you do not use. See Chapter 23, "Handling PC Maintenance."

- To add desktop content such as your home page, weather information, sports scores, or a stock ticker, click the **Web** tab (see Figure 15.5). Consult Windows XP's online help for the exact steps on how to add, modify, remove, and synchronize Web content on the desktop.

tip

What's gone? Patterns are gone. Did anyone ever bother with patterns? I doubt it. And what about Active Desktop? It's not exactly called that and you don't activate it via the desktop shortcut menu. Instead, it's buried a little within the Display Properties tab. See the previous section, "Customizing Desktop Icons."

tip

You can remove default desktop icons by unchecking their check boxes. But what about icons you have added yourself? **Delete** them by dragging the icon to the Recycle Bin; by selecting the icon, pressing **Delete**, and clicking **Yes** to confirm the deletion; or by right-clicking the icon, selecting **Delete**, and confirming the deletion by clicking **Yes**.

FIGURE 15.5

You can add Web content to your desktop using the options on this tab.

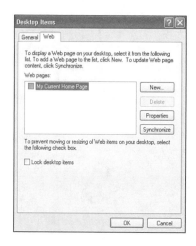

Using a Screen Saver

Screen savers are another desktop option. Are they necessary? Not really. On older monitors, an image could be burned into the monitor if the same text or image was displayed for long periods of time. This is not a problem with current monitors. Screen savers simply provide some pizzazz and a small bit of security for your computer when it is idle.

To use a screen saver, follow these steps:

1. From the Display Properties dialog box, click the **Screen Saver** tab.

2. Display the Screen Saver drop-down list and select the image you want to use. Figure 15.6, for instance, shows a preview of the Beziers screen saver.

FIGURE 15.6

You can use a screen saver that will automatically turn on when your computer is idle.

3. Set the time limit using the Wait spin boxes. When your computer is idle for the time limit you selected, the screen saver image will be displayed.

4. Click **OK**.

When a screen saver is activated, you can stop its display and redisplay your desktop by moving the mouse or pressing a key.

Changing the Color Scheme

Windows XP enables you to change the sets of colors used for certain onscreen elements such as the title bar, background, and so on. These sets of colors are called *schemes*, and you can select colors that work best for you and your monitor. Lighter colors might, for example, make working in some Windows applications easier on your eyes. On the other hand, you might prefer bright and lively colors. You can also select an option for Windows and buttons as well as a font size.

To make a change to the desktop color scheme, follow these steps:

1. From the Display Properties dialog box, click the **Appearance** tab.

2. Display the Windows and buttons drop-down list and select either Windows Classic style or Windows XP style. Classic style has many more color scheme options; the color scheme options for Windows XP style are limited.

3. Display the Color Scheme drop-down list and select the scheme you want to apply. (The schemes that appear depend on the Windows and buttons style you have selected.)

4. Display the Font size drop-down list and select a font size. You may, for instance, use a larger font size if you find the text onscreen

You can also create your own custom color scheme. To do so, select the scheme that is closest to the style you want. Then click the **Advanced** button. Use the options in the Advanced Appearance dialog box to make changes.

difficult to read. You see a preview of all your selections. Figure 15.7 shows Windows Classic style with the Lilac color scheme. The font size has also been changed to large.

FIGURE 15.7

You can tinker with the colors and fonts used to display programs and windows on your desktop.

Setting Resolution and Color Settings

The term *resolution* refers to many different things that relate to computer and computer equipment. You might hear resolution as a measure of the quality of a printer or scanner or camera, for instance. Resolution, in terms of your display, means how big or small the images are, and these are measured in pixels, such as 800 × 600. The larger the number, the smaller (and finer) the image. You can change the resolution as another desktop option.

In addition, you can change the number of colors displayed onscreen. To make these changes, follow these steps:

1. From the Display Properties dialog box, click the **Settings** tab. You see the options shown in Figure 15.8.

FIGURE 15.8

Yet another desktop option is to change its resolution and color settings.

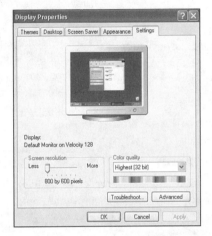

2. To change the resolution, drag the lever in between Less (bigger) and More (smaller).

3. To change the number of colors that can be displayed, display the Color quality drop-down list and select the color quality. My options were Medium (16 bit) and Highest (32 bit). Depending on your video card (also called adapter), your options will vary.

4. Click **OK**.

Customizing the Mouse

Most PC mice have at least two buttons: a left and right button. The buttons are used for different purposes. The left mouse button is used for most tasks: clicking, dragging, opening menus,

If you are having problems with your monitor, you can start the Troubleshooter from the Settings tab. To do so, click the **Troubleshoot** button, which starts the Video Display Troubleshooter. You can select from several different display problems, and Windows XP Troubleshooter will suggest possible remedies.

selecting commands, selecting text, and so on. The right mouse button is used for less-common tasks. A common use of the right mouse button is to display a shortcut menu.

If you are left-handed, you can change your mouse so that the buttons are reversed: Right does the main options, left does the shortcut menu. You can also make other changes to the mouse, including adjusting its double-click speed or changing how the cursors appear. Again, these changes are a mix of practical issues (such as the left-handed change) as well as personal issues (such as the pointer schemes).

To customize your mouse, follow these steps:

1. Click **Start** and then **Control Panel**. You see the Control Panel options.

2. Click **Printers and Other Hardware**.

3. In the lower part of the window that lists Control Panel icons (see Figure 15.9), click **Mouse**. You see the Mouse Properties dialog box.

> **tip**
>
> The following steps assume that you are using the Category View of the Control Panel options. You can also click **Classic View**. Use this if you have upgraded and are more comfortable with the Classic View. Or, you may select this option if you are having trouble finding the Control Panel icon you want to use.

FIGURE 15.9

Select the Mouse Control Panel icon to make changes to how the mouse works.

4. Do any of the following:

    To change the button configuration (a common change for left-handed users), go to the Buttons tab and check Switch primary and secondary buttons (see Figure 15.10). You can also adjust the double-click speed. If you have trouble double-clicking, you might want to either increase or decrease the speed to suit how you double-click. You can test the speed by double-clicking the folder in that area of the dialog box.

FIGURE 15.10

You can change the behavior of the mouse buttons and the double-click speed.

To change the appearance (shape and size) of the various mouse pointers that appear, click the **Pointers** tab and then select a scheme from the Scheme drop-down list. The dialog box displays a preview of your selections.

To add visual pointer clues such as indicating motion, snapping to the default button in a dialog box, or displaying a trail, click the **Pointer Options** and make your selections.

For hardware changes, click the **Hardware** tab. You learn more about hardware changes in Chapter 23.

5. Click **OK**. Your changes are put into effect.

note

The Control Panel is the main tool for all setup and customization changes. Other options are covered throughout this book. For instance, setting up printers and installing fonts are covered in Chapter 5, "Printing." User Accounts are covered in Chapter 26, "Setting Up Windows XP for Multiple Users." For less common options, either consult online help or click a link and experiment.

Customizing Sounds

Windows plays certain sounds for key system events, such as exiting windows, new mail, log on and log off, and others. You can change these sounds as well as adjust the volume using the Sounds and Audio Devices Control Panel.

To select or adjust the speaker volume and/or use a different sound scheme, follow these steps:

1. Click **Start** and then **Control Panel**. You see the Control Panel options.

2. Click **Sounds**, **Speech**, and **Audio Devices**.

3. In the lower part of the window that lists Control Panel icons, click **Sounds and Audio Devices**. You see the Sounds and Audio Devices Properties dialog box.

4. Do any of the following:

   To adjust the volume of your speakers, use the Volume tab, dragging the volume bar between low (quieter) and high (louder).

   To use a different sound scheme, click the **Sounds** tab. Display the Sound scheme drop-down list and select a scheme.

   You can also change the sound for individual events by selecting the Program event from the list and then displaying the Sounds list and selecting the sound to play (see Figure 15.11).

tip

If an event does not have a sound icon next to it, a sound is not played. You can assign sounds to these items by selecting them and then selecting a sound.

FIGURE 15.11

You can customize the sounds played for program events.

The other tabs help you troubleshoot and upgrade audio equipment as well as voice recognition features. These topics are not covered in this book, although you can find out information about hardware settings in Chapter 23.

5. Click **OK**. Your changes are put into effect.

THE ABSOLUTE MINIMUM

This chapter covered some of the many changes you can make to personalize Windows to suit your preferences. In particular, keep the following tips in mind:

- Making a change to the desktop is most often just for the look of it. You make all of these changes in the Display Properties dialog box. You can display this dialog box by right-clicking a blank part of the desktop and selecting Properties. You can select a theme for the display, choose a background image, use a screen saver, or change the appearance (color, font, placement) of window elements.

- If you want to put the **My Computer** and **My Documents** icons back on the desktop, do so by clicking the **Customize Desktop** button on the **Desktop** tab. You can then check the desktop icons to display, change the appearance of icons, and have Windows get rid of desktop icons that haven't been used. To get rid of unused icons, use the Desktop Cleanup Wizard, covered in Chapter 23.

- On the Settings tab of the Display Properties dialog box, you can change the resolution and also the color quality.

- You can change both how the mouse works and how the mouse pointers appear by using the **Mouse Control Panel** icon.

- Another common change is using a different sound scheme or selecting different sounds for key system events such as logging on or logging off. To do so, use the Sounds and Audio Devices Control Panel.

16

Setting Up Programs

In Chapter 3, "Starting Programs," you learned the basics of how to start a program. In addition to using the **Start** menu to start programs, you can create shortcut icons to programs. You also can change the **Start** menu, for example, *pinning* commonly used programs to the main menu (the left side of the menu, with Internet and Email). Finally, you can install new programs and uninstall programs you do not use. This chapter covers all these methods for customizing and setting up programs on your computer.

Creating a Shortcut to a Program

You can create shortcuts and place them on the desktop to provide quick access to programs. You can then double-click a program shortcut to quickly start that program. Creating the shortcut is easy; finding the program file is the most difficult part. Perform the following steps:

1. Display the program file for which you want to create a shortcut. For help on navigating among your drives and folders, see Chapter 6, "Understanding File Management Basics." Usually most programs are stored within folders in the Program Files folder. Try looking there. For instance, to find Office files, look in Program Files and then Office.

2. Right-click the file and then click the **Send To** command. From the submenu, click the **Desktop (create shortcut)** command (see Figure 16.1).

note

You can also update Windows and add Windows components. See Chapter 24, "Upgrading Windows."

FIGURE 16.1

Here the Excel program file is selected and a shortcut to this program will be added to the desktop.

Windows adds the shortcut to your desktop (see Figure 16.2). Notice that it has a small arrow in the left corner. This indicates the icon is a shortcut icon. The icon is not the program itself, but a link to the program.

FIGURE 16.2

The icon is
added to your
desktop.

After you add the shortcut icon, you can do any
of the following:

- Windows XP uses "Shortcut to" plus the
  program file name for the shortcut name.
  For instance, a shortcut icon to Excel is
  named "Shortcut to Excel." You can
  change this name to a more descriptive
  one. To do so, right-click the shortcut,
  select **Rename**, type a new name, and
  press **Enter**.

- Remember that you can move icons
  around on the desktop. See Chapter 2,
  "Getting Started with Windows XP," for
  more information.

- You can delete a program shortcut icon.
  Right-click the icon and select **Delete**.
  Confirm the deletion by clicking **Yes**. Keep
  in mind that when you delete the shortcut
  icon, you are not deleting the program
  itself, just the pointer to the program. If
  you want to get rid of the program (remove it from your computer), you must
  uninstall the program. See "Uninstalling Applications" later in this chapter.

> **tip**
>
> You can follow these same
> steps to create a shortcut to
> a file or folder. Open the
> drive and folder where the
> folder or file is stored. Then
> right-click and select **Send
> To**, **Desktop (create
> shortcut)**. When you double-click
> a file shortcut, that file is opened
> in the associated program. For
> instance, if you double-click a
> shortcut to a Word file, the docu-
> ment is opened, and Word is
> started. If you double-click a
> folder shortcut, the contents of
> that folder are displayed.

■ Some programs add shortcut icons to your desktop automatically when you install the program. You have the same options for working with these icons: You can rename them, move them, delete them, and double-click them.

■ The purpose of the desktop is to provide quick access to your most commonly used programs (files and folders also). If your desktop becomes too cluttered with icons, you defeat the purpose of having fast access. You can clean up your desktop, getting rid of program icons you don't use that often. You can find information on this process in Chapter 23, "Handling PC Maintenance."

Customizing the Start Menu

In addition to adding desktop icons, you can also add programs to the **Start** menu, and you can change how the **Start** menu looks. For instance, you may prefer the **Classic Start menu** (one from previous Windows versions). You may prefer to list more or fewer programs on the left pane. You can also select whether to list the Internet and E-mail programs, as well as select which programs are used for these commands. This section covers these topics.

Pinning a Program to the Start Menu

When you install most programs, they are added automatically to the **Start** menu. You can then start programs by clicking **Start** and then **All Programs**. Windows XP also enables you to *pin* a program to your **Start** menu. When you pin a program, it is always listed at the top left of the **Start** menu (with the Internet and E-mail programs).

To pin a program to the **Start** menu, follow these steps:

1. Display the program for which you want to create a shortcut. You don't have to find the actual program file. You can use the program name listed in the **Start** menu, either on the left side (commonly used programs) or on the All Programs list. Figure 16.3, for instance, shows Word selected on the left side of the **Start** menu.

2. Right-click the program name and click the **Pin to Start menu** command (refer to Figure 16.3). The program is added to

tip

When you pin a program to your **Start** menu, it is placed in the left pane of the menu. You can drag the pinned program to the **My Documents**, **My Pictures**, or **My Music** folder, but nowhere else within the **Start** menu.

your **Start** menu. Figure 16.4, for instance, now shows Word listed on the top left part of the **Start** menu. Word will always be listed here for fast access until you delete or unpin it.

Unpinning a Program to the Start Menu

If you don't want the program listed anymore (at least on the top part of the **Start** menu), you can remove it by unpinning it. To unpin a program, follow these steps:

1. Click **Start** to display the **Start** menu.

2. Right-click the program you want to unpin. You see the shortcut menu.

3. Click **Unpin from Start** menu. The program is no longer listed on that part of the **Start** menu. (The program name still appears in the All Programs list.)

Note that you cannot unpin Internet or E-mail, but you can hide them by customizing the Start menu (covered in "Changing the Appearance of the Start Menu").

Rearranging Programs on the Start Menu

Another way to change the **Start** menu is to change the order of the programs listed. You can rearrange the order of the programs. To do so, click the item you want to move and then drag it to the new location in the **Start** menu.

Changing the Appearance of the Start Menu

You have more options on how the **Start** menu appears. For instance, if you have upgraded from a previous version of Windows, you may prefer the old (called Classic) style. You may want to change the number of programs listed on the left pane. You may choose not to list the Internet or E-mail programs, or you may want to use programs for these tasks other than the defaults. (Internet Explorer is the default program for the Internet command. Outlook Express is usually the default program for E-mail command.)

Follow these steps to make a change to the **Start** menu:

1. Right-click a blank part of the taskbar and select **Properties** from the shortcut menu.

2. Click the **Start Menu** tab. You see the General tab (see Figure 16.5).

FIGURE 16.5

Here you can select **Classic Start menu** and access customizing features.

3. To use the Classic Start menu, click **Classic Start menu**. To use the regular, default menu, click **Start** menu. After you select the menu style, you can then click the **Customize** button to make further changes.

4. If that's the only change you want to make, click **OK**. You can skip the remaining steps.

Or

If you want to make additional customizing changes, click the **Customize** button. You see the Customize Start Menu dialog box (see Figure 16.6).

tip

For information on customizing the taskbar, see Chapter 15, "Customizing Windows XP."

FIGURE 16.6

This figure shows the options for customizing the Windows XP style **Start** menu.

5. From this dialog box, you can do any of the following:

Windows XP uses large icons. If you have several programs, making the **Start** menu long, you can choose to use small icons. Click **Small Icons** in the first part of the dialog box.

Select the number of recently used programs to list on the left side of the **Start** menu.

tip

To clear the list of programs on the Start menu, click Clear List.

To turn off the commands for starting your Internet or E-mail program, uncheck the option(s). To use a different program for either, display the drop-down list next to the program type and then select the program to use.

6. Click **OK** to put your changes into effect.

Installing Programs

When you bought your computer, it most likely came with certain programs already installed. Depending on the brand and model, you might have received some free programs—an antivirus program, for example. These programs should already be installed and set up on your computer.

> **tip**
>
> For more advanced options, click the Advanced tab in the Customize Start Menu dialog box and then make any changes. Here you can add a list of recently opened Documents (as in past Windows versions). You can select which items are listed. As a beginner, it's best to stick with the defaults, but you may want to click this tab and view the options so you know what's available.

If you want to add new programs, you can purchase the programs you want and then install them on your system. Most programs provide an installation program that automatically checks your system (to see if you have room for the new program and to see whether you have an existing version), copies the appropriate files, and sets up its related program icons on the **Start** menu. You can just sit back and click, click, click through the installation routine. Different programs employ different installation processes. That is, the steps will vary from one program to another. But installing programs is usually fairly automated.

The first thing to do is start the installation program. Depending on your particular program, this might happen automatically. If not, you can use Windows Add or Remove Programs Control Panel icon to start the installation. Both methods are covered here.

Using the Automatic Install

To start the installation automatically, insert the program disc. Usually, the program has an autoplay feature that automatically starts the setup or installation process and displays your options. You should see a menu or dialog box with options for installing the program. Skip to the section "Completing the Installation."

Using the Add or Remove Programs Control Panel Icon

If the installation program is not automatically started, you can use the Windows XP's Add or Remove Programs feature. Follow these steps:

1. Click the **Start** button and then click **Control Panel**.

2. Click **Add or Remove Programs**. You see the Add or Remove Programs window (see Figure 16.7).

3. Click the **Add New Programs** button in the taskbar. You see the choices for installing the program (see Figure 16.8).

4. Click the **CD or Floppy** button. Doing so starts the install wizard.

note

You learn how to uninstall programs later in this chapter. See Chapter 24 for information on adding Windows components.

FIGURE 16.7

Use this Control Panel feature to change or remove programs, install new programs, or add or remove Windows components.

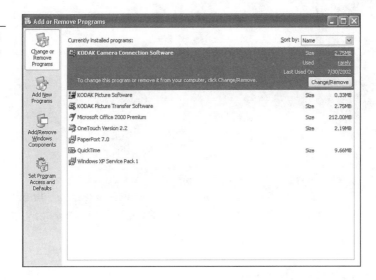

5. Insert the program's CD-ROM or floppy disk, and click the **Next** button. Windows XP checks the floppy disk drive and then the CD drive for installation programs. It then automatically selects the appropriate file, which is listed in the Run Installation Program dialog box (see Figure 16.9).

FIGURE 16.8

When installing programs, select **CD or Floppy**. (Updating Windows, the other option, is covered in Chapter 24.)

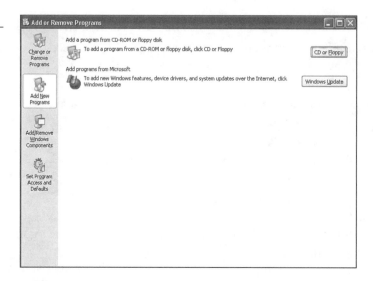

FIGURE 16.9

Click **Finish** to run the appropriate installation file, usually named install or setup.

6. Click **Finish**. What happens next depends on the software you are installing; follow the onscreen directions. See "Completing the Installation." The program is then installed, and the installation program usually adds program icons to the **Start** menu.

Completing the Installation

The installation program will prompt you to make selections, which vary from program to program. Here are some basic choices you can expect:

■ You may be asked to accept the license agreement before proceeding with the installation. This is a legal document that says how you can use the program, under what circumstances, and so on. (Basically you are agreeing to use the program on one PC and not to make illegal copies or share it with others.) Accept the agreement by clicking the appropriate option.

■ You may be prompted to select a type of installation. You can usually select a standard or customized installation. With a customized installation, you can select, for instance, which program components are installed. Most of the time the standard installation is good enough. As you use and learn more about the program, you can always add other program components (that might not have been installed with the standard installation).

■ You may be prompted to select the drive and folder used to store the program files. You may also be selected to pick or create a new program folder for the program icons.

Each installation is different. Make your choices and click **Next** to go from one step to the next.

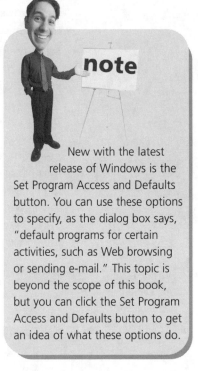

New with the latest release of Windows is the Set Program Access and Defaults button. You can use these options to specify, as the dialog box says, "default programs for certain activities, such as Web browsing or sending e-mail." This topic is beyond the scope of this book, but you can click the Set Program Access and Defaults button to get an idea of what these options do.

Uninstalling Applications

If you don't use a program, you can remove it from your system. Doing so frees up disk space. You could simply delete the program file(s), but these files are not always stored in one location. A program installation may store files in other places on your hard drive: for instance, in the Windows folder. Therefore, uninstall the program using the Add or Remove Programs Control Panel. This removes the program and all its related files and folders from your hard disk.

Removing Programs

Follow these steps to uninstall or remove a program:

1. Click the **Start** button and then click **Control Panel**.

2. Click **Add or Remove Programs**. You see the Add or Remove Programs window (refer to Figure 16.7).

If you have any folders that contain your documents within the program folders, be sure to move them to another folder or drive so that they are not deleted with the program.

3. Click the **Change or Remove Programs** button if necessary. Usually these options are displayed by default.

4. Select the program you want to remove (see Figure 16.10). Windows XP provides you with some information to help you decide whether to uninstall. First, you see the size of the program (the amount of disk space you will gain by removing the program). Second, you see a rating of how often the program is used. If the rating is "rarely," you know you don't use that program often, so it's most likely safe to remove it. Third, you may see the date the program was last used.

tip

Some programs enable you to change their setup, adding optional items that may not have been installed. If you see both a Change and a Remove button, you can click the Change button to change the program's setup.

FIGURE 16.10

Use the information listed for each program to get an idea of how often you use the program.

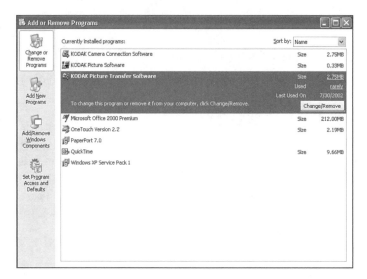

5. Click the **Remove** button. (This button may be called Remove or Change/Remove.) Windows XP then removes the program. The steps will vary from program to program. Simply follow the onscreen instructions.

Removing Programs Manually

If your program is not listed in the Add or Remove Programs area of the Control Panel, you have to use a different method to remove it. You can try one of two methods: using the program disc or deleting the program folder.

You may be able to run an uninstall program from the program disc. Insert the disc and see whether options for uninstalling the program are displayed on the install menu. If so, use these. If the program disc doesn't automatically display your install options, insert the disc, click **Start**, and then click **My Computer**. Double-click the icon for the drive that contains the program disc. Then look for a Setup, Install, or Uninstall icon. Double-click this icon and follow the steps for uninstalling. (Sometimes the Install and Setup programs will display a menu, and one of the choices will be to uninstall the program.)

If the program doesn't have an uninstall program, you can delete its files manually. This method does not always remove all of the program files. It's common for programs to place certain program files within the Windows folder, for instance. But you can get rid of the main files.

Click **Start** and then **My Computer**. Double-click the drive icon that contains your Programs folder. Then open the My Programs folder. Then look for the program folder (usually named the same as the program). Delete the program folder by selecting it and pressing **Delete** or by clicking **Delete this folder**. Confirm the deletion by clicking **Yes**.

tip

You can purchase programs to keep track of what programs you have installed, where they are, and what changes they have made to your system. You can use such a program to uninstall programs not listed in the Windows Add or Remove Programs Control Panel.

More Tips on Starting Programs

In addition to these common methods for customizing programs, you have some other options for installing, running, and switching among programs. This hodgepodge of options is the focus of this section.

Starting Programs When You Start Windows

If you shut down and restart each time you use the computer, you can have Windows start a program each time Windows starts by adding the program to your Startup Folder. Any program placed in this folder will be started each time you start Windows.

Follow these steps to start a program with Windows:

1. Right-click the **Start** button.

2. Select the **Open** command. You see the Start Menu folder.

3. Double-click the **Programs** folder. You see the Programs folder, which includes a folder called Startup (see Figure 16.11).

4. Drag the program icon you want to start with Windows to the Startup folder. You may have to open another program window to display this program icon. Use the links under Other Places to find and display the program icon.

5. Click the **Close** button to close the Programs window.

If you *don't* start Windows each time, say you leave it running, you may wonder why the program didn't start when you sat down to work. Well, the program only starts automatically when you start Windows (that is, turn off and then on the PC). Don't fret. You can still start the program. Do so with any of the other methods: shortcut icon, **Start menu** command, or keyboard shortcut.

FIGURE 16.11

Put programs you want to start when you start Windows in the Startup folder.

The next time you start Windows, the program(s) you added to the Startup folder will be started also.

If you change your mind and want to remove the program from the Startup folder (preventing it from starting all the time), you need to delete it from the Startup folder. Open the Startup folder. You should see icons for any programs you have added. Figure 16.12, for instance, shows Outlook Express added to the Startup folder. Select the icon, press the **Delete** key, and click **Yes** to confirm the deletion.

FIGURE 16.12

You can remove any programs you have added to the Startup folder.

Tips for Switching Among Programs

After you have programs running, you can switch among them. Why switch programs? Well, you are talented and capable of multitasking, and so is Windows. Windows can run a word processor and a spreadsheet at the same time, for instance. As you've seen so far, you can use the mouse or the keyboard for most tasks. The same is true for switching programs.

To use the mouse method, click the taskbar button for the program you want. Remember that Windows displays a taskbar button for each program or window that is open on your system.

If you have multiple documents open in the same program and there's not enough room on the taskbar, Windows stacks the documents together into one button. You can tell if this has occurred by looking at the button. It should have a little arrow, plus the number of documents open in that program. You can click the button to display the various document windows and then click the window you want (see Figure 16.13).

FIGURE 16.13

If the taskbar gets too crowded, Windows XP stacks similar windows together.

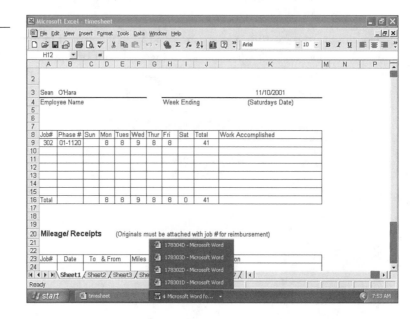

To use the keyboard method to switch programs, press **Alt+Tab** to cycle through the programs running on your computer. When the one you want is selected, stop pressing **Alt+Tab**.

Using the Run Command

Another way to start a program is using the **Run** command. You may have to do this to install older programs (DOS programs or programs without automated installations, for instance). How do you know when this is your only alternative? When you've tried the others or when the program's installation instructions specifically tell you to use this method.

In this case, follow these steps to use the **Run** command:

1. Click the **Start** button.

2. Click the **Run** command.

3. Type the name of the program you want to start (see Figure 16.14). Or to run the installation or setup program, type its name. If you don't know the program name, click the **Browse** button and browse through the drives and folders until you find the right file.

FIGURE 16.14

Use the **Run** command as a last resort to get finicky programs to start.

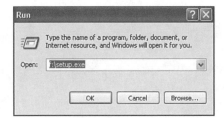

4. Click **OK**. The program starts.

THE ABSOLUTE MINIMUM

This chapter covered some of the ways you can customize the **Start** menu as well as how to install new programs and get rid of programs you no longer need. Here are the key points to remember from this chapter:

- For fast access to commonly used programs, files, or folders, add a shortcut icon to the desktop. When you double-click a program shortcut icon, you start the program. When you double-click a file shortcut icon, you open the associated program and that document. Double-clicking a folder shortcut icon displays its contents.

- You can change how the **Start** menu appears. You can pin commonly used programs to the top left pane. You can select whether the Internet and E-mail commands are listed, as well as select which program is used for these commands.

- If you have upgraded to Windows XP and prefer the classic Windows style, you can change the desktop to this style. Right-click the taskbar, select **Properties**, and then click the **Start Menu** tab to view your customization options.

- When you purchase a new program, you can run the installation program to install the program onto your system. Most programs provide a step-by-step guide for installing the program, and this installation program copies the files to your computer, as well as adds the program to the **Start** menu.

- You can start the installation program manually using the Add or Remove Programs Control Panel icon. Use this same icon to delete or uninstall programs you no longer use.

17

CUSTOMIZING EMAIL AND INTERNET EXPLORER

Windows XP is versatile and provides many options for changing how it works. For instance, you can customize how your email is handled. As another example, you can make changes to how Internet Explorer works. Like other chapters in this part, this chapter covers customization. In this particular case, you learn how to customize Outlook Express as well as Internet Explorer.

Setting Mail Options

As mentioned in Chapter 9, "Sending and Receiving Email," you have several options for controlling how messages are sent, received, formatted, and so on. To access all these settings, follow these steps:

1. Start Outlook Express.

2. Click **Tools** and then click the **Options** command. You see the General tab of the Options dialog box (see Figure 17.1). From this tab, you can select to go directly to your Inbox, play sounds when messages arrive, and other options. You can also select how often Outlook Express checks for new messages.

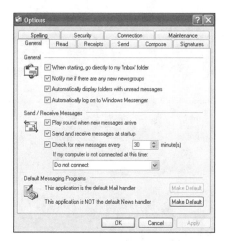

3. Make your selections.

4. Click any of the other tabs and then make additional selections. You can do any of the following:

   Click the **Read** tab and select read options such as how long messages are displayed in the preview pane before the message is marked read and how messages are downloaded.

   You can request a receipt that confirms that a recipient has received a message. Set receipt options from the Receipts tab. You can, for instance, request a receipt for all sent messages.

   Click the **Send** tab (see Figure 17.2) and specify whether a copy of all sent items are stored in the Sent Items folder, when messages are sent (for instance, immediately), the format for your messages (HTML or Plain Text), and other options.

   Use the Compose tab to select formatting options for your email. You can select a particular font. You can also use stationery (basically a pattern or style for the message).

   To select whether messages are automatically spell checked, as well as set your spell check options, use the Spelling tab.

FIGURE 17.2

Use the Send tab to select options about how messages are sent.

Use the Security tab to set security options such as message encryption.

On the Connection tab, you can, as just one example, have Outlook Express hang up or end your connection after messages are sent and received.

Use the Maintenance tab to control options such as whether deleted messages are placed in the Deleted Items folder or deleted for good, and to clean up old messages (see Figure 17.3).

5. When you are finished making changes, click **OK** to close the dialog box.

You can only use fonts or stationeries if you use HTML mail, and some recipients may not prefer this email format. Therefore use formatting with caution.

FIGURE 17.3

The Maintenance tab enables you to control how messages are handled.

Working with the Address Book

One of the most useful things you can do to customize your email is to set up your Address Book. Rather than type an address each time, you can display the Address Book and select a name from the Address Book. This method is not only easier and quicker, but also less error-prone.

You can also use the Address Book to set up a contact group so that you can easily send one message to several people without creating multiple messages or selecting several addresses.

Finally, you can, if you want to put in the effort, store a lot more information for a contact with the Address Book. And if you do so, you can then use this address book in mail merges in Word, or in Access also.

The following sections cover these Address Book options.

Adding Addresses

The easiest way to add an address to your Address Book is to pick up the address from an existing message. This saves you from having to type the information. To add an address from a mail message, follow these steps:

1. Display the message with the name you want to add to your address book.

2. Right-click the name and then select **Add to Address Book**. You see the Properties dialog box (see Figure 17.4).

3. To simply add the name, click **OK**. You can also add other contact information. See "Using the Address Book as a Contact List" later in this section.

> **tip**
>
> You can also change what items are displayed in the Outlook Express window. Use the commands on the View menu to turn on or off the various program window features.

> **tip**
>
> If you upgraded to Windows XP and have your old Address Book (either on another computer or stored as a file on your PC), you can import it to Windows XP. Then you don't have to re-create the list you so painstakingly created before.
>
> To import an Address Book, from the Address Book window, open the **File** menu and select **Import**. From the submenu, select **Address Book (WAB)**. In the Select Address Book File to Import From dialog box, select the file to import and click **Open**. Your addresses are imported into the new Address Book from the Outlook Express in Windows XP.

FIGURE 17.4

You can add names to your address book.

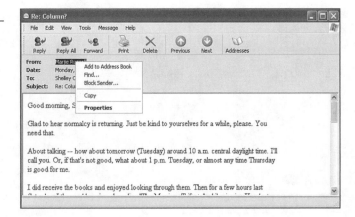

If you don't have an email message from the person you want to add, or if you prefer to type the address book entry, you can do so. Follow these steps:

1. From the Outlook Express main window, click **Address Book**. You see a list of entries you already have in your Address Book (see Figure 17.5).

FIGURE 17.5

You can display the entries in your Address Book at any time.

2. Click the **New** button and then select **New Contact** from the drop-down options. You see the Properties dialog box for a new contact (see Figure 17.6).

3. The first tab contains the basic contact information. Complete the entries on this tab. At the minimum, type the first and last name as well as the email address. You can also type any title or assign a nickname.

tip

A nickname is a shorthand reference to a contact. You can type this shorter name when creating a new mail message.

FIGURE 17.6

Complete the
information for
the contact you
want to add.

4. Complete any of the other information (see the section "Using Your Address Book as a Contact List.")

5. Click **OK** to add the contact.

Setting Up Contact Groups

If you commonly send a message to a group of people, you can set up a group rather than select each person in the mail message. Then when you want to send a message to that group, you select the group name and each person in that group receives the message. You can create groups from the Address Book. Follow these steps:

1. Open the Address Book by clicking **Start**, **All Programs**, **Accessories**, and then **Address Book**. You see the list of contacts in the Address Book window (refer to Figure 17.5).

2. Click **New** and then select **Group**. You see the Properties dialog box.

3. Type a name for the group.

4. Add the members to the group. To add a member, click **Select Members** and then select any contacts already in your address book. Or type the name and email address for the person and click **Add** (see Figure 17.7).

5. When you have added all the members, click **OK**.

Now when you want to send a message to all members in this group, you can click the **To** button in the new mail message window and then select the group from the Address Book.

FIGURE 17.7

You can add names to a group by selecting them from the Address Book or by typing the address for each person.

Using the Address Book as a Contact List

In addition to keeping track of email addresses, you can also add other information for each contact, including address, phone numbers (phone, fax, cell), business information (company, title, web page), personal information (spouse, children, birthday), and notes. To add other information, follow these steps:

1. Open the Address Book by clicking **Start**, **All Programs**, **Accessories**, and then **Address Book**. You see the list of contacts in the Address Book window.

2. Double-click the contact for which you want to add more information. The Properties dialog box for that contact is displayed. The first tab includes summary information. The Name tab includes email information.

3. Click the **Home** tab. You see the various fields of information you can enter (see Figure 17.8). Complete any or all of the fields.

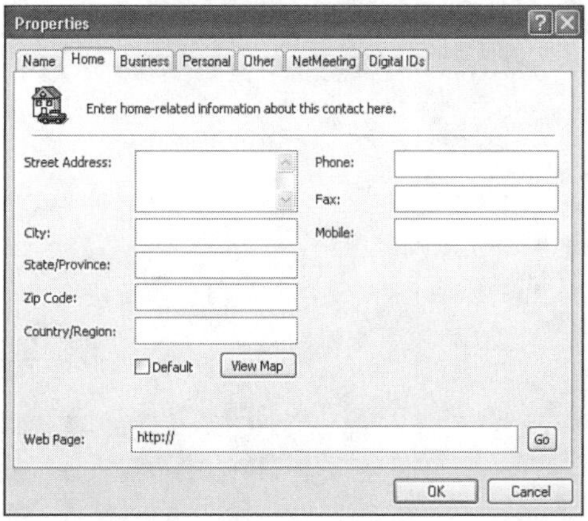

FIGURE 17.8

You can keep track of other information, such as mailing addresses, company information, and other data in your Address Book.

4. Click any of the other tabs and complete any or all of the fields for that category. For instance, click **Business** to enter company information.

5. Click **OK** when you are finished entering information.

Customizing Internet Explorer

In addition to customizing email settings, you also have a variety of options for customizing Internet Explorer. As one common example, you can change your home page. You can also organize your list of favorite sites, breaking it into folders of related sites rather than one long list. This section covers these common changes. See also the later section "Setting Internet Security Options" for more information on setting Internet security and privacy settings.

Setting Your Home Page

You are not stuck with the home page set up by your Internet provider or by Microsoft (MSN). You can use any page as your home page. For instance, you may prefer to use a search site so that you start with tools for finding information. Or if you have your own Web site, you may want to make this your home page. You can select any site for your home page by following these steps:

1. Start Internet Explorer.

2. Click **Tools** and then select **Internet Options**. You see the Internet Options dialog box (see Figure 17.9).

FIGURE 17.9

You can customize your home page as well as make other changes from this dialog box.

3. Do any of the following:

   Type the address to the page you want as your home page in the Address text box.

   To use the current page as your home page, click **Use Current**.

   To use the default home page, click **Use Default**.

4. Click **OK**. Now when you start Internet Explorer, the home page you selected is displayed. Also, when you click the **Home** button, this is the page that is displayed.

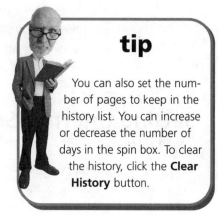

tip

You can also set the number of pages to keep in the history list. You can increase or decrease the number of days in the spin box. To clear the history, click the **Clear History** button.

Organizing Your Favorites List

In Chapter 10, "Browsing the Internet," you learned how to add sites to your Favorites list. If you add several sites, the list can become too long and unwieldy. To make it easier to find a site when using this list, you can organize your Favorites list into folders.

Start by clicking **Favorites** (the menu command, not the button) and then clicking the **Organize Favorites** command. You see the Organize Favorites dialog box (see Figure 17.10).

FIGURE 17.10

You can organize your list of favorite sites using this dialog box.

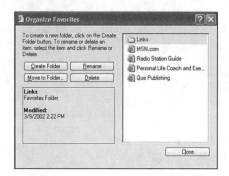

From the Organize Favorites dialog box, you can do any of the following:

- To create a new folder, click the **Create Folder** button and then type the folder name.
- To move sites to a folder, select the site in the list, click **Move to Folder** and then select the folder from the list and click **OK**. You can also drag the site in the list to the folder.

■ To rename a site or folder, select it in the list and then click **Rename**. Type a new name and press **Enter**.

■ To delete a site or folder, select it and click **Delete**. Click **Yes** to confirm the deletion.

Setting Internet Security Options

To further customize Internet Explorer, you can set security features. For instance, many home users these days use a cable Internet connection. Because these types of connections are connected 24/7, it's important that you protect your computer from outsiders. To do so, you can use Windows firewall protection. This section covers security features as well as privacy options.

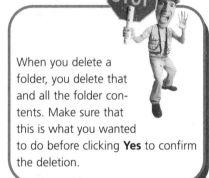

When you delete a folder, you delete that and all the folder contents. Make sure that this is what you wanted to do before clicking **Yes** to confirm the deletion.

Turning On Windows XP Firewall Systems

If you want to prevent access to your computer from the Internet, you can activate Windows XP's new firewall system. As defined by Windows XP online help, "a firewall is a security system that acts as a protective boundary between a network and the outside world." To activate the firewall, follow these steps:

1. Click the **Start** button, select **Connect To**, and then select your Internet connection. You see the status for that connection.

2. Click the **Properties** button. You see the General tab, which lists the general settings, including the modem and phone number (see Figure 17.11).

3. Click the **Advanced** tab, and then check the **Internet Connection Firewall** check box (see Figure 17.12).

4. Click **OK**.

note

If you have a home network and used the Home Networking Wizard to set it up, Internet Connection Firewall is turned on automatically. You can get more information on home networking in Chapter 28, "Setting Up Windows XP on a Home Network."

The General tab lists the basic setup options.

FIGURE 17.12

Turn on (and get information about) the new Internet Connection Firewall from this dialog box.

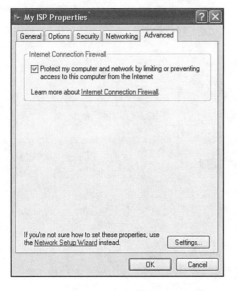

If you aren't sure how this feature protects your Internet use, you can click the link for more information. That link gives you all the technical details about how the firewall monitors incoming, unsolicited traffic from the Internet.

Setting Privacy Options

Privacy is one of the key issues of debate about the Internet. How do you take advantage of all the Internet has to offer, while still retaining some privacy? To address this concern, Windows XP includes a Privacy tab that you can use to set the level for privacy. You have various zones including the Internet, Local intranet, Trusted sites, and Restricted sites. You can then add sites to each of these zones. Follow these steps to select the level of privacy:

Both cable and DSL connections have more security issues than systems that use dial-up access. Why? Because they are connected 24/7 and usually have a static (unchanging) IP address. Dial-up access is connected only when you are online and uses a temporary IP address, making them much more difficult to crack into.

1. Open the **Tools** menu and click the **Internet Options** command.

2. Click the **Privacy** tab (see Figure 17.13).

FIGURE 17.13

When you drag the lever to high, medium, or low, the dialog box explains how privacy is handled with that setting.

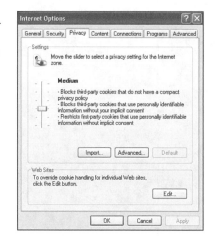

3. Select the privacy level you want.

4. Click **OK**.

If you set privacy on a high setting, you may have problems visiting or displaying information at some sites.

If you have children, you might also use the Content Advisor on the Content tab of the Internet Options. You can also set up special security zones (trusted sites and restricted sites). You do this from the Security tab of the Internet Options dialog box, selecting the type of site (trusted or restricted), manually typing in the addresses of the sites in that category, and then adding them to the list.

> **tip**
>
> If you are an online shopper, be sure to read that site's privacy statement before entering any information. Most reputable sites provide a link that specifically outlines their privacy rules. Also, watch out for check boxes for automatic alerts, new products, or joining mailing lists. Often these are checked (turned on), and if you don't make a change, you are placed on that mailing list and receive constant messages about "special" offers "just for you!"

THE ABSOLUTE MINIMUM

This chapter covered the many ways you can customize both email and Internet access to suit your preferences. In particular, keep these main points in mind:

- You can control how messages are sent, received, and handled using the Outlook Express mail options.

- To make addressing email messages easier, use the Address Book. Also, if you frequently send email messages to a set of people, create a contact group.

- You can select a different page for your start page using the Internet Options dialog box.

- To keep your favorites list organized, create folders and then organize sites by category.

- The Internet Options dialog box also enables you to set privacy and security settings.

- If you have a 24/7 connection (a connection that is always connected), turn on firewall protection to prevent unauthorized access to your computer.

18

CUSTOMIZING YOUR PRINTER

Chapter 5, "Printing," covered the basics of setting up a printer and printing. As you use your printer more often, you may want to tinker with its setup. You might, for instance, change the way the page is printed on the page (*portrait*, down the long side of the page, or *landscape*, across the long side of the page). Another common change is to add additional fonts to your computer so that you have more of a selection in changing how text and other data appear in your printed documents.

This chapter focuses on the common printer customization changes you can make.

Setting Printing Preferences and Properties

After you have installed a printer (see Chapter 5), you can adjust the printer preferences and properties. Preferences are things such as the default orientation (portrait or landscape), page order, pages per sheet, and paper/quality options(including size, copy count, print quality, and other settings). Properties are things such as printer sharing, device settings, and other more techie printer-related features. You can make changes to either set of options. Look first at the preferences; these are things you are more likely to change. Look second at properties; these are things you may change if you are a control freak or if you are having printer problems.

Changing Printing Preferences

Printing preferences are settings such as the order pages are printed (beginning to end of document, or end to beginning), orientation (portrait or landscape), and paper source. If you always print a certain way, you can change these settings.

Changing the printer's preferences changes them for all documents you print on this printer. If you want to change settings for just one document, change the setting in that document instead.

> **tip**
>
> The default printer is indicated with a checkmark. To select another printer as the default, right-click the icon for that printer and select **Set as Default Printer**.

To change the printing preferences for all print jobs, follow these steps:

1. Display the printer icon by clicking the **Start** button and then clicking **Control Panel**. Click the **Printers and Other Hardware** category. Click the **Printers and Faxes Control Panel** icon. You see a list of all the installed printers and faxes (see Figure 18.1).

2. Select the printer you want to modify.

3. Click **Select printing preferences** in the Task pane. You see the Printing Preferences dialog box (see Figure 18.2).

4. On the Layout tab, select a default orientation and a default page order.

5. Click the **Paper/Quality** tab. Select a default paper source.

6. Click **OK**.

FIGURE 18.1
To customize your printer, first display the Printers and Faxes Control Panel.

FIGURE 18.2
Use the options in this dialog box to control the orientation, page order, and paper source for all print jobs printed with this printer.

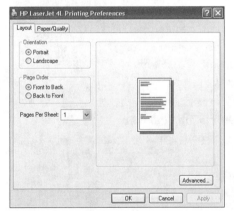

Changing Printing Properties

In addition to printing preferences, you can also view and change printer properties. These are more technical details of how your printer works—for instance, when the printer is available, the port to which the printer is attached, whether printer sharing is enabled, and other options. Follow these steps to modify printing properties:

1. Display the printer icon by clicking the **Start** button and then clicking **Control Panel**. Click the **Printers and Other Hardware** category. Click the **Printers and Faxes Control Panel** icon. You see a list of all the installed printers and faxes (refer to Figure 18.1).

2. Click the printer you want to customize and then select **Set printer properties**. You see the Properties dialog box for your particular printer (see Figure 18.3).

FIGURE 18.3

On the General tab, you can see which features your printer supports as well as the printer speed.

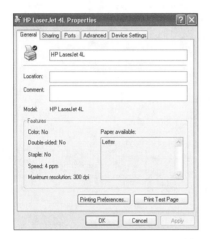

3. On the General tab, change the printer name. If the printer is used on a network, you can also type a location and comment used to identify the printer.

4. To change the port to which the printer is connected, click the **Ports** tab, and then select from the available ports listed.

5. To set printer sharing options (more for network printers), use the Sharing tab.

6. To change technical details such as when the printer is available, the driver that is used, how spooling is handled, and other technical aspects of the printer, use the Advanced tab.

7. Click the **Device Settings** tab to make changes for the paper trays, for printer memory, and for font substitution.

8. Click **OK** to confirm your changes.

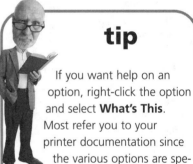

tip

If you want help on an option, right-click the option and select **What's This**. Most refer you to your printer documentation since the various options are specific to the printer itself.

Viewing and Installing Fonts

One of the most common formatting changes you make is changing appearance of the text by using a different font. You can select from business fonts to calligraphy fonts, from fancy fonts to silly fonts. The fonts that are listed within the program are the fonts you have installed in Windows XP. How do they get there and what fonts do you have? This section answers these questions.

Where Do Fonts Come From?

Most people have no idea how they get the fonts that are listed within a program. They also don't realize that not all computers have the same fonts and if you have used a font that the computer does not recognize, you'll most likely see gibberish.

Fonts come from several sources, and the first source is the printer itself. Every printer comes with built-in fonts that it can print, and these are usually indicated with a printer icon in font lists.

In addition to the built-in fonts, Windows itself includes some built-in fonts; these fonts are actually TrueType files and they tell the printer how to print that particular font. Other TrueType fonts are installed when you install some programs; the programs themselves also include fonts and when you install the program, you also install the fonts.

As another source, you can purchase fonts and install them within Windows. Once installed, they become available to all programs.

Viewing Your Installed Fonts

Windows XP lets you view which fonts you have as well as install new fonts. You do so using the Fonts Control Panel. Follow these steps:

1. Click **Start** and then select **Control Panel**.

2. In the Control Panel window, select Appearance and Themes.

3. In the See Also area, click **Fonts**. You see the Fonts folder, which displays file icons for all the installed fonts (see Figure 18.4).

note

Spooling is when Windows XP takes the request for a print job and then stores the document on your hard disk so that you can continue working. The spooler then sends the document temporarily stored on the hard drive to the printer.

tip

You'll have to look pretty hard to find Fonts in Windows XP. They aren't listed in the category view of the Control Panel. You find them in the See Also area of the task pane for other Control Panel options (as covered here). Or you can switch to Classic View and use the regular Font Control Panel icon.

FIGURE 18.4

Fonts are stored as files on your computer and indicated with a font icon.

4. To view a font, double-click the file. You see a sample of the font in various sizes, as well as information about the font (its name, type, version, and file size). Figure 18.5, for instance, shows the information for Bauhaus 93. When you are done viewing the font, click the **Done** button or the **Close** button for the font window.

FIGURE 18.5

You can see how each letter of the alphabet appears in the font as well as a sample sentence in various sizes.

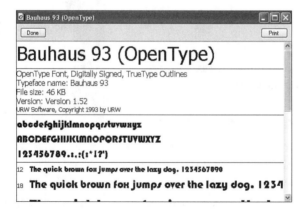

5. Click the **Close** button to close the Font Control Panel.

Installing New Fonts

If you purchase new fonts, you can install them in Windows. To do so, follow these steps:

1. Click **Start** and then select **Control Panel**.

2. In the Control Panel window, select **Appearance and Themes**.

3. In the See Also area, click **Fonts**.

4. Open the **File** menu and select **Install New Font**. You see the Add Fonts dialog box.

5. Select the drive that contains your font files from the Drives drop-down list.

6. If the files are stored within folders, select the folder from the Folders list. When you open the drive and folder, all the available fonts are listed in the List of fonts list (see Figure 18.6).

tip

It can be overwhelming to see all the fonts and each variation (bold, italic, bold italic). You can select different views from the View menu. For instance, to group similar types of fonts together, click **View** and then click **List Fonts by Similarity**. To hide all variations of a font (bold, italic, and so on), click **View** and then click **Hide Variations**.

FIGURE 18.6

Many font collections include so many fonts that you probably don't want to install them all. Instead, select the fonts from the collection that you do want to install from this dialog box.

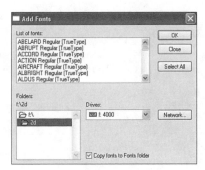

7. Select the font(s) to install. To select multiple fonts, **Ctrl+click** each font you want to select. To select all fonts, click the **Select All** button.

8. Click **OK** to install the selected fonts. The files are copied to the Fonts folder and are then available in all Windows programs.

9. Click the **Close** button to close the Fonts window.

THE ABSOLUTE MINIMUM

As you look into customizing your printer, keep these main ideas in mind:

- Most of the time you don't need to make that many adjustments to how your printer works. But, if needed, you can set certain options for a printer, including page layout options (the default orientation) as well as technical details.

- The printer customization options that are available will vary from printer to printer.

- Fonts enable you to change the appearance of text within a document. The fonts available in your programs are the fonts you have installed through Windows, or that were included with your printer.

- You can view the fonts as well as add new fonts using the Font Control Panel icon.

PART V

EVERYDAY PC MAINTENANCE

IN THIS CHAPTER

- Working with Folders and Files
- Saving Space by Compressing Files

19

ORGANIZING FILES

In Chapter 6, "Understanding File Management Basics," you learned the basics of handling files—how to create folders, rename files, delete and undelete files, and other key file-related tasks. This chapter builds on these skills and covers some additional file-related tasks to help you keep your computer organized.

Keeping your files organized provides many benefits. First, you can more easily find the folder or file you want. Second, you can keep your disk running in good shape by periodically weeding out old files (the topic also of Chapter 22, "Improving Your Computer's Performance"). Third, with a good setup, backing up files (the topic of Chapter 20, "Viewing and Finding Files") is easier.

Working with Folders and Files

As you read in Chapter 6, you can create, delete, and rename files and folders. You also have some other options for working with folders and files as covered here in this section. This section also contains a mini-review of folder basics.

A Quick Review Course on Files and Folders

Here are some quick reminders of the main folder-related tasks:

■ You can open a folder to view its contents. You can start from several commonly used folders listed on the **Start** menu, including My Documents, My Pictures, My Music, and My Computer (see Figure 19.1). Click one of these folders from the **Start** menu to display its contents.

FIGURE 19.1
The **Start** menu lists commonly used folders.

■ To open a folder, double-click it. For instance, in Figure 19.2, you see the My Documents folder. You can double-click any of the folder icons to view its contents. For instance, double-click **Books** to see the files (and subfolders) within this folder.

■ You can navigate to other folders using the **Back**, **Forward**, and **Up** buttons.

note

You can change how the contents of the file window are displayed. See Chapter 20, for more information.

Forward

Back   Up

FIGURE 19.2

To open any
listed folders,
double-click the
folder icon.

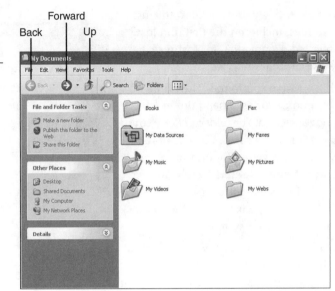

- To create a new folder, open the folder in which you want to place the new one. Then click **Make a new folder** in the task pane. Type the folder name and press **Enter**.

- To select a folder, click it.

- To delete a folder, select it, and then click **Delete this folder** in the Task pane or press the **Delete** key on your keyboard. Click the **Yes** button to confirm the deletion.

- To rename a folder, select the folder and then click the **Rename this folder** link. The current name is selected. Type the new name and press **Enter**.

Moving Folders and Files

As you create more and more documents, you may need to do some rearranging. For example, say you have several documents all within one folder, and you decide it would make sense to create subfolders to further organize and categorize the files. You can create a new folder and then move files (or folders) to this new folder.

To move a file or folder, follow these steps:

1. Select the file or folder. You can select multiple files by **Ctrl+clicking** (hold down the Ctrl key and click the mouse button) on each file. To select a group of files next to each other, click on the first file and then **Shift+click** (hold

down the Shift key and click) on the last file. All files, including the first and last, are selected. Figure 19.3, for instance, shows several files selected.

2. Click the **Move** command. The name of the command varies depending on what you have selected. For folders, click **Move this folder**. For a single file, click **Move this file**. For several files and/or folders, click **Move the selected items**. You see the Move Items dialog box (see Figure 19.4). This dialog box lists all the drives and folders on your system.

3. Display the folder or drive you want. If an item has a plus sign beside it, that item (drive or folder) contains other folders. You can click the plus sign to expand the list to show subfolders.

FIGURE 19.3

You can select folders, files, or both for moving.

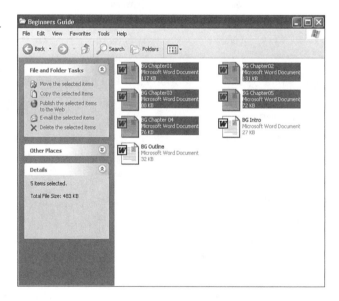

FIGURE 19.4

Select the drive and folder to which to move the selected item(s).

Check out the Details area of the file window. It shows the number of items selected as well as the total file size.

4. Click the folder from the list and then click **Move**. The selected items are deleted from the original location and moved to the new location. Keep in mind that if you moved a folder, you moved not just the folder, but its contents as well.

Copy Folders and Files

In addition to moving folders and files, you can also copy files. You may want to keep an extra copy of files or folders. (You will learn about backing up files in the next chapter.) A quick-and-dirty way to back up files is to simply copy them to another drive. You may copy files to a floppy disk, for instance, to share with others or to bring home from your office. You can even copy files to a CD-R disc. You can use either the **Copy** command or the **Send To** command, as covered in this section.

To create a new folder in which to place the selected item(s), select the folder in which you want to place the new folder. Then click **Make New Folder**. Type a folder name and press **Enter**.

Copying with a Command

To copy a file or folder, follow these steps:

1. Select the file or folder. You can select multiple files by **Ctrl+clicking** (hold down the Ctrl key and click the mouse button) on each file. To select a group of files next to each other, click on the first file and then **Shift+click** (hold down the Shift key and click) on the last file. All files, including the first and last, are selected.

2. Click the **Copy** command. The name of the command varies depending on what you have selected. For folders, click **Copy this folder**. For a single file, click **Copy this file**. For several files and/or folders, click **Copy the selected items**. You see the Copy Items dialog box (see Figure 19.5). This dialog box lists all the drives and folders on your system.

FIGURE 19.5

The Copy Items dialog box is the same as the Move Items (from the previous section), only you are copying the items to the selected drive or folder rather than moving them.

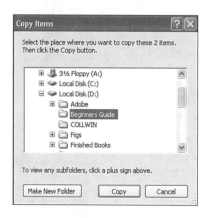

3. Display the folder or drive you want. If an item has a plus sign beside it, that item (drive or folder) contains other folders. You can click the plus sign to expand the list to show subfolders.

4. Click the folder from the list and then click **Copy**. The selected items remain both in the original location and the new location. Keep in mind that if you copied a folder, you copied not just the folder, but its contents as well.

Copying with the Send To Command

Because it's common to copy a file to another disk, Windows XP also provides the **Send To** command, another quick way to copy a file to a floppy drive. Follow these steps to copy a file or folder with the **Send To** command:

1. Select the file(s) or folder you want to copy.

2. Right-click any of the selected items and then select the **Send To** command. You see the Send To options (see Figure 19.6).

3. Select the drive from the shortcut menu. The file(s) or folder are copied.

FIGURE 19.6

For a fast way to copy files or folders to a floppy drive, use the **Send To** command.

Burning Files onto a CD

Most new CD drives enable you to both read and write information to the CD drive. Because a CD drive can hold lots of information, it makes a good medium for making a copy of files you want to save. Copying files to a CD disc is often called "burning" a CD. You must have a CD-R (stands for CD Recordable drive; you can only write data to this disk once) or a CD-RW (stands for CD ReWriteable; you can read and write to the disk) drive to copy files. If you have a CD-ROM drive, you can only read information from the drive; you cannot record information.

> **tip**
>
> You can also use the **Send To** command to compress files (see "Saving Space by Compressing Files" later in the chapter). You can also create a desktop shortcut, send the files via email, or send them to the My Documents folder.

To copy files or folders to a CD disc, follow these steps:

1. Display the file you want to copy.

2. Do one of the following:

   Display Folders bar by clicking **Folders**. Then drag the selected file(s) or folder to the CD drive icon.

   Right-click the selected item(s), select **Send To**, and then select your CD drive from the submenu.

The files are copied to the disc.

Saving Space by Compressing Files

You'll be surprised how quickly your computer fills up with files. And some files will fall into the category "I want to keep it, but I don't really use it." For these types of files, you can store them in a compressed folder, kind of like those magic shrink wrap storage devices they advertise on TV. The files are shrunk down in size and stored in a folder so that they don't take up so much space. These are often called zip files, and the folder icon includes a little zipper to indicate that the folder contains compressed files. When you need the files again, you can uncompress them.

Because reading files from a CD drive is slower, don't use this as a primary storage device. But use it for big files you want to keep. It's a great way to make a backup copy of important files without having to use a ton of floppy or zip disks. Also, note that some disks created on CD-RW drives can't be read in some CD players.

Compressing Files

Follow these steps to compress files:

1. Select the file(s) or folder you want to compress.

2. Right-click any of the selected items and then select the **Send To** command. You see the Send To options (see Figure 19.7).

FIGURE 19.7

You can create a compressed folder from the **Send To** menu.

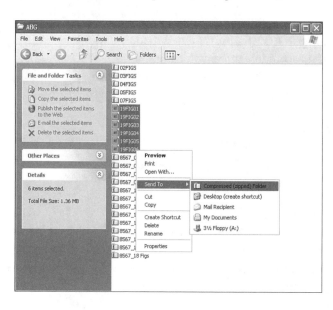

3. Select Compressed (zipped) folder. The files are zipped up and stored in a folder with the default name of the first file you selected. The files still appear in the folder (see Figure 19.8).

4. To regain the disk space, delete the original files by right-clicking them, selecting **Delete**, and confirming the deletion by clicking **Yes**.

5. It's also a good idea to rename the compressed folder to a more descriptive name rather than the default filename. Right-click the folder, select **Rename**, type a new name, and press **Enter**.

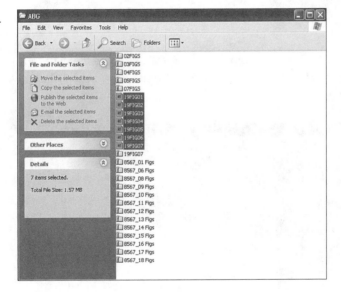

tip

If you are sending several files via email, compress them first. Doing so makes the file transfer quicker for both you and the recipient.

FIGURE 19.8

You see the compressed (or zipped) folder with the default name.

Uncompress Files

If you need to access these files again, you can uncompress or unzip them and then copy them back to your hard drive. To do so, follow these steps:

1. Open the drive and folder that contains the compressed folder. Note that the folder icon has a little zipper indicating that it is a compressed folder (see Figure 19.9).

FIGURE 19.9

You can uncompress files stored in a compressed folder.

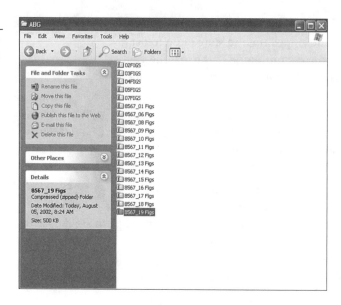

2. Double-click the compressed folder. You see the files within this folder (see Figure 19.10). Note that the files are not uncompressed until you follow the next steps.

FIGURE 19.10

When you open a compressed folder, you see the contents of that folder.

3. Select the file(s) you want to unzip and then select the **Copy** command. You can right-click and select **Copy**, or you can click **Copy** the selected items in the task pane.

4. Open the folder where you want to place the uncompressed files. Usually you can click **Back** to go back to the original folder (the one that contained the compressed folder).

5. Copy the files by right-clicking a blank area of the file window and selecting **Paste**.

tip

You can add additional files to the compressed folder. Drag the file icon to the folder icon. The file is added but also appears listed. You can delete the file since it is now stored in the compressed folder.

The file(s) are uncompressed, and you can now open and work with them as needed.

The Absolute Minimum

As you become more proficient with your computer and create more documents, you need to remember to use good file-management skills. This chapter built on the basics covered in Chapter 6, but also highlighted other features you can use to keep your files organized. Keep in mind the following key points:

- You can create, delete, rename, and select both folders and files. You start by opening the file window. You can open common folders (My Documents and My Computer, for instance) from the **Start** menu.

- You can create new folders and select, rename, and delete both files and folders.

- If you need to change the location where a file or folder is stored, you can move the file(s) or folder.

- You can copy your folders or files to keep an extra copy, or to take a copy of a file(s) or folder to another location. For copying, you can use the **Copy** command or the **Send To** command.

- To save disk space, you can compress files you need to save, but don't need readily available. When you do need these files again, you can uncompress them.

20

VIEWING AND FINDING FILES

Even if you are fairly organized with your files, you can still easily misplace a file or forget where a file is stored. Windows XP provides methods for viewing and sorting files to help you locate a particular file. In addition, you can search for a file based on name, creation date, or other file properties. This chapter covers these options for viewing, sorting, customizing, and finding files.

Viewing and Sorting Files

It is pretty common to save a file and then not be able to find it again. Either you didn't save it to the location you thought, or you cannot remember in which folder you saved it. Sometimes you don't remember the exact filename. One way to find files is to change how they are displayed in the folder window. You can view the contents of a window in a variety of ways. You can also sort the contents so that files are listed in alphabetical order, by date, or by type. A new command in Windows XP lets you group similar files together. All these viewing and sorting options are covered in this section.

Changing the View

You have several choices for how the contents of a window are viewed: thumbnails, tiles, icons, list, and details. Changing the view can help you better locate the item you want. Each view has its advantages. For instance, if you want to see more of a window's contents at one time, you can change the view to List. Figure 20.1 shows files in List view.

FIGURE 20.1

List view is the bare bones—a simple compact list of the file-names.

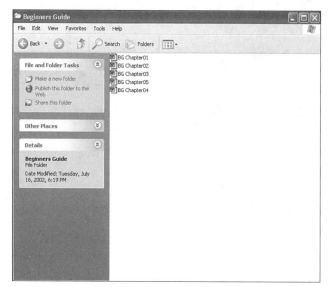

Another simple view is Icon view, which displays the filename and icon (see Figure 20.2).

As another alternative, you can add a little more information by changing to Tiles. In this view, you see the file icon, plus the document type and size (see Figure 20.3).

Want still more information? Change to Details view to see the size, name, type, and modification data. Figure 20.4 shows Details view.

tip

When you want to select a group of files, List view is the best view to work in.

FIGURE 20.2

In Icon view, the filename and icon are listed left to right across the window.

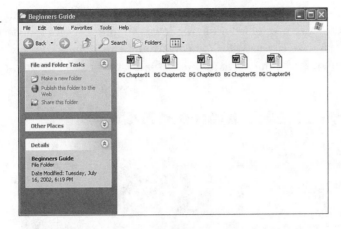

FIGURE 20.3

Use Tiles to view the filename, file type, and file size.

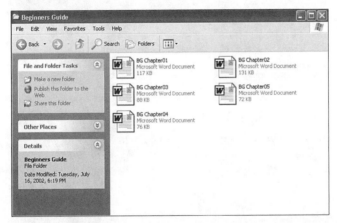

FIGURE 20.4

If you want detailed file information, change to Details view.

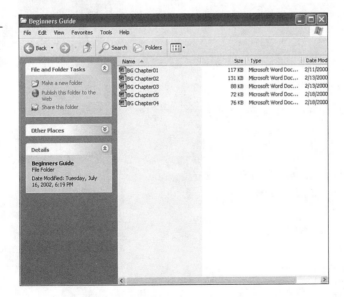

You can also select **Thumbnails**, useful for pictures. You see a thumbnail image of each picture. Also available for file windows with graphic files is a view called Filmstrip view (see Figure 20.5). You can scroll through the pictures, seeing both the selected image in the main area as well as other picture files along the bottom (or filmstrip).

FIGURE 20.5

For picture files, you can use Thumbnails or Filmstrip (shown here).

To change to a different view, follow these steps:

1. In the window you want to change, click the **View** menu. The current view is indicated with a dot (see Figure 20.6).

FIGURE 20.6

You can see the current view selection as well as select another view from the **View** menu.

2. Select the view you want. The window displays the contents in that view.

tip

Another helpful way to find a file is to view the file properties. Right-click the file and then select **Properties**. Some files may have several tabs with identifying information. When you are done reviewing the file properties, click **OK**.

Also remember that when a file is selected, you can view the Details section in the task pane for information about the type and size of the selected file.

Sorting Files

In addition to changing the view, you can also sort the contents of a folder window so that you can more easily find the folders and files you want. Windows enables you to arrange the contents of a window by name, type, date, and size. Your sorting will be visible in all views, but the change is most apparent in Details view since this view includes columns for size, date, and type.

Follow these steps to sort files:

1. Open the window you want to sort.

2. Click **View** and then click the **Arrange Icons By** command. The current sort order is indicated with a dot. For instance, if you see a dot next to Name, you know the contents are sorted by filename.

3. Select the sort order you want. Windows XP sorts the files in the selected order. For example, Figure 20.7 shows the files sorted by size (smallest to largest). Note that the sort column is indicated with a very faint shading and an icon in the heading.

FIGURE 20.7

You can sort files to make it easier to find the file you need.

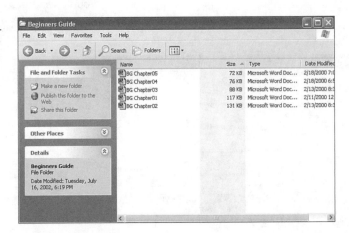

To change the order (ascending to descending or vice versa), select the same command again. Doing so reverses the sort order.

Grouping Files

New with Windows XP is the capability to group file icons. The grouping depends on how the items are sorted. If you sort by name, the contents are grouped alphabetically. If you sort by type, the contents are grouped by type. Grouping enables you to work with a select group of files or folders more easily.

To start, sort first and then group. You can group in any view. Follow these steps to group files:

1. Sort the contents by how you want them grouped. For instance, to group by type, sort by type.

2. Click **View**, **Arrange Icons By**, **Show in Groups**. Windows groups the icons by the sort order. Figure 20.8 shows the files sorted and then grouped by type.

tip

In Details view, you can also click the column heading as a shortcut for sorting. For instance, to sort by Date Modified, click this column header.

Grouping does not work in List view. Change to one of the other views (**Thumbnails**, **Tiles**, **Icons**, or **Details**) if you want to group a window's contents.

FIGURE 20.8

You can group files to keep similar file types together.

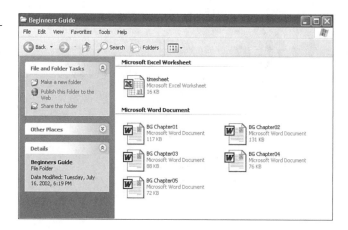

Setting Up Folder Options

In addition to viewing, sorting, and grouping, you can customize the appearance of your folders. Basically, you can change the way you open or display contents. Rather than double-click to open a folder, you can make the folder contents more "Web-like" and single-click. You can also hide the task pane. For instance, if you have upgraded to Windows XP, you may prefer the "classic" window style. You can change the folder options to more closely resemble previous versions of Windows.

tip

To undo the grouping, select the command again to remove the checkmark next to **Show in Groups** and remove the grouping in the file window.

To set folder options, follow these steps:

1. In the folder you want to change, open the **Tools** menu and select the **Folder Options** command.

   You see the General tab of the Folder Options dialog box (see Figure 20.9).

FIGURE 20.9

The General tab, as its name suggests, sets general options for how folders are displayed, browsed, and opened.

2. Make any changes to these options:

   To hide the task pane, select **Use Windows classic folders**. To display the task pane, select **Show common tasks in folders** (the default).

   By default, when you open a folder, the contents are displayed within one window (the new contents replace the existing contents), not separate windows. If you prefer to open each folder in its own window, select this option: **Open each folder in its own window**.

By default, you double-click to open an item. If you want to single-click, select **Single-click to open an item** (point to select) and then select how the underlining appears (either consistent with your Internet browser settings or underlined only when you point at them). Figure 20.10, for instance, shows the single-click option selected, with underlining consistent with the browser.

3. Click **OK**. Your changes are put into effect.

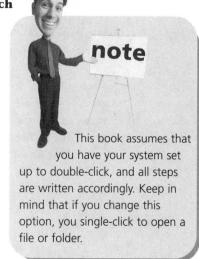

note

This book assumes that you have your system set up to double-click, and all steps are written accordingly. Keep in mind that if you change this option, you single-click to open a file or folder.

FIGURE 20.10

You can single-click rather than double-click to open a file or folder.

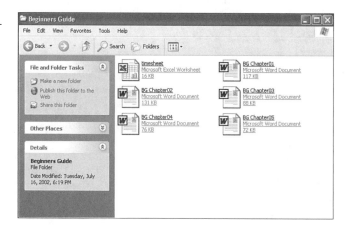

Searching for Documents

If you cannot find a particular file by browsing, even after changing the view or sorting, you have other options: You can search for it. You can search for several different file types. From the search results, you can then open, print, copy, or move the file.

Follow these steps to search for a file:

1. Click the **Start** button and then click the **Search** command. Or click the **Search** button in a file window. You see the various search options (see Figure 20.11).

2. Select the type of file you want to find. You can search for pictures, music, or video files; documents (word processing, spreadsheet, and so on); or all files and folders.

3. Enter the search criteria. The available options vary depending on what you selected to search for. Figure 20.12 shows searching for all files or folders. You can type all or part of the filename, search for a word or phrase in the file, and select the disk to look in, as well as set other search options including the last time the file was modified, the approximate size of the file, and still other options.

tip

The other tabs are more useful for reviewing information and making advanced changes. For example, you can click the **View** tab to select advanced settings for file view (such as displaying the full path for files or folders in the address or title bar, or selecting whether hidden or system files are displayed). Use the **File Types** tab to review the various file types with the associated program. This information is important because if you double-click a file icon, Windows uses the associated program to open that file. You can view the extensions, file types, and details from the **File Types** tab.

FIGURE 20.11

Help Windows XP narrow your search by selecting the type of file that you want to find.

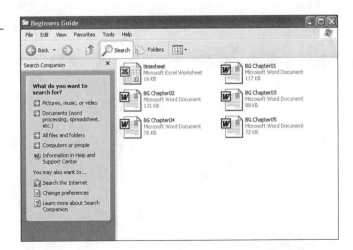

FIGURE 20.12

To search, enter
the search crite-
ria that you
think will best
help Windows
XP find a match.

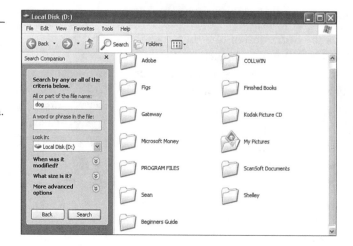

4. Click the **Search** button. Windows
   searches and displays a list of found files
   in the right pane of the window (see
   Figure 20.13). You can open, move, copy,
   or delete any of the listed files. For
   instance, you can double-click any of the
   listed files or folders to open that file or
   folder.

5. To close the search window, click its **Close**
   button.

> **tip**
>
> You can also use the
> **Search** command to search
> the Internet or to search for
> people (addresses or email
> information). See Chapter
> 11, "Searching the
> Internet," for more infor-
> mation on this type of search.

FIGURE 20.13

The results of the
search are dis-
played in the
right pane of the
Search Results
window.

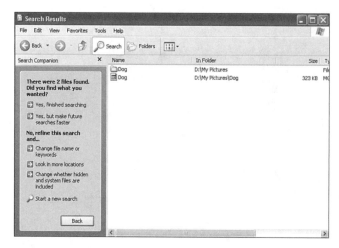

tip

To use additional search criteria click the link **More advanced options**. You can then limit the search to particular folders, choose whether subfolders (folders within the current folder or drive) are searched, select whether the search is case sensitive (whether capitalization has to match the word or phrase exactly as you've typed it), and more.

The Search bar lists the number of files found as well as options for refining the search. If the results did not turn up the file you want, search again. Some options for refining the search include changing the filename or keywords, looking in more locations, and changing which files and folders are searched.

THE ABSOLUTE MINIMUM

It's easy to misplace a file. Luckily, Windows XP has several ways to help you locate a file, including changing how the contents are displayed, sorting files, grouping files, and finally searching for files. For finding lost files, use the following guidelines:

- The view of a file window can help you find a particular file. For instance, if you are looking for a picture, use Thumbnail to view a small image of the picture. If you are looking for a particular type of file, use Details view.

- To change the view, display the **View** menu and select the view. Or use the **View** button in the file window's toolbar.

- You can sort files by name, type, size, or modification date. To do so, use the **Arrange Icons By** command in the **View** menu.

- Another handy feature for working with files of the same type (or other grouping) is to sort and then group the files. For instance, you can group all worksheet files together, all word processing documents together, and so on.

- To further fine-tune how you work with a file window's contents (whether you single- or double-click for instance), change the folder options.

- You can also search for a file, and Windows XP provides many search options. You can search for a file by type, modification date, name, or contents. You can also limit the search to a particular drive or folder.

21

Securing Your PC

Many beginning computer users are skittish about using the computer. They think they are going to "break" it. Really, there's not much you can do to ruin your computer, but you should take some precautions to guard your data—that is, the document files stored on your computer. Another safety issue is virus protection. You should periodically check your computer for viruses. This chapter defines what a virus is as well as gives advice on how to handle this security issue.

Finally, you learn about using System Restore, useful for going "back in time" on your computer. You can use this to troubleshoot any problems that might pop up when you make changes to your computer.

Back It Up!

The most important thing you can do to safeguard your data is to back it up! Yes, it can be time-consuming. Yes, it is a hassle. But the most valuable thing isn't the computer itself, but the data on it. Re-creating the data is not easy and in some cases not possible. Say, for instance, you store all your chapters for your next great book. Can you re-create them? Say, as another example, that you store all your contact information about your company on your computer. Can you re-create that data from a hodge-podge of business cards you might be able to round up?

tip

Another important security issue is protecting your computer while using the Internet. Internet security issues are covered in Chapter 17, "Customizing Email and Internet Explorer."

You take for granted the accessibility of your data. Take your Address Book. With it, you can easily send email to all your friends, colleagues, and relatives. Without it, do you really know by heart all the email addresses in that simple file?

That's why backing up your data is so critical. You should get in the habit of backing up your entire system at regular intervals and backing up your documents (data files) even more frequently.

Selecting Backup Programs and Equipment

To back up your files, you need backup media and a backup program. Media is the type of item you use to store your backup. Before the hard drives on computers got so big, you commonly backed up your data to floppy disks. Now backing up your system to floppy disks would be ludicrous (although you can use floppy disks as a quick method to back up important data files). Instead, you most commonly back up to a CD-R or CD-RW drive. Or you may purchase a special backup media called a tape drive. You can then back up using the tape drive.

To perform the backup, you need a backup program. The program not only performs the backup, but also provides options for selecting which files are backed up. Windows XP includes a backup program, but this program is not installed and is not easily accessed. (The program is stored on a folder on your Windows XP CD. See the following tip.)

You can also purchase backup programs. If you purchase a tape backup system, for instance, it usually comes with software for backing up. Also, some utility programs (sets of programs handy for maintaining and troubleshooting your computer) include backup programs.

You can find many—sometimes even free—backup programs by visiting any of the freeware or shareware sites on the Internet. Some popular programs include Back it Up, Monday Backup, Winbacker, Sysback (for backing up system files), and Backup Pro.

Tips for Backing Up

Here are some tips to make backing up more efficient:

- If you don't perform routine backups, you should at least make manual copies of all your data files. You can make a backup of important data files by copying them to floppy disk or to a CD drive (if you have a CD drive that can read and write data). See Chapter 19, "Organizing Files," for information on copying and compressing data.

- Consider doing a complete backup at least once a year and before any major system change (such as upgrading to a new operating system).

- You don't have to back up your program files (except during your complete system backup) since you can always reinstall them from the original program discs. Do, though, back up your data files more than once a year. You might consider daily or weekly intervals. I guarantee you the minute you think you don't need a backup will become the minute you do.

- To facilitate backing up data files, create and store files in a solid organizational structure. You might store all data files within subfolders in the My Documents folder. You can then concentrate on this folder when creating data file backups.

tip

Finding the Windows XP backup program isn't easy since it is not listed as an optional component to install on the installation program. (Chapter 24, "Upgrading Windows," explains how to install additional Windows components.) But you can find it by browsing your Windows XP CD. Insert your Windows XP disc into the drive. You should see the installation options. Click Perform additional tasks. Then click Browse this CD. Double-click the VALUEADD folder to open it. Double-click the MSFT folder to open it. Double-click the NTBACKUP folder to open it. Finally, double-click the NTBACKUP setup icon to install the Windows Backup program.

Checking a Disk for Errors

In addition to backing up your data, you should also periodically check your disk for errors. It's not uncommon for parts of your hard disk get damaged. When this happens, you might see an error message when you try to open or save a file.

To scan the disk for damage and fix any problems, you can use a handy system tool called Check Disk that is included with Windows XP. Follow these steps to use this program:

1. Open My Computer. You can do so by clicking **Start** and then **My Computer**. Or if you have added a desktop icon for My Computer, double-click this icon to open the drive window. You should see each of your drives listed.

2. Right-click the drive you want to back up and select **Properties**. If you have just one hard drive, it is named drive C. Some computers have more than one hard drive. If so, right-click this drive to select it.

   You see the General tab which gives you useful information about the status of this drive (see Figure 21.1).

FIGURE 21.1

You can display the properties dialog box for the hard drive(s) on your computer.

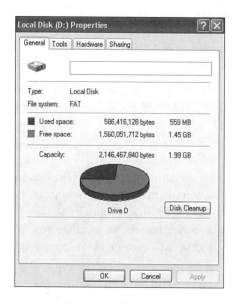

3. Click the **Tools** tab. You see the system tools for working with hard drives (see Figure 21.2).

tip

You can use this same dialog box to clean up your disk (get rid of files you don't need). For information on disk-performance options, see Chapter 22, "Improving Your Computer's Performance."

FIGURE 21.2

You can access the Check Disk program from the Tools tab.

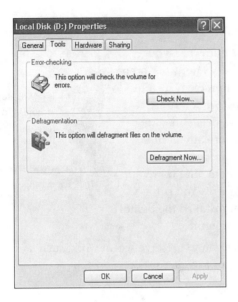

4. Click the **Check Now** button on the **Tools** tab. You see the available options for running the scan (see Figure 21.3). You can select whether errors are automatically fixed and whether the scan checks and repairs bad sectors.

FIGURE 21.3

Select how to perform the disk check.

5. Click **Start** to start the check.

6. If Check Disk finds an error, a dialog box appears explaining the error. Read the error message and choose the option you want to perform. For instance, the check might find errors in how data is stored (such as sector errors, invalid file dates, and bad sectors). Click **OK** to continue. Do this for each message.

7. When the Disk Check is complete, click **OK**.

note

To store data, your computer divides your disk into parts called sectors. It's not uncommon for a hard drive to have some bad sectors. You can check and repair these sectors, but note that this type of scan takes much longer.

Using System Restore

If you add new programs or hardware, you might find that your system does not work properly. Trying to troubleshoot a problem such as this can be difficult. To help, Windows XP includes System Restore. If needed, you can go back to any point in time before any of these restore points were set. For instance, suppose that you added a digital camera, and now your computer is not working properly. You can go "back" in time to before you installed the digital camera to troubleshoot the program.

Using System Restore enables you to preserve recent work, such as saved documents, email messages, history lists, or favorites lists.

Understanding Restore Points

Instead of relying on you to create backups, System Restore monitors changes to your system, and creates *restore points* each day by default. There are several types of restore points:

- The *initial system checkpoint* is created the first time you start your computer after Windows XP is installed (don't select this restore point unless you want to wipe your computer clean of everything you've done on it since installing XP).

- *System checkpoints* are created by Windows every 24 hours, and every 10 hours your computer is turned on.

- *Program name installation restore points* are created automatically when you install a program using one of the latest installers. Select this restore point to remove installed programs and other settings.

- *Manually created restore points* are those restore points you create yourself (covered later in this section).

- *Restore operation restore points* track restoration operations themselves, enabling you to undo them.

- *Unsigned driver restore points* are created any time System Restore determines that you are installing an unsigned or uncertified driver.

Setting a System Restore Point

In addition to those restore points set by the system automatically, you can also manually set a restore point. Then you are guaranteed a go-back-in-time point to when you know things were working. To set a system restore point, follow these steps:

1. Click **Start**, **All Programs**, **Accessories**, **System Tools**, and finally, click **System Restore**. You see the Welcome to System Restore window. You have the option of restoring your computer or creating a restore point (see Figure 21.4).

FIGURE 21.4

Start System Restore to set a restore point or go back to a restore point.

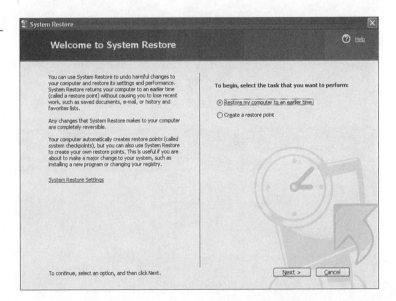

2. Select **Create a restore point** and click **Next**. You are prompted to type a name or description for the restore point (see Figure 21.5).

3. Type a description for the restore point and click **Create**. The point is created with the date and time you set the restore point (see Figure 21.6).

4. Click **Close** to close the System Restore window.

FIGURE 21.5

To keep track of the different restore points, type a descriptive name.

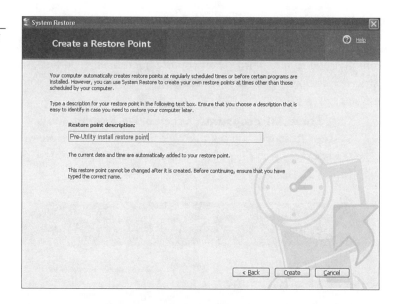

FIGURE 21.6

When you click **Create**, you see your new system restore point added.

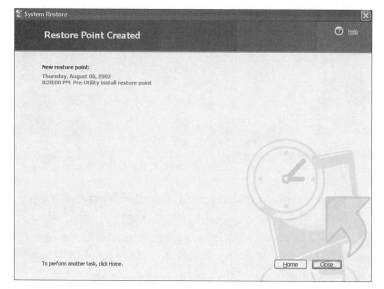

Restoring Your System

When something does go wrong and you wish you could get in a time machine and go back to happy times when you could check your email and you could use your printer, you can go back in time to a restore point, one set automatically or by you manually. Follow these steps to do so:

1. Click **Start**, **All Programs**, **Accessories**, **System Tools**, and finally, click **System Restore**.

2. Select **Restore my computer to an earlier time** and click **Next**. You see a calendar. Any dates that are bold have restore points (see Figure 21.7).

FIGURE 21.7

You can go back days or months using System Restore.

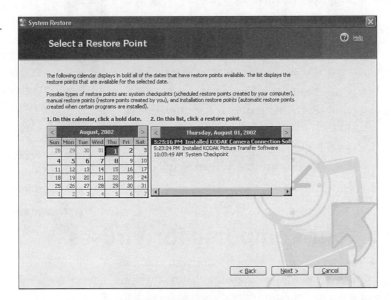

3. Click the date in the mini-calendar. You can use the scroll arrows to scroll backward or forward to other months. When you click a date, the available system restore points for that date are listed (see Figure 21.8).

FIGURE 21.8

Select the restore point by first selecting the date and then selecting the restore point on that particular date.

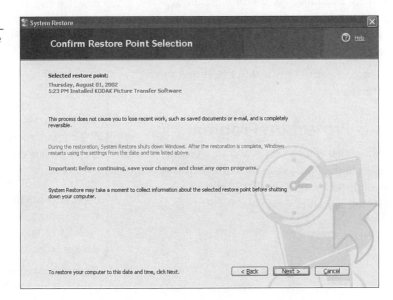

4. Select the restore point in the list and then click **Next**. You see a description of what happens. Note that saved documents and email are not affected, and you can reverse the actions of a system restore. As described in the dialog box, Windows is shut down, restored, and then restarted using the settings from the date and time of the system restore point.

5. Click **Next**. As described, the system is shut down and restored. You are returned to the System Restore window with a message saying the restoration is complete.

6. Click **OK** to close the System Restore window.

tip

If you want to undo the restore, you can do so. Follow the same steps to open the System Restore window (**Start**, **All Programs**, **Accessories**, **System Tools**, **System Restore**). You now have an option for undoing the restore. Select this option and then follow the onscreen prompts, clicking Next to go from step to step.

Checking Your Computer for Viruses

Just like you can get a virus, so can your computer. Computer viruses range from simple, mischievous programs that might display a stupid message to really dangerous ones that can wipe out all the data on a drive. How does your PC get infected? Well, you can get a virus from any number of sources, including the Internet, email attachments, and opening a file that happens to be infected from a floppy disk or other removable media (like a CD drive).

To protect yourself, you should get and use a virus scan program.

Using a Virus Protection Program

With a virus protection program, you can periodically check your system for known viruses, scan incoming files, and warn you before any infected files are copied to your system.

You might think you are safe by scanning just program files. (Usually these files have the extension .exe and are called .exe files.) It's a common myth that you can only get a virus from this type of file. Not true. You can get viruses from documents with macros, as in recent outbreak of Word viruses that you could get simply from opening the infected document.

Don't just scan program files; be careful with other documents also, especially if they contain executable modules such as macros.

Popular antivirus programs include Norton's AntiVirus (visit www.symantec.com for more information) and McAcfee VirusScan (visit www.mcafee.com for product information).

Antivirus programs each work differently. Most are started automatically when you start Windows and then scan your computer at a set interval. You can also set them up to scan every file you open. Finally, you can also start them and run them at any time by double-clicking the program icon for the antivirus program or by selecting it from the **Start** menu.

For instance, you can set up the program to scan all floppy disks inserted in your system and to scan files that are downloaded to your system, including email attachments. Check your particular antivirus program's manual or online help for information on setting virus options.

Handling an Infected File

When you scan for viruses, the program identifies any files that have been infected by any virus it recognizes, and usually offers you the option to repair the file if it can. In some cases infected files can be "cleaned" by your virus protection software; in others, the files will have to be discarded. For really lethal viruses, you may have to reformat your hard disk and start over from scratch. In this case, you will be glad if you backed up your data (covered earlier in this chapter).

You need to update your antivirus program periodically. New viruses are created all the time, so if you don't have the latest upgrade, you can get a virus even if you are checking for viruses.

Your antivirus program has a database of problems, viruses, and fixes. To make sure your program is working from the most recent list of viruses and fixes, you need to periodically update your program. Many programs offer free updates for a period of time after their purchase. You can then subscribe to additional upgrades, and you should!

tip

It's embarrassing, but when you do find out you have a virus, you should notify anyone whom you've had contact with and whom you might have unintentionally infected. Send them the fix if possible. If not, at least alert them so that they can check their own systems.

THE ABSOLUTE MINIMUM

This chapter focused on how to keep your data and computer secure using a variety of Windows XP tools as well as other programs, including a backup program and a virus program. In particular, keep these main points in mind:

- Back up your data: It is the most important and valuable thing on your computer. A computer can be replaced; your data sometimes cannot.

- To back up, you need a backup program as well as backup media (tape drive, or CD-R or RW drives). You can select how often to perform the backup as well as which files are backed up.

- You should periodically scan your computer for errors. You can use Windows XP's Check Disk to do so.

- Viruses are programs that unbeknownst to you can infect your computer and can wreak havoc. Use a virus protection program to scan files and email attachments for viruses and warn you of any viruses.

- You should also put into place Internet privacy and security settings, especially if you have a 24/7 connection. This topic is covered in Chapter 17.

22

IMPROVING YOUR COMPUTER'S PERFORMANCE

When you first start using your computer, it will seem pretty quick, especially if you have not used a computer before. But as you use the computer more often, you might notice that the performance is a little sluggish. As another example, you may find that your desktop is cluttered with too many icons. To keep your computer working as efficiently as possible, every now and then you should use some tools to check and, if needed, optimize the computer's performance. This section covers how to display disk information; the rest of the chapter covers how to use Windows XP's tools to enhance your computer's performance.

Displaying Disk Information

To get an idea of the size of your hard disk and how much space is used, you can display disk information. This is handy if you think you are running out of room for your files. You also access several of Windows XP's disk tools from this dialog box.

To display disk information, follow these steps:

1. Open the My Computer window. You can click **Start** and then **My Computer**. Or if you added the My Computer icon to your desktop, you can double-click it.

2. In the My Computer window, right-click the disk for which you want information and click the **Properties** command. The disk's Properties dialog box is displayed. On the General tab, shown in Figure 22.1, you can see the total disk space, disk space used, and free space.

3. Click **OK** to close the dialog box.

FIGURE 22.1

This hard disk is dangerously full. There is very little free space for storing files.

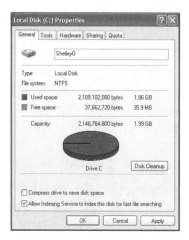

Other sections of this chapter cover how to use the tools in this dialog box to improve performance.

Cleaning Up Your Disk

Like any storage place (think closets, garages, basements), eventually the clutter starts to overwhelm you, and you need to get rid of stuff you don't need. The same is true for your hard disk(s). You should periodically clean out files you don't need. To help with this task, you can clean up some temporary files, empty your Recycle Bin, and find some other hidden nooks and crannies of Windows that take up storage space.

Windows makes it easy to get rid of files that you don't need with the Disk Cleanup Wizard. When you use this wizard, Windows XP recommends some files for deleting as well as lists the disk space you'll gain. You can select from the list of items suggested for deleting and then have Windows XP remove these items and regain that disk space.

To clean up files using the Windows XP Disk Cleanup Wizard, follow these steps:

1. Open the My Computer window by double-clicking this icon on your desktop or by clicking **Start** and then clicking **My Computer**.

2. Right-click the disk you want to check and then select **Properties**. You see the General tab of the Properties dialog box for that disk (refer to Figure 22.1). From this tab, you can view the total capacity of this disk drive, the used space, and the free space.

3. To clean up files, click the **Disk Cleanup** button. The Disk Cleanup tab displays files for deletion (see Figure 22.2). Any items that are checked will be deleted. For instance, notice that in Figure 22.2 temporary files take up quite a bit of space. You can regain this space by removing these files.

One of the first places Windows looks for space is in the Recycle Bin. Before you permanently delete those files, take a quick peek to make sure that the Recycle Bin doesn't contain any files you need. To view the particular files, select the item in the list and then click the **View Files** button. You can then confirm that they can be deleted.

FIGURE 22.2

You can select which files are removed using Disk Cleanup.

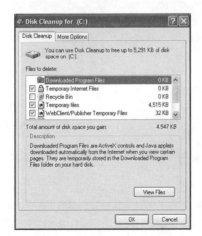

4. Check the items you want to delete. Uncheck items you do not want to delete.

5. Click **OK**.

6. Confirm the deletion by clicking **Yes**. The files are permanently deleted and that disk space regained.

For access to additional cleanup options, click the More Options tab in the Disk Cleanup dialog box. From here, you can select to remove optional Windows components, remove programs you don't use, or remove all but the last restore point (see Figure 22.3).

FIGURE 22.3

If you want to gain more space, use the **More Options** button to display other space-gaining options.

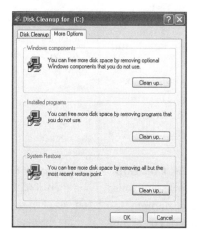

For instance, if you are running out of room, you can remove programs you do not need. For more information on adding and removing programs, see Chapter 16, "Setting Up Programs." You can also remove Windows components that you do not use. For information on this process, see Chapter 24, "Upgrading Windows." For information on what a system restore point is, see Chapter 21, "Securing Your PC."

> **tip**
>
> You can also run this program from the **Start** menu. Click **Start**, **All Programs**, **Accessories**, and then **System Tools**. In the System Tools menu, click **Disk Cleanup**.

Increasing Performance by Defragmenting Your Disk

Another way to improve performance is to *defragment* your disk. To understand how this process improves your disk performance, you first need to have a short introduction to how data is stored. Basically, when you defragment a disk, you rearrange how the files are stored so that Windows XP can open and display a file more efficiently.

The Basics of Disk Storage

When you store a document, the data in that document is written to your disk and saved as a file with a specific name in a specific location on your disk. To keep files organized, your disk is divided into sections called *sectors*, which are broken down into smaller sections called *clusters*. Each cluster can hold a certain amount of data.

A file is often larger than one cluster. Therefore, when you give a command to save a file, Windows takes the file and stores the file in a cluster. If the file is too big to fit in one cluster, Windows goes to the next available cluster, stores more of the file in that cluster, and so on until the entire file is stored on the disk.

Windows keeps a little cheat sheet that tells it where all the chunks of each file are stored.

When you want to open that file again, Windows checks its file system, its map of the disk, and collects all the pieces of the file, basically putting all the pieces together again, and displays it onscreen.

Initially, this storage does not cause performance problems because your disk is empty, and files are usually stored sequentially. But over time, your disk files become fragmented. And you might find that it takes a long time to open a file or start a program.

To speed access to files and to help prevent potential problems with fragmented files, you can use Disk Defragmenter to *defragment* your disk. Defragmenting basically reorders the files on the disk, putting file parts next to each other if possible and putting all the empty, available clusters together so that when new files are saved, they get a block of

Probably the biggest complaint and most noticeable performance issue is with online connections. Logging on to the Internet or displaying Web pages can take a long time, but this slowness is related to the type of Internet connection you have. For instance, dial-up accounts are limited to the speed of the modem, and modem speed is also limited in speed because of the phone lines.

To get better Internet performance, you usually need to get a different type of connection, commonly called a *broadband connection*. The most common broadband connections for home users are cable connections (through your cable provider) and DSL connections (a special type of phone line). You can learn more about connection types in Chapter 10, "Browsing the Internet."

clusters together. Defragmenting your disk is a general-maintenance job that you should perform every few months for best results.

How to Run Disk Defragmenter

You can run the defragmentation program on your hard disk by following these steps:

1. Open the My Computer window by double-clicking this icon on your desktop or by clicking **Start** and then clicking **My Computer**.

2. Right-click the disk you want to check and then select **Properties**. You see the General tab of the Properties dialog box for that disk.

3. Click the **Tools** tab. You see the available system tools for disks (see Figure 22.4).

> **tip**
>
> Here's a little history note. Older Windows versions used a file allocation table (called FAT or FAT32) for file management as the "cheat sheet." Newer Windows versions, including Windows XP, use a more advanced file system called NTFS. This new file system lets you use huge storage media and long filenames. This file system also automatically replaces bad clusters.

FIGURE 22.4

Use the Tools tab to access disk tools.

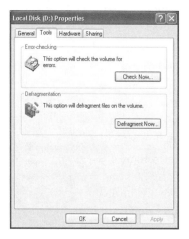

4. Click the **Defragment Now** button. You see the Disk Defragment window.

5. To see whether the disk requires defragmenting, click the **Analyze** button. Windows analyzes the data on the drive and makes a recommendation on

> **tip**
>
> For information on checking a disk for errors, see Chapter 21.

whether you should defragment the drive (see Figure 22.5). You can view the report, start defragmenting, or close the recommendation alert box.

6. Click **Close** so that you can view a detailed map of the drive. You see this map in the Disk Defragmenter window (see Figure 22.6). The legend at the bottom of the Disk Defragmenter window helps you understand the map and identify the various file types (fragmented, contiguous, unmovable, and free space).

tip

You can also run this program from the **Start** menu. Click **Start**, **All Programs**, **Accessories**, and then **System Tools**. In the System Tools menu, click **Disk Defragmenter**.

FIGURE 22.5

Before you defragment, analyze your drive to see whether defragmenting is necessary.

FIGURE 22.6

In the analysis, you can see how the files are stored, which ones are contiguous (next to each other) and which are fragmented. You can also see where you have free space.

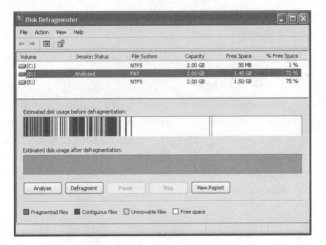

7. Click the **Defragment** button to defragment the drive. As the files are rearranged, you see the progress of the defragmentation (see Figure 22.7).

FIGURE 22.7

You can view the progress of the defragmentation.

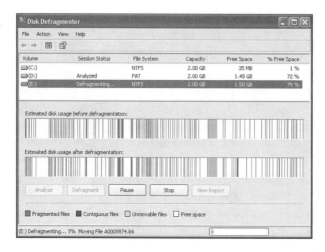

Disk Defragmenter may take a while to defragment your disk, depending on the size of the disk, the number and size of files on the volume, the extent of fragmentation in the disk, and available system resources. Disk Defragmenter's progress is indicated by the progress bar in the Disk Defragmenter window.

When the process completes, Disk Defragmenter displays the results. You can choose to display a report on the process; this report displays detailed information about the disk that was defragmented. Click the **Close** button to close the report and then the Defragmenter window. Or you can click **OK** to close the Disk Defragmenter window without viewing the report.

Cleaning Up the Desktop

In addition to cleaning up files, you may also want to tidy up your desktop. Doing so won't necessarily improve the system performance, but it may help *your* performance—that is, help you find and access the icons on your desktop more efficiently. To help you determine which icons you really use and which can be deleted, you can use the Desktop Cleanup Wizard.

Follow these steps:

1. Right-click a blank part of the desktop. You see the Display Properties dialog box.

2. Click the **Desktop** tab.

3. Click the **Customize Desktop** button. You see the Desktop Items dialog box (see Figure 22.8).

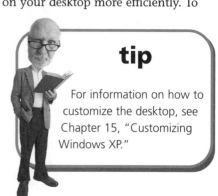

tip

For information on how to customize the desktop, see Chapter 15, "Customizing Windows XP."

FIGURE 22.8

You can access the Desktop Cleanup Wizard from this dialog box.

4. Click **Clean Desktop Now** to start the wizard.

5. Follow the steps in the Desktop Cleanup Wizard, clicking **Next** to move from step to step. The first window displays a welcome that explains the purpose of the wizard. When you click **Next**, you see a list of desktop icons. You can see the date the icon was last used (see Figure 22.9). If you do not use an icon, Windows XP checks its box and recommends it for deleting. Check any icons you want to remove; uncheck any icons you want to leave as is. Click **Next**.

6. Click the **Finish** button to finish the cleanup.

FIGURE 22.9

You can decide whether the icon is moved or left on the desktop.

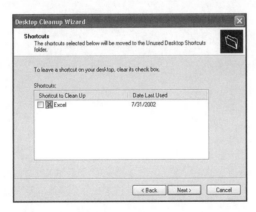

If you select to remove an icon, it is not deleted, but moved to the Unused Desktop Shortcuts folder. You can always add back the icon if needed.

THE ABSOLUTE MINIMUM

In this chapter you learned how to improve the performance of your computer using some of the built-in tools in Windows XP. You may not need to use these tools if you have a new computer, but keep them in mind as you use the computer more and more. If you notice a drop in performance, take a look at some of the changes you can make to regain that performance. In particular, keep these main points in mind:

■ You can view the disk properties of your hard disk to see how much total space you have, how much is used, and how much is free.

■ If your drive is becoming too full and you want to remove files, you can help Windows select some commonly unneeded files for removal. To do so, use the Disk Cleanup Wizard. You can access this wizard from the disk properties dialog box.

■ When performance is really slow, you may need to defragment the drive, rearranging the data stored on the drive to optimize the performance. You can start the defragment process from the Tools tab of the disk properties dialog box.

■ If your desktop becomes cluttered with too many icons, you can run the Desktop Cleanup Wizard to have Windows suggest icons to be removed.

23

HANDLING PC MAINTENANCE

So far in this part you have learned some particular tools and tasks for keeping your computer in tip-top shape. Chapter 19 "Organizing Files," and Chapter 20, "Viewing and Finding Files," covered how to keep your files and folders organized. Chapter 21, "Securing Your PC," explained how to secure your data by backing up, checking for viruses, and so on. Chapter 22, "Improving Your Computer's Performance," covered how to check and improve disk performance.

This chapter adds to this list of maintenance chores but covers tasks you need to do less frequently such as adding new hardware and troubleshooting hardware problems.

Scheduling Maintenance Tasks

If you are not good at remembering things, you can set up Windows XP to perform scheduled tasks on a set interval. These can include maintenance tasks as well as other tasks including checking and downloading mail. You basically can run any program at the time and interval you select.

Adding a New Task

To set up a scheduled task list, follow these steps:

1. Click **Start**, **All Programs**, **Accessories**, **System Tools**, and finally, click **Scheduled Tasks**. You see the Scheduled Tasks window listing any tasks that you have set up (see Figure 23.1).

FIGURE 23.1

You can add and change scheduled tasks using the Scheduled Tasks window.

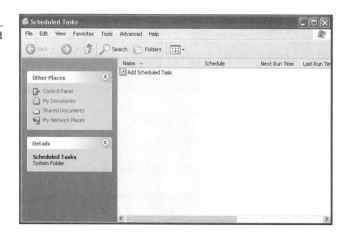

2. Double-click the **Add Scheduled Task** item to start the Scheduled Task Wizard. The first screen introduces this feature.

3. Click **Next** to move to the next step. You are prompted to select the program you want to run (see Figure 23.2).

FIGURE 23.2

You can select to schedule and run any installed and registered programs on your computer.

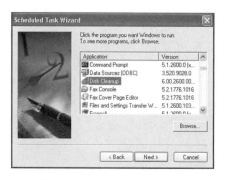

4. Click the program to select it and click **Next**. You are prompted to type a name for the task. This is the name that appears in the scheduled task list. You also select an interval for running this program. You can select daily, weekly, monthly, one time only, when my computer starts, or when I log on (see Figure 23.3).

FIGURE 23.3

Select how often you want to run this scheduled task.

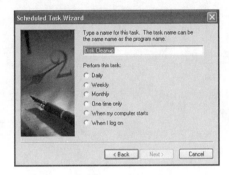

5. Select the interval for running the selected program and then click **Next**. You next set the schedule for the task (see Figure 23.4). The options for setting the schedule vary depending on the interval you select.

FIGURE 23.4

Here you see the options for running the selected program monthly.

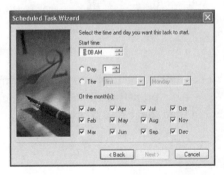

6. Select the start time and date(s) to run the program and then click **Next**.

7. If required, type the username and password. You must type the password twice—once to enter it and again to confirm it. Click **Next**.

The final screen displays all your entries—the selected program and when the program is scheduled to run (see Figure 23.5).

8. Click **Finish**. The task is added to the Scheduled Tasks list and will run at the interval you selected.

FIGURE 23.5

You see the
details of the
scheduled task.

9. Click the **Close** button to close the
   Scheduled Tasks window.

Modifying Scheduled Tasks

If needed, you can delete or adjust any of the
scheduled tasks. To do so, follow these steps:

1. Click **Start**, **All Programs**,
   Accessories, **System Tools**, and finally,
   click **Scheduled Tasks**. You see the
   Scheduled Tasks window listing any tasks
   that you have set up.

2. Do any of the following:

   To edit an item—for instance, to change how often the program is run—
   double-click the item. You see the properties dialog box for that program.
   Click the **Schedule** tab and then make any changes (see Figure 23.6).
   Click **OK**.

> **tip**
>
> If more than one person
> uses your computer, you can
> set up multiple users. Step 7
> lets you select the user under
> which the task is run. See
> Chapter 26, "Setting Up
> Windows XP for Multiple
> Users."

FIGURE 23.6

You can change
when the sched-
uled item is run.

To delete a scheduled item, select it and then click **Delete this item** in the task pane or press the **Delete** key. Confirm the deletion by clicking **Yes**.

3. Close the Scheduled Tasks window by clicking its **Close** button.

Setting Up New Hardware

As you use your computer, you may find that you want to add new components to your system. You may purchase a digital camera or scanner. You may add a DVD drive or a CD-R drive (a recordable drive). As another example, you may add one of the many digital music add-ons such as MP3 or other portable music devices.

In any case, setting up new hardware can be straightforward. In the best-case scenario, you simply attach or install the new device, and Windows XP sets it up automatically. If that doesn't happen, you can always install the device manually. Both methods are covered in this section.

Setting Up New Hardware Automatically

To set up hardware automatically, simply follow the installation instructions for your particular device. For some add-on components, you simply connect the device to an available port. For example, most scanners plug into a USB port. (USB is short for *universal serial bus*, and it is a type of port found on most computers. You can connect devices to these ports by plugging in the USB cable to the USB port on your computer.)

For other hardware, you may have to turn off your computer and remove the system case. For instance, to install network or modem cards, you have to turn off the power, remove the case, and then plug the cards into slots inside the system unit.

In either case, if Windows XP recognizes the new hardware, it automatically starts the Add Hardware Wizard and queries the device for setup information. It then installs the appropriate driver file and alerts you that the device has been found and installed. You should see alert messages in the system tray as this process is completed. You can then use your device.

Using the Manufacturer's Install Program

Usually a hardware component comes with a disk with its own driver and installation routine. A *driver* is a special type of file that tells Windows XP the details about a particular hardware device.

If your component came with a disk, use this disk to install the new hardware. Usually you connect the device and then insert the disk to start the installation process. Follow the specific instructions for your particular hardware component.

Installing New Hardware Manually

If the Add Hardware Wizard does not start and find your new hardware device automatically or if you do not have a driver from the hardware maker, you can use the Add Hardware Wizard to manually set up the device. You can then have Windows search for and install the new device. Or you can select the device manufacturer and product from a list. Windows XP includes drivers for many popular hardware components.

Follow these steps to run the Add Hardware Wizard:

1. Click **Start** and then **Control Panel**. In the Control Panel window, double-click **Add Hardware**.

2. Click **Next** to move past the welcome screen. You are asked whether the device is already connected.

3. You should have connected the device before starting the wizard, so click **Yes**, I have already connected the hardware. Click **Next** to move to the next step. You see a list of all the devices already installed (see Figure 23.7).

FIGURE 23.7

To add new hardware, select the last option in the list of hardware devices.

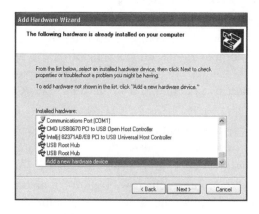

4. Select **Add a new hardware device**. (Scroll to the end of the list to find this option.) Click **Next**. You have the choice of letting Windows XP search for the new device and set it up automatically or to set up the device manually. Try searching first.

5. To have Windows XP search and install, select this option. Windows XP searches for new devices. If the device is found, Windows XP then installs the new device. Follow the onscreen prompts to install and set up the device. You can skip the remaining steps listed here.

Or

If the automatic method did not work or if you want to use the manual method, select this option. You see a list of common hardware categories (see Figure 23.8).

FIGURE 23.8

Select the type of device you are adding.

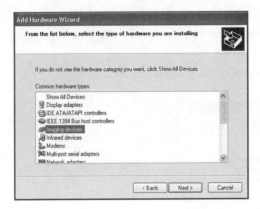

6. Select your device type and click **Next**. You are prompted to select the manufacturer and model of the device you are installing (see Figure 23.9).

FIGURE 23.9

Select the manufacturer and model of the device from this list.

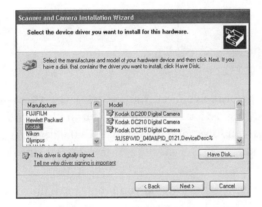

7. Scroll through the list of manufacturers until you see the manufacturer of your device. Then click it. You then see available models from this manufacturer in the Model list. Click the model and click **Next**.

8. Follow the onscreen instructions for completing the installation of your device. You can then use your new hardware device.

If your device type is not listed, click **Show All Devices**.

Troubleshooting Hardware Problems

If you are having problems with a particular hardware device, you can use one of Windows XP's troubleshooters to display common problems as well as solutions.

Follow these steps to display help on a particular hardware device:

1. Right-click the **My Computer** icon and then select **Properties** to display the System Properties dialog box.

2. Click the **Hardware** tab (see Figure 23.10).

FIGURE 23.10

You can start the Add Hardware Wizard or display installed devices from this dialog box.

3. Click the **Device Manager** button. You see the Device Manager listing the categories of hardware devices. Each category has a plus sign next to it. You can click this plus sign to expand the list and see the device(s) installed for each category. Figure 23.11, for instance, shows the Imaging devices category expanded.

4. When you see the device that's giving you problems, right-click the device name and then select the **Properties** command. You see the properties dialog box for this particular device (see Figure 23.12).

5. Click the **Troubleshoot** button in the properties dialog box. Doing so launches the Windows XP help system and displays the initial troubleshooting help window.

6. Select your device (if needed). Windows XP displays queries to try to determine the problem. Answer the questions, clicking **Next** to go to the next step. For instance, if you are troubleshooting a scanner, Windows XP prompts you to select the type of scanner.

FIGURE 23.11

Expand the hardware device list to view and select your particular device.

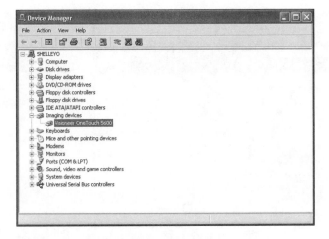

FIGURE 23.12

You can view device information from the properties dialog box.

7. Review each screen, selecting the appropriate option and clicking **Next**. Windows then lists common problems. For instance, Figure 23.13 lists some common problems for scanners. When Windows identifies the problem, it recommends some ways to solve that problem. Try any recommended fixes. You may have to step through several pages of questions and help suggestions until the problem is fixed.

tip

If you need to update the driver or make more advanced changes, you start from the properties dialog box. That particular topic is beyond the scope of this book.

FIGURE 23.13

Windows displays several options for fixing the device.

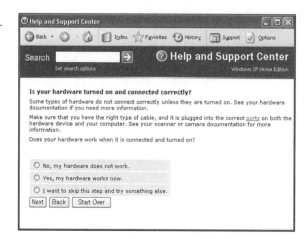

8. When you are finished troubleshooting the device, click the Help window's **Close** button.

THE ABSOLUTE MINIMUM

In this chapter you learned about some additional maintenance features available in Windows XP, in particular the following:

■ You can schedule maintenance tasks with the Scheduled Task Wizard. Do this so that you won't forget to perform regular tasks such as backing up your computer or checking your disk for problems.

■ If you add new hardware, you can install it using one of several methods: automatically, using the installation program and files provided with the hardware component, and using the Add New Hardware Wizard.

■ You can use the Device Manager to display information about installed hardware as well as troubleshoot a device if you are having problems.

24

UPGRADING WINDOWS

Windows XP is by no means perfect, so during its lifetime, Microsoft will fix problems (called *bugs*) with little programs (called *patches*). To keep your version updated, you can download updates to Windows XP. Also, depending on your Windows installation, certain components may not have been installed. You can review the list of components and add or remove as needed. That's the focus of this chapter—upgrading Windows.

Installing Windows Updates

To keep your system as up-to-date as possible, you should periodically check for and then install Windows updates. These updates, as mentioned, fix bugs and provide software patches. A bug is a problem in the software code that causes problems. A patch is a small chunk of programming code that repairs the bug or provides some additional functions for Windows.

You have two ways to perform this task. This section covers both of these methods as well as covers how to change the notification settings (how and when you are notified about updates).

Running Automatic Updates

As Windows XP is initially set up, critical updates are downloaded automatically, and you are prompted to install these updates when they are available. A little pop-up reminder will be displayed in the system tray reminding you to check for updates. From this reminder, you can select to update Windows by clicking the reminder and then following the appropriate steps.

tip

To check for and install automatic updates, you must have an Internet connection. See Chapter 10, "Browsing the Internet," for more information on this topic.

Checking for Updates

You can also check for updates at any time. For instance, in addition to critical updates, Microsoft also provides driver updates as well as updates that add new features. To check for and install other updates, follow these steps:

1. Click **Start** and then click **All Programs**. In the top section of the **Start** menu, you should see Windows Update listed.

2. Click **Windows Update**. For dial-up Internet connections, you are prompted to get connected. For cable connections, Internet Explorer is started. Windows XP checks your system against the latest updates to see which updates are applicable. This may take a while, depending on your Internet connection speed. Then you see the Windows Update page (see Figure 24.1).

Because the Microsoft page is updated frequently, what you see when you select to update will be different. Also, the process may vary some from these steps. Follow the onscreen steps or check help at the Web site if you have problems.

3. To scan for updates, click **Scan for updates**. Windows checks for updates and lists all updates (see Figure 24.2). Note that Windows categorizes the updates. Critical Updates and Service Packs are highly recommended; these updates usually fix problems that affect the safety of your computer and data. In the example in Figure 24.2, no critical updates for my version of Windows XP are needed.

To check for and
download
updates, go to
the Microsoft
Windows Update
page.

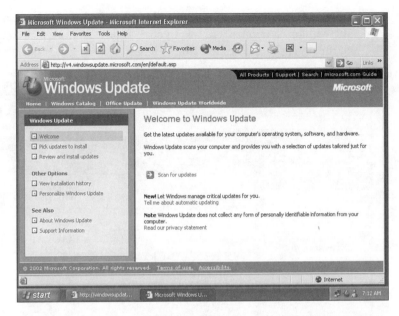

You can view
the various
updates that are
available.

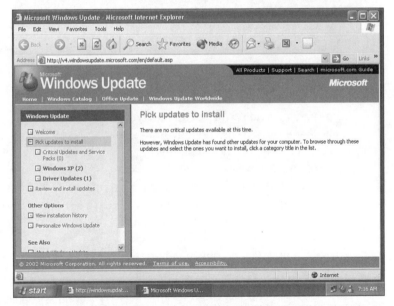

In addition to Critical Updates and Service Packs, you can display other updates for Windows. As another option, you can download new drivers for Windows XP. A *driver* is a file that tells Windows XP the details about a particular hardware component. To use the component with Windows, you install the appropriate driver file. (Chapter 23, "Handling PC Maintenance," covers installing new hardware, including drivers.)

4. Click the update you want to install in the Windows Update pane. You see the various components of this update. Figure 24.3, for instance, shows some of the optional updates for Windows XP.

5. Make your selections, following the onscreen instructions for guidance. The steps vary depending on the update type, so just read the screens carefully and make your selections based on the onscreen advice. Basically, you download (copy from this Web site to your computer) the upgrade files and then install them on your computer. Depending on the type of Internet connection and the size of the update files, downloading the update files can take a while. After the update is downloaded, you then install it, updating the Windows files on your system. Then you are usually prompted to restart Windows to put the new updates into effect. In some cases, you must restart your computer to put the new features or update into effect.

tip

From the Windows Update page, you can also review and select from a list of updates. You can view your installation history, change the settings for Windows update, and get help information on this topic. To do any of these tasks, use the links in the Windows Update pane of the window or click any links in the main area of the Update page.

Setting Automatic Update Options

If you want to review or change your update settings (when you are notified of updates, for instance), you can do so. For instance, you may want to check more frequently for updates.

1. Click **Start** and then right-click the **My Computer** icon. Select **Properties**. You see System Properties dialog box (see Figure 24.4).

FIGURE 24.4

You can control how Windows updates are handled.

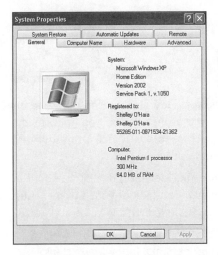

2. Click the **Automatic Updates** tab in the System Properties dialog box. You see the notification settings options (see Figure 24.5).

FIGURE 24.5

You can select when you are notified for updates.

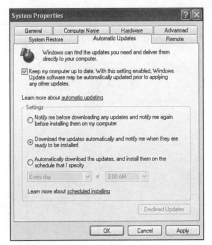

3. Select how updates are managed: download them automatically and then notify
   you, notify before downloading, or automatically download on a schedule you
   specify. If you choose this last option,
   select the frequency and time from the
   drop-down lists.

4. Click **OK**.

tip

If you have any questions
about the types of updates
or how the updates work,
click the link Learn more
about automatic updating in
the Notification Settings
Wizard page.

Installing or Removing
Windows Components

In addition to Windows updates, you may also need to add or remove Windows
components. Depending on the type of installation you performed, you may not
have installed certain features (such as fax features). Or to save disk space, you may
want to remove components you don't use.

For instance, you may read in a book (including this book) about how to use your
computer to play Solitaire. But when you look at your **Start** menu, you don't see
Solitaire listed. Perhaps the games included with Windows XP were not installed on
your computer. If so, you can install them.

To make a change to Windows components, follow these steps:

1. Click the **Start** button and then click **Control Panel**.

2. Click **Add or Remove Programs**. You see the Add or Remove Programs
   window (see Figure 24.6).

FIGURE 24.6

You can use this
Control Panel
item to add and
remove pro-
grams, including
Windows
components.

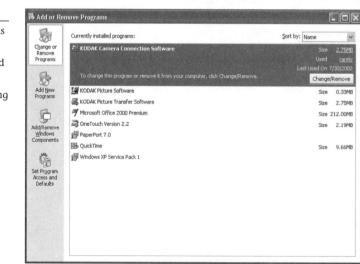

3. Click the **Add/Remove Windows Components** button. You see the Windows Components Wizard (see Figure 24.7). Items that are checked are installed. You can uncheck items to remove them from your setup. You can also check any item to add it to your setup.

FIGURE 24.7

You can select which Windows components are installed.

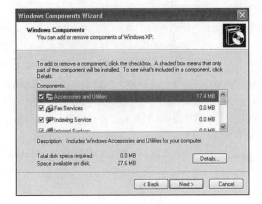

4. Check (to add) or uncheck (to remove) the components you want to change.

5. Click **Next** and then follow the onscreen instructions as Windows XP updates its installed components. Components you checked are added. You may be prompted to insert your Windows disk. Windows configures and sets up any new components. If you unchecked a component, it is removed.

6. Click **Finish** to complete the wizard. You may need to restart your computer to update Windows XP's configuration and put the update into effect.

tip

Some listed components are actually several components. To view the various components within a group, select the item (such as Accessories and Utilities) and then click the Details button. You can then check or uncheck the components listed within this group.

The Absolute Minimum

To keep your system up-to-date, you should periodically check for and install Windows updates. This chapter covered this topic as well as installing or removing Windows components. Keep these main ideas in mind:

- Usually your computer is set up to automatically scan for and install updates. You'll know when an update is installed because Windows displays a notification icon.

- To check for updates manually or to select from optional updates, use the **Windows updates** command. This command starts Internet Explorer and takes you to the Microsoft Windows Update page. Here you can review current updates and select to install those updates.

- If you prefer to control when updates are installed, you can change the notification settings for the automatic install. Click the update notification icon to start this wizard.

- To review, add, or remove installed Windows components, use the Add or Remove Programs Control Panel item.

WINDOWS XP FOR SPECIAL SITUATIONS

25

USING WINDOWS ACCESSORY PROGRAMS

Windows XP includes more than just the necessary tools and programs to be your operating system. Windows XP also comes packed with several other programs such as an email program (covered in Chapter 9, "Sending and Receiving Email"), an Internet browser (covered in Chapter 10, "Browsing the Internet"), a fax program (covered in Chapter 12, "Sending and Receiving Faxes"), a music player (covered in Chapter 13, "Playing Music and Videos"), and several others.

This chapter focuses on some of the other accessory programs included with Windows XP. Although these programs won't replace your need for full-fledged programs, they do serve some simple purposes. And they are great for tinkering around and experimenting. Many program skills—copying text, selecting a menu command, undoing changes—work the same way in all programs. Use this chapter to explore some of Windows XP's accessory programs.

Checking Out the Accessories

You can get a good idea of the accessory programs included in Windows XP by displaying the Accessories folder. To do so, click **Start**, **All Programs**, and then **Accessories**. Some programs are grouped together into a folder (such as System Tools). Others are listed on the menu (see Figure 25.1). To open a folder and display the programs, click the folder name. To start any of these programs, click its name.

FIGURE 25.1

You can view the accessory programs included with Windows XP.

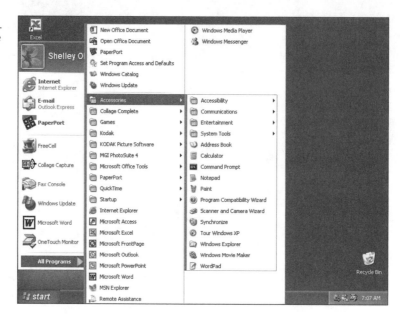

The following briefly lists the main use of the Accessories program and provides references to other chapters where these features are covered.

- Accessibility features provide special features for those with special needs. For instance, you can display an onscreen keyboard and type from that. You can magnify the screen. You can read more on these features in Chapter 27, "Using Accessibility Options."

- Communications features include the Home Networking Wizard and other networking features (covered in Chapter 28, "Setting Up Windows XP on a Home

If you do not see a Windows program listed that is covered here or in other books, this component may not have been installed. To install additional Windows components, see Chapter 24, "Upgrading Windows."

Network"), the New Connection Wizard (covered in Chapter 10), and Fax (covered in Chapter 12).

- Entertainment programs include Sound Recorder, Windows Media Player, and Volume Control. Music is covered in Chapter 13. You can also use the new Windows Movie Maker (the topic of Chapter 14, "Working with Photographs and Movies").

- System Tools includes features for checking and optimizing your computer. These topics are covered in Part V of this book.

- Address Book helps you keep track of contacts. You can find out more about using Address Book in Chapter 17, "Customizing Email and Internet Explorer."

- Calculator is a basic calculator you can use to calculate mathematical equations. This program is covered later in this chapter.

- Command Prompt is a throw-back to those DOS days (before Windows). Even within the world of Windows, you might need access to a command prompt. For instance, you might use Command Prompt to run a DOS game.

- Notepad is good for simple text files.

- Paint is fun for creating simple illustrations; this program is covered in this chapter.

- You can use WordPad to create simple text documents. Like Paint and Calculator, WordPad is described in this chapter.

- The Accessories program folder also includes programs for checking program compatibility, setting up a camera or wizard, synchronizing data from a laptop with your desktop computer, viewing a tour of Windows XP, and managing files with Windows Explorer.

> **tip**
>
> Windows XP also includes games. These programs are stored in the Games folder, not the Accessories folder. You can read more about games later in this chapter.

Using WordPad

WordPad is a simple word processing program with basic features for typing, editing, and formatting text. If you create simple documents, WordPad might suit you just fine. If you create a lot of documents, consider purchasing a word processing program with a more robust set of features. Popular word processing programs include Word for Windows and WordPerfect.

This section covers some basic features of WordPad. For more information, consult online help or experiment!

Taking a Look at the Program Window

You start WordPad as you do all other programs: click its icon in the **Start** menu. Click **Start**, **All Programs**, **Accessories**, and then click **WordPad** to start the program and display the WordPad window (see Figure 25.2).

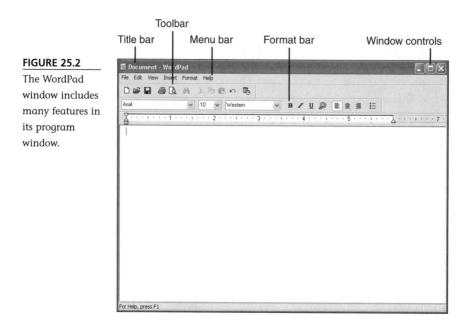

Toolbar

Title bar   Menu bar   Format bar   Window controls

FIGURE 25.2

The WordPad window includes many features in its program window.

Many onscreen features are included in WordPad. You'll find these same features in other programs. Table 25.1 describes common program elements found in WordPad and other programs.

Table 25.1 Common Program Elements

Item	Description
Title bar	Lists the name of the document and the program. If you have not saved the document, you see a generic name.
Menu bar	Lists the menu names. To select a menu command, click the menu name and then click the menu command. For more help on selecting menu commands, see Chapter 3, "Starting Programs."

Table 25.1   (continued)

Item	Description
Toolbar	As a shortcut to commonly used menu commands, most programs include a toolbar. In WordPad, for instance, you can use the toolbar buttons to open a document, create a new document, print your work, save your document, and more.
Format bar	To make formatting as accessible as possible, many programs include a second toolbar often called the Format bar or Formatting toolbar. You can use this toolbar to make changes to the appearance of your document. For instance, you can use the Font drop-down list to change the font. Use the **Bold** button to make text bold.
Window controls	In addition to the program elements, the program window also includes window controls for maximizing, minimizing, and closing the program window. See Chapter 2, "Getting Started with Windows XP," for more information on manipulating the window.

Typing and Editing Text

WordPad, as mentioned, is used to create text documents. If you want to create a simple document, WordPad has enough features and options to create a basic document. If you are new to computing, WordPad is a great place to learn skills such as entering text, copying and moving text, deleting text, changing the appearance of text, and more. The skills you use in WordPad to perform these tasks translate to other programs. That is, you follow the same basic steps to copy text in WordPad as in a full-featured word processing program such as Word for Windows. This section covers some common tasks.

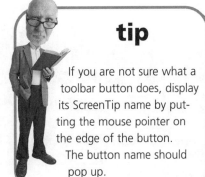

tip

If you are not sure what a toolbar button does, display its ScreenTip name by putting the mouse pointer on the edge of the button. The button name should pop up.

Typing Text

When you start WordPad, you see a blank document onscreen. You also see a flashing vertical pointer that indicates the current cursor location. Text you type is entered at this cursor location. (Later when you edit a document, you can move this insertion point to any place in the document to add or select text. When you first open WordPad, because you have not typed any text, you cannot move the insertion point.)

To enter text, just start typing. You see the text onscreen as you type. You can make editing changes as you type. Notice also that the insertion point moves to the right as you type and that WordPad automatically wraps text to the next line. You do not have to press Enter at the end of the line.

Editing Text

After you have entered text, you may need to go back and make some revisions. The following list covers the basic text-editing skills. Keep in mind that these skills work in most other text programs.

Here are the basic editing tasks:

A common mistake is to press **Enter** at the end of each line, but you should, instead, let WordPad add the line breaks. That way if you add or delete text, WordPad adjusts the line breaks as needed.

Do press **Enter** when you want to end one paragraph and start another or when you want to insert a blank line.

- To make a change to text, you start by selecting it. For instance, if you want to move a section of text, you select it. If you want to format text (covered next), you select it. To select text, click at the start of the text, hold down the mouse pointer, and drag across the text you want to select. The text appears highlighted onscreen (see Figure 25.3).

FIGURE 25.3

The first thing you do in most editing and formatting is select the text you want to modify.

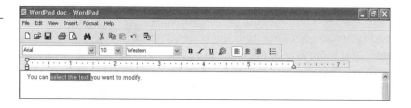

- To delete text, select the text and press the **Delete** key. Notice that WordPad adjusts the lines of text. Use this method when you want to delete more than a few characters. You can also delete characters one at a time using the Backspace key (deletes characters to the left of the insertion point) or the Delete key (deletes characters to the right of the insertion point).

- Moving and copying text uses a cut/copy and paste metaphor. You start by selecting the text you want to move or copy. Then select the **Edit**, **Cut** command (to move text) or the **Edit**, **Copy** command (to copy text). Move to the location where you want to insert the text; this might be another location in the current document, in another document, or even in another program.

Click the **Edit**, **Paste** command to paste the text in the new location. When you move text, the text is deleted from the original location and appears only in the new location. When you copy text, the text appears in both locations: the original and the new.

■ If you make a mistake, you can undo it. Suppose, for instance, that you delete text by mistake. You can undo it by selecting the **Edit**, **Undo** command or by using the Undo toolbar button. (The shortcut key for Undo is **Ctrl+Z**.)

Formatting Text

When you want to make a change to how the text appears, you can use the Format commands or the Format bar. The fastest way to make a change is to use the Format bar, but if you have many changes or if you are unsure of what each button does, use the commands in the **Format** menu.

From the Format bar or menu, you can select another typeface; change the font size; apply emphasis (bold, italic, or underline); change the text color; change the alignment of paragraph(s) to left, right, or center; and make many other changes.

Select the text to change and then click the button or select the menu command. For instance, to make text bold, select the text and then click the **Bold** button. Figure 25.4 shows just a few of the changes you can make.

Saving Your Work

As you create documents (any document, not just WordPad), you should save and save often. To save a document, use the File, Save As command. You learn more about saving and naming documents in Chapter 4, "Saving Your Work."

tip

Most programs include multiple ways to perform the same task. Is one better? Not really. You can select the one most suited to your working style. In addition to the menu commands (how most beginners learn), you can also use the **Cut**, **Copy**, or **Paste toolbar** buttons for moving and copying text. Or you can use the shortcut keys: **Ctrl+X** for Cut, **Ctrl+C** for Copy, or **Ctrl+V** for Paste.

tip

Another program for editing or viewing simple text (.txt) files is Notepad. You can start this program by clicking **Start**, **All Programs**, **Accessories**, and then **Notepad**. It has even fewer features than WordPad, but it is useful for viewing README files commonly included with programs.

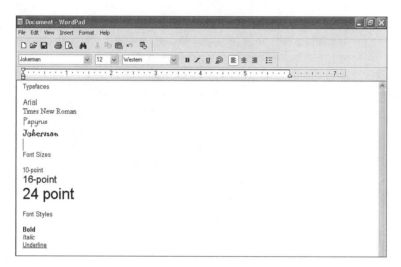

Using Paint

In addition to a word processing program, Windows XP includes a drawing program called Paint. You can use Paint to create simple drawings. You can draw lines and shapes, add text, and change the colors. If you make a mistake, you can use the Eraser to erase part of the drawing.

To start Paint, click **Start**, **All Programs**, **Accessories**, and then click **Paint** (see Figure 25.5).

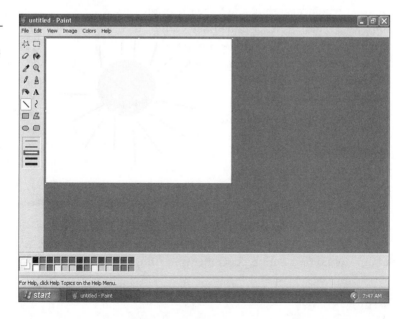

In Paint, you can do any of the following:

- To draw a shape, click the tool in the toolbar. Then click and drag within the drawing area to draw the shape.

- To add color, you can use the Fill With Color tool or the Airbrush tool.

- To draw a text box, use the Text tool. Then type the text to include. You can change the font, font size, and font style (bold, italic, or underline).

- If you make a mistake and want to get rid of something you have added, you can use the Eraser tool. Click the **Eraser** tool and click the size you want the eraser to be. Move the pointer to the drawing area. Hold down the mouse button and drag across the part you want to erase.

- If you want to save your drawing, use the File, Save As command. For more information on saving a file, see Chapter 4.

- To change the colors for an object, use the color box (at the bottom of the Paint window). Click the color you want to use for the lines used to draw the object. To change the color for the fill (for filled objects) right-click the color you want.

Using Calculator

One of my favorite accessory programs is the Calculator. It's easy to pop it open and perform calculations. You can add, subtract, multiply, divide, figure percentages, and more with this handy tool shown in Figure 25.6.

FIGURE 25.6
Use Calculator to perform basic calculations.

To use the calculator, type the first numeric entry. You can type values or operators on the Numeric keypad (press **Num Lock** first) or on the number keys above the alphabet keys. You can also click the buttons on the calculator. Type the value, operator, value, operator, and so on until you complete your equation. You can use the following mathematical operators:

-	Subtract
+	Add
*	Multiply
/	Divide

To view the results of the equation, press the equal sign on the calculator. For instance, if you type 5 * 20 and then press the equal sign, you see the results of this equation—100.

Playing Games

Windows provides several games that you can play to break up your workday with a little entertainment. Playing games is also a good way to help you get the hang of using the mouse if you are a beginner. For example, playing Solitaire can help you practice clicking and dragging. You can find the games by clicking **Start**, **All Programs**, **Accessories**, and then **Games**. Figure 25.7 shows the game Solitaire.

tip

The calculator also has memory and percentage features. If you routinely use a handheld calculator, you already know how to use these features. (If not, consult online help.) You can also use a more complex scientific calculator. Start **Calculator** and then click **View**, **Scientific**. You then can use any of these calculation features.

FIGURE 25.7

You can play one of many games, including the popular Solitaire.

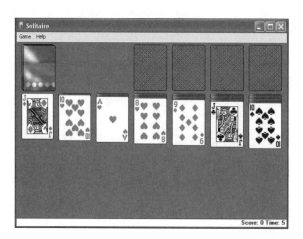

Score: 0 Time: 5

THE ABSOLUTE MINIMUM

Explore the many extra programs packed in with Windows XP including the following:

- To create simple text documents, use WordPad.
- Paint is a great way to create simple drawings or graphic documents such as party invitations. Kids also like to play around in Paint.
- For a quick mathematical problem, use Windows XP's built-in calculator.
- Playing games is a good way to practice using the mouse as well as take a break from work.
- Look elsewhere in this book for help on other accessory programs including Fax, System Tools, and others.

26

SETTING UP WINDOWS XP FOR MULTIPLE USERS

If more than one person uses your PC, you might want to personalize certain Windows settings for each person. For example, you can customize the desktop, **Start** menu, Favorites folder, My Documents folder, and more. Each person can set up Windows the way he or she wants and then create a user account. Each time that person logs on, all those settings will be used.

This chapter covers the basics of setting up accounts, logging on and off, and modifying accounts.

Setting Up a New Account

When you first install and use Windows, you are prompted to set up the names accounts for your PC. You can add names for each person using the computer (and then later go back and modify the accounts). Or you can add the accounts later, as described here.

The purpose of accounts is to let each person customize how Windows works. The user accounts also save favorite Web sites, create My Documents folders, and more. You can customize Windows and then create a new account; the new account will use these settings. Or you can create a new account. Any changes you make to certain settings (Favorites List, display, mouse, and so on) are saved with that particular account.

Follow these steps to set up a new account:

1. Click **Start** and then click **Control Panel**.

2. Click **User Accounts** in the Control Panel window. Any accounts you have created are listed (see Figure 26.1).

FIGURE 26.1

You can use this Control Panel option to modify existing accounts and set up new accounts.

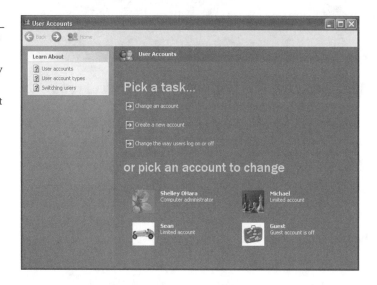

3. Click the **Create a new account** link. You are first prompted to type a name. As the prompt explains, "This name will appear on the **Start** menu as well as the Welcome screen" (see Figure 26.2).

4. Type a name for the account and click the **Next** button. You are prompted to select an account type.

5. Select what type of account you want to create: Computer administrator or Limited. When you select an account type, you see a description of what that account can and cannot do. For instance, Figure 26.3 shows what you can do with an administrator account.

FIGURE 26.2

The name identifies the account and is displayed when you start Windows XP.

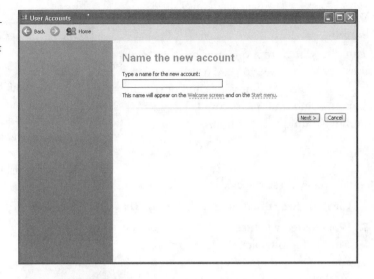

FIGURE 26.3

You can limit the types of changes a user can make to your PC using the account type.

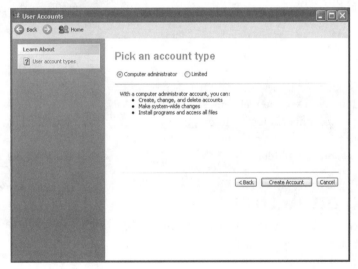

6. Click the **Create Account** button. The new account is added.

Logging In and Out

If you have set up accounts, you see the different account names when you turn on your computer. You can click your account to log on. Any personalized settings, such as a customized desktop, wallpaper, Favorites list, and others, are loaded, and you see Windows XP just the way you left it. You can get to work.

You can also switch from one user account to another. For instance, if you are finished working, you can log off so that your child or spouse can log on. Using multiple accounts lets each person have a unique, personalized setup.

Logging Off

To log off, follow these steps:

1. Click the **Start** button and click **Log Off**.

2. When asked whether you're sure that you want to log off, click the **Log Off** button. You are logged off. Windows XP also saves any settings you changed. You see the Welcome screen.

Logging On

When you log off or when you first start Windows, you see the Welcome screen that lists all user accounts. To log on to one of these accounts, click the account name. All personalized settings are loaded.

Modifying an Account

You can make changes to existing accounts, specifying a password for that account, changing the picture, and so on.

To modify an account, follow these steps:

1. Click **Start** and then click **Control Panel**.

2. Click **User Accounts** in the Control Panel window. Any accounts you have created are listed (refer Figure 26.1).

3. Select the account in the User Accounts window. You see the available options for modifying this account (see Figure 26.4).

> **tip**
>
> Consider having one person as the computer administrator. This person can create new accounts and modify and delete existing accounts. Use the limited account for those you don't want to have complete access to the computer. These users can perform all the basic computing tasks but cannot perform system tasks such as installing programs.

> **tip**
>
> You can change the way users log on or off. To do so, click **Change the way users log on or off** from the list of tasks in the first User Accounts window. You can use the Welcome screen (the default). Or if you want to keep programs running and return to them as is, you can also enable the **Fast User Switching** option. Make your choice and click **Apply Options**.

FIGURE 26.4

You can modify existing accounts as needed.

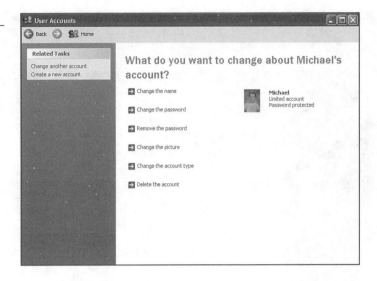

FIGURE 26.4

You can modify existing accounts as needed.

4. You can then make any of the changes as covered in the following sections.

5. When you are finished making changes, close the Control Panel windows.

Changing the Account Name

To change the name of the account, click **Change the name**. In the screen that appears, type a new name and then click the **Change Name** button. Again, this name shows up on the Welcome screen and **Start** menu.

Adding a Password

If you want to apply some security to using the computer, you can assign a password to an account. This person must type the password to log on to that account.

To create a password, click **Create a password**. You see several text boxes (see Figure 26.5). Type the password you want to use in the first text box. Type it again to confirm in the second text box. Finally, type a hint to help you remember the password. When you've completed all three text box entries, click the **Create Password** button. Now this person is prompted to type the password to gain access to this account.

FIGURE 26.5

Assign a password for one measure of security.

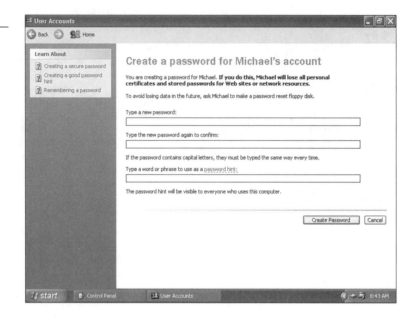

Assigning a Picture

Windows XP assigns a graphic image to each account (an airplane, butterfly, guitar, chess set, and others). If you don't like the graphics, you can use one of the other icons supplied with Windows XP. If none of these suits your fancy, you can use other graphic images. For instance, you might use actual pictures of each person for his or her account.

To use a different picture for the account, follow these steps:

1. Click **Change the picture**.

2. Select from one of the available pictures (see Figure 26.6).

   Or

   Click **Browse for more pictures** to select another picture (for instance, a photograph) stored in another location. Open the folder that contains the image (see Figure 26.7). Select the image and then click **Open**. The image is used for this account (see Figure 26.8).

FIGURE 26.6

You can select from several images included with Windows XP.

FIGURE 26.7

To use another image, change to that drive and folder.

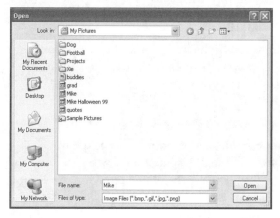

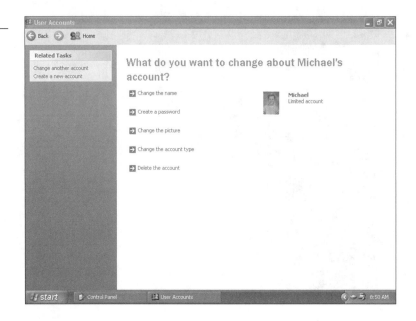

Changing the Account Type

If you want to set limits (or lift the limits) on a user account, change the account type. To do so, click **Change the account type**, select the account type, and then click the **Change Account Type** button.

Deleting an Account

If someone no longer uses the computer (perhaps he got his own!), you can delete accounts. Doing so frees up the disk space taken by this person's user account settings and documents. (You do have the option of saving the documents or deleting them.)

To delete an account, follow these steps:

1. Select the account you want to change.
2. Click **Delete the account**. You are prompted to keep or delete the files (see Figure 26.9).
3. Select whether to keep or delete the account files by clicking **Keep Files** or **Delete Files**. You are next prompted to confirm the deletion.
4. Click the **Delete Account** button.

FIGURE 26.9

You can delete
outdated or
unused
accounts.

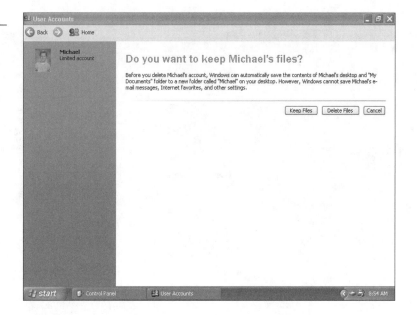

THE ABSOLUTE MINIMUM

User accounts are a handy way to let multiple users have a personalized version of Windows XP that suits how that person uses the computer (how the desktop appears, the list of favorite sites, and so on). For this purpose, Windows enables you to create user accounts. You can use this feature to do the following:

- You can set up accounts for each person who uses the computer, selecting an account name, picture, and type.

- When you turn on the computer, all user accounts are displayed. You can log on to your account.

- When you want to log off one person so that another user can log on, the current person logs off. Then the new person can log on. Use the **Log Off** button on the **Start** menu to log off.

- Any changes made to Windows settings are saved each time a person logs off.

- You can modify user accounts as needed, changing the name, type, or picture. You can also assign a password and delete unneeded accounts.

27

USING ACCESSIBILITY OPTIONS

If you or someone else in your family has special needs, you should look into Windows XP's Accessibility Options. Windows XP includes two sets of accessibility tools: those listed on the **Accessories** menu plus a set of Control Panel options. These features make using the computer easier for those with special needs. For instance, you can magnify the screen. You can display visual warnings for system sounds. You can customize the keyboard as well as type using an onscreen keyboard and your mouse or other pointing device.

This chapter covers these special need features of Windows XP.

Using the Accessibility Accessory Programs

In addition to the accessory programs covered in Chapter 25, "Using Windows Accessory Programs," Windows XP includes a set of accessibility accessory programs. These programs make it easier for those with disabilities to use the operating system and include the following:

- Magnifier magnifies the contents of your screen.
- Narrator reads the contents of your screen aloud.
- On-Screen Keyboard enables users who have limited mobility to type onscreen using a pointing device.

To start any of these accessory programs, follow these steps:

1. Click the **Start** button, select **All Programs**, **Accessories**, and then click **Accessibility**.
2. Click any of the programs: Magnifier, Narrator, or On-Screen Keyboard. The particular program is started.

When you start each program, you see a dialog box that provides information about the program you opened. When this appears, read over the contents of the dialog box and click **OK** to close it.

You can also use the Accessibility Wizard to set up and turn on any of the programs. The wizard is covered later in this chapter.

Finally, to keep the program open but remove the program's dialog box from view, click the **Minimize** button in the top-right corner of the dialog box.

The following sections discuss how to use each of the accessibility accessory programs.

Using Magnifier

Magnifier magnifies part of your screen so that you can better see the screen. The top part of the screen shows the location of the mouse pointer. The rest of the screen shows the "regular" view of the window. In Figure 27.1, for instance, you see the Display Properties dialog box open. The magnification area shows the location of the mouse pointer. You can use this tool to better see and select options.

FIGURE 27.1

You can magnify
the current loca-
tion of the
mouse pointer so
that you can
better see and
select options.

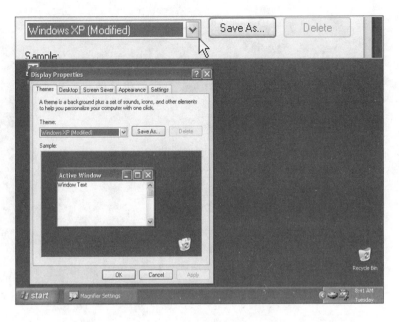

To fine-tune this program, you can use the Magnifier Settings dialog box, shown in
Figure 27.2. This dialog box appears when you start the program. From this list of
options, you can do any of the following:

- To change the magnification level, display the drop-down list and select a different level. The higher the level, the bigger the current pointer location
  appears.

- By default, Magnifier automatically follows the mouse cursor, keyboard focus,
  and text editing. To turn off any tracking
  options, uncheck them.

- By default, the Magnifier Settings dialog
  box is displayed. You can choose to start
  the program minimized. You can also
  invert the colors. To do so, check any of
  these options in the Presentation area of
  the dialog box.

To exit Magnifier, click the **Exit** button in the
Magnifier Settings dialog box.

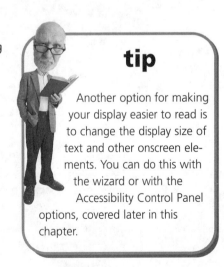

tip

Another option for making
your display easier to read is
to change the display size of
text and other onscreen elements. You can do this with
the wizard or with the
Accessibility Control Panel
options, covered later in this
chapter.

FIGURE 27.2

Use the
Magnifier
Settings dialog
box to make
changes to how
this program
works.

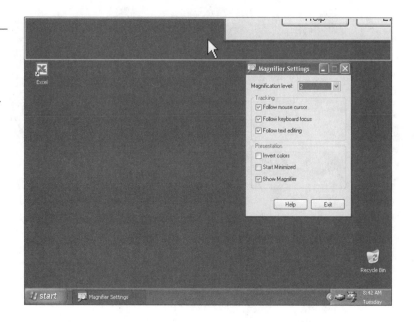

Using Narrator

When you start Narrator, you see the opening screen. Click **OK**. You see the Narrator
dialog box, shown in Figure 27.3, and the Narrator reads events onscreen and typed
characters.

FIGURE 27.3

Use Narrator to
have the pro-
gram announce
events including
reading dialog
box options as
well as typed
characters.

You can also have Narrator move the mouse pointer to the active item. As another
option, you can start the program minimized. Check any of the desired options in
the Narrator dialog box.

You can select a voice you want to use for Narrator, as well as the speed, volume,
and pitch of that voice. To do so, click the **Voice** button in the Narrator dialog box.
A Voice Settings dialog box opens; select your settings and then click **OK**.

To exit the program, click **Exit**. Then click **Yes** to confirm that you want to exit.

Using On-Screen Keyboard

When you start On-Screen Keyboard, you see the welcome screen, which describes its use. Click **OK** to close the dialog box. You can then use the On-Screen Keyboard, shown in Figure 27.4, to type.

FIGURE 27.4

You can use On-Screen Keyboard to type using your mouse.

You can type by clicking the onscreen keys with your mouse pointer. If you prefer a different method, you can click **Settings** and then **Typing Mode** to select another method: hover or scanning. In hovering mode, you use a mouse or joystick to hover the pointer over a key; the selected character is then typed. In scanning mode, On-Screen Keyboard scans the keyboard, highlighting letters; you press a hot key or use a switch-input device whenever On-Screen Keyboard highlights the character you want to type.

Using Accessibility Control Panel Options

In addition to the accessory programs, you can also use one of several Control Panel options. You can adjust settings such as the size of the text display. You can also use the Accessibility Wizard to select options suited for particular needs. This section covers both.

Using the Accessibility Wizard

To start the Accessibility Wizard, follow these steps:

1. Click **Start** and then click **Control Panel**. You see the various Control Panel options (see Figure 27.5).

2. Click **Configure Windows** to work for your vision, hearing, and mobility needs to start the Accessibility Wizard.

3. Click **Next** to move past the welcome screen. You see the first screen, which lets you select the text size. If larger text would, for instance, make the computer easier to use, select one of the various text size options (see Figure 27.6).

FIGURE 27.5

Use the
Accessibility
Options Control
Panel to set
options and use
the Accessibility
Wizard.

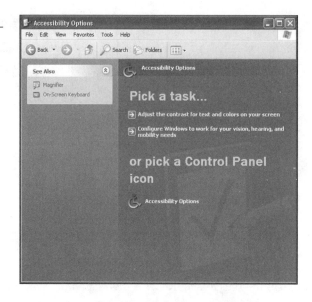

FIGURE 27.6

Select a different
text size to make
text easier to
read.

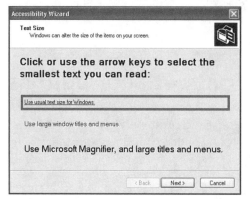

4. Select a text size option and then click **Next**. You see additional options for the display including changing the font size, using Magnifier (covered earlier in this chapter), and disabling personalized menus (see Figure 27.7).

5. Select the display options that control the size of text and other items and then click **Next**. You see additional special needs (see Figure 27.8).

FIGURE 27.7

You can select additional display options.

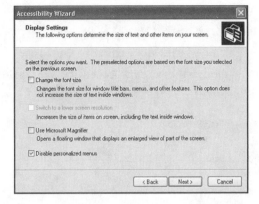

FIGURE 27.8

You can select additional display options.

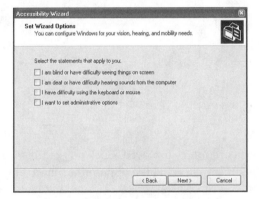

6. Complete the wizard, turning on various features for a particular special need and clicking **Next** to move through these options. For instance, if you have problems with the keyboard, the wizard prompts you to turn on StickyKeys (covered later).

7. After making your selections, click **Finish**.

The options you selected are put into effect.

Modifying Accessibility Options

In addition to the wizard, you can view and select other accessibility options. These are the same options that appear in the wizard when you select your special needs in step 6. The wizard simply selects the most appropriate options for you. With the dialog box method, you can select from all the options.

To view and select these options, follow these steps:

1. Click **Start** and then click **Control Panel**.

2. In the Control Panel window, click **Accessibility Options**.

3. In the Accessibility Options window, click **Accessibility Options** again. You see the Accessibility Options dialog box (see Figure 27.9).

4. By default, the Keyboard tab is displayed. Click any of the tabs and turn on any additional options by checking the appropriate check box.

5. Click **OK**.

You can select the following options:

- On the Keyboard tab, you can turn on **StickyKeys** (allows you to press one key at a time instead of simultaneous keystrokes), **FilterKeys** (ignores brief or repeated keystrokes), or ToggleKeys (plays tones when you press **Caps Lock**, **Num Lock**, or **Scroll Lock**).

- On the Sound tab, you can turn on the **SoundSentry** (displays visual warnings in conjunction with playing system sounds) or **ShowSounds** (instructs programs to display captions for sounds). Figure 27.10 shows these options.

- On the Display tab, you can turn on **High Contrast** (uses alternative colors and font sizes to improve screen contrast). You can also select the blink rate for the cursor as well as its width.

FIGURE 27.10
Use this tab to
select sound
options.

■ On the Mouse tab, you can turn on MouseKeys if you want to control the
mouse pointer using the keys on the numeric keypad.

■ On the General tab, you can set general options such as whether a feature
is turned off after being idle for a set amount of time, whether you see or
hear a sound when a feature is turned on or off, and other options (see
Figure 27.11).

FIGURE 27.11
The General tab
controls options
such as when
notification
warnings sound.

The Absolute Minimum

If you have special needs, it's worthwhile to explore the many features designed to make the computer as accessible as possible. You can use any of the following features:

■ Windows XP includes several accessibility programs including Magnifier (enlarges the view of your screen), Narrator (reads the contents of your screen aloud), and On-Screen Keyboard (enables you to type onscreen using a pointing device).

■ In addition, you can use the Accessibility Wizard to turn on additional features such as enlarging the text size.

■ You can also access accessibility options that control your hardware (sound, keyboard, mouse, display) from the Control Panel. Use these options to make these components more suited to your needs.

28

SETTING UP WINDOWS XP ON A HOME NETWORK

It used to be that setting up a network was a stupendous task, requiring all kinds of special wiring and special devices. A network still requires these basic features (some type of connection and some networking hardware, a network card), but the process of setting up a network and using the networking are dramatically easier. This chapter touches on the basics of home networking.

Home Networking Basics

If your household contains multiple computers (one equipped with Windows XP and Internet access, and at least one more equipped with XP, Windows ME, Windows 98, or Windows 95), you can connect them to create a home network. Doing so enables you to share an Internet connection, hardware (such as a printer, scanner, and so on), and files and folders. Networking the computers in your home also enables members of your household to play multicomputer games.

Setting up a home network involves three basic steps:

1. Planning your network.
2. Installing and configuring the appropriate network hardware on each computer on the network.
3. Running the Windows XP Network Setup Wizard.

This section provides a brief overview of steps 1 and 2. You also learn about using the wizard (step 3). Keep in mind that an in-depth discussion of the first and second steps is beyond the scope of this book, but you can find ample information about it in Windows XP's Help area (click the **Networking** and the **Web** link in the main Help and Support page).

Planning Your Network

When planning your network, you must determine what type of network you want to build. Your options are mostly determined by how the computers are connected. You may use telephone cabling for instance. Or as is more common in recent years, you may set up a wireless network. This type of network has a hub, and as its name indicates, the other computers communicate without wires.

You also need to decide which machine will serve as your host or main computer. This main computer is usually called the *network server*. The computer you designate as the server should run Windows XP and be connected to the Internet.

Installing and Configuring Network Hardware

In terms of installing and configuring the appropriate network hardware, you must equip each computer on your network with a network interface card (often referred to as a NIC or a *network adapter*).

Additionally, if you want to network more than two PCs, you will need a *hub*, which is a separate box into which cables from each network card connect. Many retail home networking kits contain the cards and the hub, as well as setup instructions.

Again the details for installing and configuring vary depending on the type of setup, the number of computers, and many other factors.

Running the Windows XP Network Setup Wizard

After you have installed the necessary networking hardware, you can configure each computer to use the network by working through the Network Setup Wizard. This wizard automates several procedures that were once done manually in earlier versions of Windows, including configuring your network adapters, configuring all your computers to share a single Internet connection, naming each computer, setting up file and printer sharing, installing a firewall, and more.

Follow these steps to run the Network Setup Wizard:

1. Click **Start**, **All Programs**, **Accessories**, **Communications**, and finally **Network Setup Wizard**.

2. Click **Next** to begin setting up your home network. Make sure that you've installed all network cards, modems, and cables; turned on all computers, printers, and external modems; and connected to the Internet (see Figure 28.1). Then click **Next**.

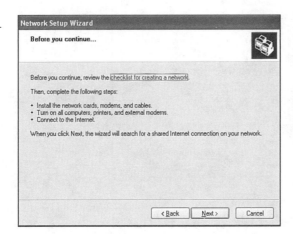

3. Complete each step in the wizard, answering the questions based on your particular setup and clicking **Next** to move to the next step. You can expect to select the type of computer you are configuring, enter a name and description of the computer, name the network you are creating, confirm the settings for this network, set up the Internet connection (see Figure 28.2), and then configure all other computers hooked up to the network.

4. When the setup is complete, click the **Finish** button (see Figure 28.3). You then need to restart to finish the setup and start the configuration setup for all other connected computers.

FIGURE 28.2

As one step for setting up the network, select your Internet connection type.

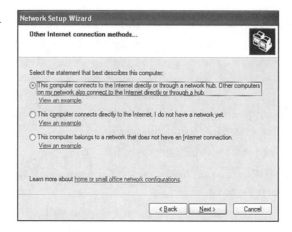

FIGURE 28.3

The last step is to click the **Finish** button.

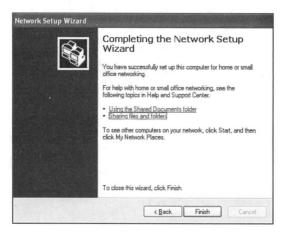

Sharing Resources on a Network

The purpose of a network is to make sharing information and hardware components (such as a printer) easier. This section focuses on common networking tasks including sharing files, sharing printers, and setting up network security.

Enabling File Sharing

By default, certain folders are made available to all computers on your network. To make other folders available to other computers on your network, you must enable file sharing for those folders. (You'll also need to perform this task on all networked computers that contain folders that you want to make available over the network.)

To enable file sharing, follow these steps:

1. Right-click the folder you want to share on your network and click the **Sharing and Security** command. The folder's Properties dialog box opens, with the Sharing tab displayed (see Figure 28.4).

2. Check the Share this folder on the network check box.

3. If you want users on other machines to be able to change the contents of this folder, check the Allow network users to change my files check box.

4. Click **OK**.

Enabling file sharing could make your computer vulnerable to outside users unless you have a firewall. Be sure to turn on firewall protection.

FIGURE 28.4

Use this dialog box to enable file sharing for the selected folder.

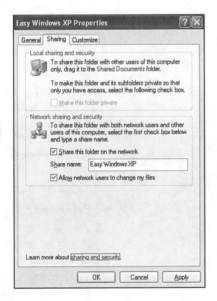

Browsing Shared Files

You can browse shared files on the network through My Network Places. It works just like My Computer, except that it shows you files on the other network computers.

tip

In addition to sharing folders and files, you can share drives and devices, such as printers, scanners, and so on. Follow the same steps, but instead of right-clicking a folder, right-click the drive or device instead.

To view these files, follow these steps:

1. Click the **Start** button and then click **My Network Places**. The My Network Places window is displayed, listing all shared folders on the network (see Figure 28.5).

FIGURE 28.5

You can open any shared folders on the network.

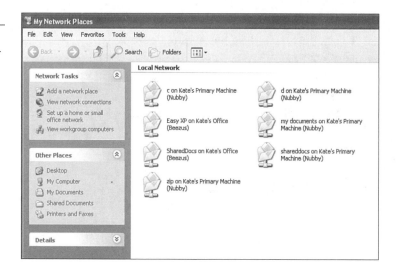

2. Double-click a folder icon to open that folder. You see the contents of that folder.

3. To open a document, double-click the document. You can then edit, print, and save the document as needed.

Sharing Printers

You can connect and set up a printer to the main network server. When you add the printer using the Printer Wizard, you can select network printer as the type. Once set up and set as a shared device, you can print to this printer from any of the other networked computers.

> Depending on the file-sharing properties, you may only be able to view certain files. To make changes, the **Allow network users to change my files** check box for this folder/file must be checked.

To do so, select **Network the printer** from the Print dialog box in whatever program you are printing from. For more information about printing, refer to Chapter 5, "Printing."

Sharing Internet Connections

You can also share an Internet connection. You set up your Internet access for the main computer (server) using the Network Wizard. You can then connect to the Internet from any of the networked computers.

You have several options for how the connection is made. You can use one of the machines as the gateway, you can use a special Windows XP feature (Internet Connection Sharing or ICS), or you can purchase and set up a broadband router.

If you use one of the machines on the network as the gateway, the network's performance will be slowed based on the amount of traffic you're sending through it.

You could share a modem connection on a single machine with others on the network using ICS (Internet Connection Sharing). This, again, is not the fastest method, but it does work transparently.

Finally, you can purchase and install a broadband router instead. This component allows you to share the connection without having one of your machines do the job. The router also can act as a firewall for your network.

Some versions of AOL do not allow you to share a single Internet connection among multiple machines; contact AOL for more information. Likewise, other ISPs may charge you extra to use a single Internet connection for multiple computers.

Controlling Network Security

If your home network is connected to the Internet, you suffer an increased risk of hackers obtaining access to the computers on that network. One way to obstruct unauthorized users is to erect a *firewall*. Windows XP ships complete with a firewall that is installed automatically when you run the Network Setup Wizard on a machine with a direct connection to the Internet.

You can also view and change security options as needed. Follow these steps:

1. Open the My Network Places window.

2. Click the **View network connections** link in the task pane (see Figure 28.6).

3. Right-click the icon for your network and then click the **Properties** command. You see the General tab of the network properties dialog box (see Figure 28.7).

FIGURE 28.6

To set security options, first display the network connections.

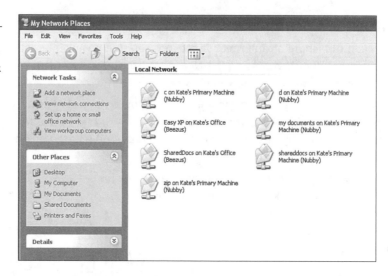

FIGURE 28.7

The network properties dialog box provides several tabs with useful connection and security options.

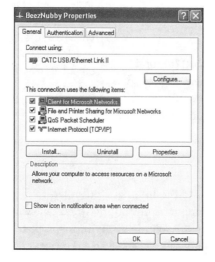

4. Review or make any changes to the General options.

5. Click the **Advanced** tab to check that firewall protection is on (see Figure 28.8).

6. Click **OK**.

tip

The network properties dialog box includes many more features for controlling your connection, network use, security, and other settings. Consult online help or consider purchasing *Absolute Beginner's Guide to Computer Basics* (ISBN# 0-7897-2899-6), which has some coverage on home networking.

FIGURE 28.8

You can use the Advanced tab to check your network's firewall protection.

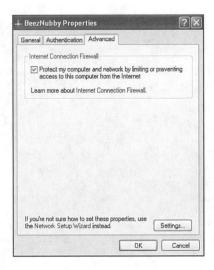

THE ABSOLUTE MINIMUM

If you have more than one computer, it's worthwhile to set up a home network so that you can more easily share data and hardware components (such as a printer or Internet connection). Setting up a home networking has been greatly simplified in Windows XP. In particular, look into the following features:

- To set up a network, you need a main computer (usually called the server or host). You also need a connection type; common connection types include phone lines or wireless connections. Also, each computer on the network must have a network card. Setting up and installing the individual hardware components of a network are beyond the scope of this book. Try online help for more detailed information.

- Windows XP includes a Network Setup Wizard that guides you step-by-step through the process of setting up a home network.

- After a network is set up, you can share files. To do so, you must enable file sharing. After you have done so, you can open and work with any shared files on the network.

- You can also share a printer, printing to the network printer, and an Internet connection.

- Security is a big issue for networking. Make sure that you turn on and keep on firewall protection. You can also investigate additional security and network options from the network properties dialog box.

Index

How can we make this index more useful? Email us at indexes@quepublishing.com

How can we make this index more useful? Email us at indexes@quepublishing.com

Y - Z

How can we make this index more useful? Email us at indexes@quepublishing.com

Your Guide to Computer Technology

www.informit.com

Sams has partnered with **InformIT.com** to bring technical information to your desktop. Drawing on Sams authors and reviewers to provide additional information on topics you're interested in, **InformIT.com** has free, in-depth information you won't find anywhere else.

ARTICLES

Keep your edge with thousands of free articles, in-depth features, interviews, and information technology reference recommendations—all written by experts you know and trust.

POWERED BY
Safari

ONLINE BOOKS

Answers in an instant from **InformIT Online Books'** 600+ fully searchable online books. Sign up now and get your first 14 days **free**.

CATALOG

Review online sample chapters and author biographies to choose exactly the right book from a selection of more than 5,000 titles.

 www.samspublishing.com